# PETER JENNINGS

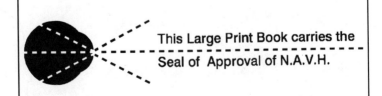

This Large Print Book carries the
Seal of Approval of N.A.V.H.

# PETER JENNINGS

## A REPORTER'S LIFE

## *Edited by*
# KATE DARNTON,
# KAYCE FREED JENNINGS
# & LYNN SHERR

**THORNDIKE PRESS**

*An imprint of Thomson Gale, a part of The Thomson Corporation*

**THOMSON**
**GALE**

Detroit • New York • San Francisco • New Haven, Conn. • Waterville, Maine • London

**THOMSON**

**GALE**

**LIBRARY OF CONGRESS CATALOGING-IN-PUBLICATION DATA**

Peter Jennings : a reporter's life / edited by Kate Darnton, Kayce Freed Jennings, and Lynn Sherr.
    p. cm.
    "Thorndike Press Large Print Nonfiction."
    Includes bibliographical references.
    ISBN-13: 978-1-4104-0271-4 (hardcover : alk. paper : lg. print)
    ISBN-10: 1-4104-0271-1 (hardcover : alk. paper : lg. print)
    1. Jennings, Peter, 1938-2005. 2. Television journalists — Canada — Biography. 3. Large type books. I. Darnton, Kate. II. Jennings, Kayce Freed. III. Sherr, Lynn.
PN4913.J46P48 2007b
070.1'95092—dc22
    [B]
                             2007038015

# PETER JENNINGS

# CONTENTS

# INTRODUCTION

*Lynn Sherr*

This book would have been anathema to Peter Jennings. I can hear his usually well-honed skepticism now: "A biography? Of me? Whatever for? Surely there are more important subjects."

Not this time.

For more than four decades on American television, Peter Jennings reported the news that defined our lives, a reliable authority who earned our trust with his constant search for the truth. As the sole anchor of ABC's *World News Tonight* for his last twenty-two years, he cemented that bond with a presence so commanding and a face so familiar that dedicated viewers placed their confidence in him to convey everything from the muddle of Middle East politics to the thrill of the millennium, from the purity of a child's question to the horror of 9/11.

9

He informed us and calmed us and led us on grand adventures, a lifetime of service that helped shaped the perceptions of tens of millions of Americans. Peter's death from lung cancer in 2005 silenced a mighty voice. But his impact is indelible.

The principles that made Peter a broadcasting legend still reverberate along the corridors of ABC News, informing the program that he led and energizing the people who worked with him. His legacy is our commitment to serious journalism, a goal that he fought for daily, and tenaciously, pitting his dynamic presence against the increasing commercial challenges of a rapidly changing business.

Outside the office, the magic of his friendship continues to brighten the lives of everyone lucky enough to have connected with him personally. And for those who knew him only as the suave TV anchor who reported the news every night and made the world understandable, the memory of what we had — and what we've lost — has not disappeared. You cannot work for ABC News without having someone, somewhere, come up to you and say, "I miss Peter Jennings."

We all do.

Here, then, is a chance to remember him; to celebrate his life, and to learn about this man who was, in heart and soul, a reporter.

For those of us who worship the same career gods, that is the ultimate compliment. Peter Jennings was curious and insatiable in his drive to uncover the facts. He never took anything at face value and regularly challenged the status quo. He was fiercely competitive, but at the core a softie whose concern for the most vulnerable beings on the planet could dissolve him into tears. Even on the air.

Especially when the subject was his children. Nothing could make Peter smile more brilliantly or show more concern than the mention of Lizzie and Chris, the twin suns illuminating his personal universe. He cherished their innocence as youngsters, then respected their individualism as adults, a doting dad whose love knew no bounds.

The still point at the center of it all was his wife, Kayce. Their shared passion — for life, for each other, for telling stories that make a difference, and opening doors for those less fortunate — created an enviable partnership that is reflected in the family's decision to channel proceeds from this project into the Peter Jennings Foundation, so that the dreams of others can be realized as well.

That, too, is Peter Jennings' legacy.

The words that follow come from his

friends and family and colleagues and competitors, and from some who got to know him as the questioner on the other side of the camera. Most were recorded in the sorrow and shock of the period between August 7, 2005 — when Peter left us — and August 10, 2005, when ABC News aired a two-hour tribute to the man who had so gracefully led our network. Because the interviews were conducted so quickly, the voices are unusually raw — barely edited — captured in candor and honesty, and reproduced here almost exactly as they were spoken. They are by no means the only people whose lives intersected Peter's. But they produce a remarkably similar narrative with many recurrent themes, a universality of perception that arises from uncommonly gifted storytellers. Also included are some excerpts from the memorial service for Peter one month later, when those who knew him best had a chance to consider his life even more thoughtfully.

Some of Peter's own words are here too, culled from the many scripts, speeches, and letters he wrote over the decades and selected from some interviews he reluctantly gave to the reporters who could convince him that his thoughts were, in fact, important to record.

The intimate portrait they paint is a triumph of collective memory — a non-revisionist history of an era, of a profession, and, ultimately, of a most astonishing human being. Think of it as a conversation, a conversation about Peter Jennings and the reporting that he championed.

People were Peter's touchstones. As you'll read within, he connected with every person he met. He didn't use them. At a big event, Peter Jennings' eyes never roamed the room for someone more important to buttonhole. He zeroed in on you and made you believe that you were the only person on the planet. He dazzled. He surprised. He worked his tail off to get it right. And he understood the privilege and responsibility that come from being a television star.

Not that he was a saint. He was not. Peter Jennings could be a pain in whatever part of your anatomy is most vulnerable. He judged our words, our clothes, our beaux, our goals. He could make you nuts. And yet, in the end, he was often (no, Peter, not always, but often is pretty good) right.

Peter was our anchor in every sense of the word: as a loyal pal, a caring colleague, the strongest link in our effort to chronicle the times that we live in. For some of us, going out on assignment, or risking our careers, or lives, on an event, made sense in part because we knew that he would put it into context by introducing our reports perfectly, by making everyone understand why this piece really mattered. Secretly, some of us even took comfort in believing that if it came to the end, Peter would secure our place in heaven by highlighting what made us special, as he recounted our lives' accomplishments to the world.

Who ever thought we would be doing it for him?

# CONTRIBUTORS

*Editorial note: All of the reflections on Peter Jennings' life in this book come from the individuals listed below, either drawn from transcripts of the interviews conducted for the ABC News program "Peter Jennings: Reporter" or from his memorial service a month later. Quotations have mostly been left intact, with the interviewees' occasional mismatch of present and past tense that characterized their inability to deal immediately with the loss. To make the reading easier, there are few indications of the minor editing inevitably required to continue the conversational flow. And, very occasionally, sentences have been gently rearranged to make the point clearer. But nothing has been taken out of context, only a word added here or there that the speaker inadvertently left out. What you read is what they said; these people, who knew Peter best, described him impeccably.*

**Alan Alda** is an actor, director, and writer who was Peter's friend and neighbor.

**Jonathan Alter** is a senior editor and columnist for *Newsweek* magazine who writes frequently about media issues, and a contributing correspondent for NBC News.

**John and Hilary Andrews** met Peter in the early 1970s in Lebanon, where John was teaching at the American University of Beirut. Peter hired him as a soundman, and John went on to report for the *Guardian,* NBC News, and the *Economist.*

**Hanan Ashrawi** got to know Peter in 1968, when he was covering the Middle East and she was an undergraduate at the American University of Beirut and a member of the General Union of Palestine Students. She is an academic and a member of the Palestinian Legislative Council.

**Ken Auletta** is a writer for the *New Yorker* magazine and the author of several books on the media, and he was Peter's friend and neighbor.

**Gretchen Babarovic** was Peter's executive assistant for more than twenty years.

**Lauren Bacall** is an actress, and she was a friend and neighbor of Peter's.

**Jon Banner** was the executive producer for *World News Tonight with Peter Jennings,* beginning in 2003. He continues as Executive Producer of *World News with Charles Gibson*.

**Bill Blakemore** was teaching in Beirut when Peter recruited him as a soundman. He later became ABC's Rome bureau chief and Vatican correspondent. He's been in New York for ABC News since 1984.

**Todd Brewster** was co-author with Peter of *The Century* and *In Search of America,* and editorial producer of the ABC television series of the same names. He is director of the Peter Jennings Project for Journalists and the Constitution at the National Constitution Center in Philadelphia, Pennsylvania.

**Tom Brokaw** was a reporter for NBC News in 1966 when he first ran into Peter. He became the solo anchor of *NBC Nightly News* in September 1983 at the same time Peter became the solo anchor of *World News Tonight*. He retired as anchor in December 2004.

**Hilary Brown**, a fellow Canadian, met Peter at his parents' home in the mid–1960s when she was reporting and anchoring for CBC Radio. She was hired by ABC and overlapped with Peter when both were based in London. She has worked out of Tehran, Paris, Washington, New York, and Cyprus.

**Hal Bruno** began covering national elections in 1960 and served as ABC News political director for nineteen years. He became Peter's political tutor when Peter returned to the United States shortly before the 1984 presidential campaign.

**Karen Burnes** was a child when she met Peter, shortly after he arrived in New York. Her father and Peter were friends and colleagues. She became a correspondent, then a producer, and she is now Supervising Editorial Producer for ABC's news magazines.

**Marc Burstein** is Executive Producer of Special Events for ABC News. He was a voice in Peter's ear on dozens of breaking news stories, including the Gulf War, the war in Iraq, and 9/11, and special events, such as the millennium, presidential elections, and President Reagan's funeral.

**Michael Clemente** wrote for Washington anchor Frank Reynolds during the triple anchor era of *World News Tonight*. He became Peter's writer when Peter became the solo anchor and was then named a senior producer. He is now Senior Executive Producer of ABCNews.com. Peter was godfather to Mike's daughter, Noelle.

**President Bill Clinton** shared the stage with Peter for two town meetings titled "Answering Children's Questions." The last time Peter interviewed him was at the opening of his presidential library in November 2004.

**John Cochran** was an NBC correspondent in London — and Peter's direct competitor — when they first met in 1978. John joined ABC News in 1994 and is now Senior Washington Correspondent.

**Jeanmarie Condon** produced several of Peter's documentaries, including "Jerusalem Stories," "The Search for Jesus," and "Jesus and Paul: The Word and the Witness." She is now Senior Producer for ABC News' *Nightline*.

**John Cooley** met and first worked with Peter in Lebanon. At the time, he was writing for the *Christian Science Monitor*. He later became a radio correspondent and off-air reporter for ABC News, specializing in the Middle East. He is the author of several books on the region.

**Walter Cronkite** was the anchor of the *CBS Evening News* when Peter was made the ABC anchor for the first time. Cronkite remained the CBS anchor until he retired in 1981, two years before Peter took the ABC anchor job for a second time.

**Sam Donaldson** was ABC News' Chief White House Correspondent from 1977, when Ronald Reagan took office, until 1989. He was a weekend anchor, co-anchor of *Prime Time Live,* a regular on *This Week with David Brinkley,* and then co-anchor of

*This Week with Sam Donaldson and Cokie Roberts.*

**Barrie Dunsmore** shared an apartment with Peter when both were based in Rome. He reported on foreign affairs for ABC News from Rome and the Middle East, from Washington as the State Department correspondent, and from ABC's London bureau. Peter was the best man at his wedding.

**Dick Ebersol** was Peter's producer at the 1972 Olympics in Munich. He is now chairman of NBC Universal Sports and Olympics.

**Tom Fenton** was a foreign correspondent at CBS news for more than thirty years and a journalistic competitor of Peter's when he was in London.

**Linda Bird Francke**, a journalist and author, was a longtime friend of Peter's and a neighbor on Long Island.

**Paul Friedman** first worked with Peter at ABC News in London, where he became the director of overseas news coverage. He was the executive producer of *World News Tonight* twice (1988–1993 and 1997–2000) and then executive vice president of news coverage. He is now Senior Vice President of CBS News.

**David Gelber** was the executive producer of a number of Peter's documentaries, including reports on Haiti, the decision to drop the atomic bomb, and two on the Bosnian crisis.

**Charlie Gibson** encountered Peter for the first time in 1968. He joined ABC News in 1975, covering the White House and Capitol Hill. He became the co-anchor of *Good Morning America* in 1987 and, in 2006, the anchor of *World News with Charles Gibson*.

**Rudy Giuliani** was the mayor of New York City on September 11, 2001.

**Charles Glass** met Peter in Beirut in 1972. He became an ABC News correspondent and is now a journalist and writer specializing in the Middle East. Peter was the best man at his wedding.

**Roger Goodman** first worked with Peter at the Munich Olympics in 1972. After that, he directed virtually all of Peter's major breaking news coverage and news specials, including elections, political conventions, the children's specials, weddings and funerals, the millennium broadcast, and 9/11.

**Jeff Gralnick** was the executive producer of *World News Tonight* during the triple anchor era, when Peter anchored from London. He worked with Peter again as vice president and executive producer of special events.

**Dan Harris** has been a correspondent for

ABC News since 2000. He has anchored *World News Sunday* since November 2006.

**Don Hewitt** is the creator of CBS News' *60 Minutes,* and he served as its longtime executive producer. He was also the executive producer of the *CBS Evening News* with Walter Cronkite from 1960 to 1965.

**Bob Iger** was a young programming executive at ABC Sports when he first met Peter, who was then based in London. He is now President and CEO of the Walt Disney Company, which owns ABC.

**Chris Isham** first worked with Peter in 1983, when he was a producer of the documentary "War and Power: The Rise of Syria." He moved to *World News Tonight* in 1988 and became chief of investigative projects. He is now Washington Bureau Chief for CBS News.

**Christopher Jennings** is Peter's son.

**Elizabeth Jennings** is Peter's daughter.

**Sarah Jennings** is Peter's sister, a journalist, and a writer.

**Timothy Johnson** is Medical Editor for ABC News, a physician, an ordained minister, and an author.

**Gil and Lena Kaplan** are longtime friends of the Jennings family. Gil is the founder of *Institutional Investor* magazine and a scholar of the composer Gustav Mahler.

He was on the Carnegie Hall board of directors with Peter.

**Ted Koppel** was hired by ABC News in 1963, one year before Peter came to the network. Ted, Peter, and the News Division grew up together, with Peter ultimately anchoring *World News Tonight* and Ted anchoring *Nightline*. He joined the Discovery Channel in 2006.

**Yael Lavie** was a producer in the ABC Jerusalem bureau. She is now Middle East Bureau Chief for Sky News.

**Mike Lee** has been a London-based correspondent for ABC News since 1980. Peter was godfather to Mike's first child, Jenny.

**John Leo**, a journalist and syndicated columnist, was a friend and neighbor of Peter's. He often served as Peter's sounding board.

**Lauren Lipani** was Peter's assistant at *World News Tonight*.

**Elmer Lower**, then president of ABC News, brought twenty-six-year-old Peter down from Canada and put him in the anchor chair for the first time.

**Vinnie Malhotra** produced many news stories with Peter and accompanied him on numerous overseas trips, including Peter's final visit to Iraq. He is now Executive Producer for the weekend editions of *World News*.

**Michele Mayer** is Stage Manager for *World News*.

**Cynthia McFadden** has been with ABC News since 1994, first as legal correspondent and then as a correspondent and co-anchor for *Prime Time*. She is now Co-anchor of *Nightline*.

**John McWethy** was the national security correspondent for ABC News for almost twenty years.

**Jenna Millman** was an associate producer on Peter's documentary "Jesus and Paul: The Word and the Witness."

**Matthew Myers** is President of the Campaign for Tobacco-Free Kids. He was interviewed by Peter for the documentary "From the Tobacco Files: Untold Stories of Betrayal and Neglect."

**Tom Nagorski** first met Peter in 1990, just before going overseas as a producer for ABC News. He returned to New York three years later to become the foreign editor of *World News Tonight,* where he remains as Senior Broadcast Producer.

**Peter Osnos** was a foreign correspondent with the *Washington Post* when he first encountered Peter overseas in the late 1970s. After becoming a foreign and national editor, he left journalism for the book business, first as publisher of Times Books and then as founder and publisher of PublicAffairs, which published this book.

**Vincent Perry** is an audio engineer at *World News* who worked with Peter on every election and political convention since 1984.

**Colin Powell** was the U.S. secretary of state from 2001 to 2005, which included the first years of the war in Iraq.

**Martha Raddatz** became the State Department correspondent for ABC News in 1999 and then senior national security correspondent in 2003. In 2005, she was named Chief White House Correspondent.

**Dan Rather** replaced Walter Cronkite as anchor of the CBS *Evening News* in 1981, two years before Peter became the sole anchor at ABC. He stayed in the job until March 2005.

**Condoleezza Rice** first met Peter in the mid–1980s when she was a professor at Stanford University and appeared on ABC News as an analyst of Soviet affairs. She succeeded Colin Powell as U.S. Secretary of State in January 2005 after serving as President Bush's national security advisor.

**Cokie Roberts** has covered politics for ABC News since 1988 as a reporter, analyst, and commentator. She was a co-anchor of *This Week with Sam Donaldson & Cokie Roberts* from 1996 to 2002. She is now Senior News Analyst for National Public Radio.

**Brian Ross** joined ABC News in 1994. He is ABC's Chief Investigative Correspondent.

**Diane Sawyer** first remembers meeting Peter in 1968 while working for the ABC affiliate in Louisville, Kentucky. She joined ABC News in 1989 as a co-anchor of *Prime Time Live* and became a co-anchor of *Good Morning America* in 1999. She worked with Peter on many special events and breaking news stories.

**Antonin Scalia** is Associate Justice of the U.S. Supreme Court. He and Peter took in the occasional Baltimore Orioles game together.

**Stu Schutzman** traveled the country and the world with Peter, first as his producer and then as a senior producer for *World News Tonight,* where he remains.

**Al Sharpton**, minister, activist, and one-time presidential candidate, was interviewed by Peter on many occasions — extensively for a film on Gary, Indiana, which was part of the *In Search of America* series.

**Peter Shaw** was Peter's writer in London during *World News Tonight*'s triple anchor era in the late 1970s and early 1980s.

**Lynn Sherr** first met Peter in 1968 while

she was with the Associated Press. She joined ABC News in 1977, where she covered politics and the space program among many other stories. She worked with Peter at political conventions and on election nights as well as on the *Challenger* explosion and the millennium. Since 1986, she has been a Correspondent at *20/20*.

**Pete Simmons** was one of Peter's producers in the 1970s, when both were based in London. When Peter became the London anchor, they continued to work together, as they did on the occasional special or documentary after both moved back to New York.

**George Stephanopoulos**, who was a former senior advisor to President Clinton, joined ABC News in 1997. He is Chief Washington Correspondent and Anchor of *This Week with George Stephanopoulos*.

**Mary Brosnahan Sullivan** is the Executive Director of the Coalition for the Homeless.

**Keith Summa** was Peter's guide through New York's homeless shelters and encampments. He left the Coalition for the Homeless and joined ABC News in 1992, where he produced documentaries with Peter on subjects including tobacco, guns, and the healthcare industry. He is now Senior Investigative Producer for CBS News.

**Elizabeth Vargas** was named co-anchor of *World News Tonight,* along with Bob Woodruff, following Peter's death. She is now Co-anchor of *20/20.*

**Rupen Vosgimorukian** covered the world with Peter. Beginning in Lebanon, he was Peter's primary cameraman for several years. He continued working with Peter on many overseas assignments, even after Peter relocated to the United States.

**Barbara Walters** shared anchoring duties and air time with Peter on many news specials, breaking news stories, and special events, including Egyptian President Anwar Sadat's funeral, "Liberty Weekend," the British royal wedding, and the millennium.

**Peggy Wehmeyer** was hired by ABC at Peter's urging to be the first full-time religion correspondent on network TV. She was at ABC from 1994 to 2002.

**David Westin** replaced Roone Arledge as president of ABC News in 1997. He was division president when Peter anchored the millennium broadcast, 9/11, and two election cycles. He remains President of ABC News.

**Alexandra Wolfe** has been a friend of Elizabeth Jennings, Peter's daughter, since they were children.

**Tom Wolfe** is a writer and Alexandra

Wolfe's father.

**Bob Woodruff** was a London-based foreign correspondent for ABC News before moving to New York in 2002. He was named co-anchor of *World News Tonight* following Peter's death. One month later, while covering the war in Iraq, he was severely injured by a roadside bomb. He is back reporting for the network.

**Tom Yellin** was the executive producer of dozens of Peter's documentaries and news specials. He also produced *The Century* and *In Search of America* series. Together, he and Peter created the *Peter Jennings Reporting* series and PJ Productions. Tom is currently President and Executive Producer of The Documentary Group, the production company he founded in 2006 with Peter's wife, Kayce.

*Both my parents taught me that station in life really didn't make very much difference. . . . My mother was just plain giving and genuine. My father was, I think, my only hero.*
*—Peter Jennings*

# 1
## A CANADIAN CHILDHOOD

*Peter Charles Archibald Ewart Jennings was born in Toronto, Ontario, in 1938. He and his younger sister, Sarah, were the children of Elizabeth Osborne and Charles Jennings. His father was a prominent radio broadcaster for the Canadian Broadcasting Corporation (CBC), and Peter called him the most influential person in his life. Peter Jennings started his broadcasting career hosting* Peter's People, *a half-hour, Saturday morning CBC Radio show for children.*

SARAH JENNINGS: Peter was a naughty little boy, a very mischievous, very high spirited little boy. As a consequence, he was constantly getting into trouble. I don't suggest he was delinquent. I don't mean that at all. I mean he was into mischief.

PETER JENNINGS: *One of my earliest mean-*

*ingful memories is in Toronto . . . lighting the family crèche on fire, for reasons I've never fully understood, and my mother coming up to the top of this tiny little house where we lived, totally puzzled as to why her son would do this. . . . I suppose I was doing what little boys of seven or eight do — playing with matches.*

SARAH JENNINGS: In those days, polio was a threat in the urban centers, so people who could manage it would get out of the city and take their children to the country. We would go up to a beautiful lake called Stoney Lake, about an hour or two north of Toronto, where our grandfather had a cottage. When I say we, that meant my mother and Peter and I, because Dad would work six days a week and try to get up on Sundays to see his family.

My poor mother had these two naughty, mischievous children in tow. But Peter was a good person. He never did anything bad, or malicious, or mean. He was just full of high spirits.

SARAH JENNINGS: I think Peter was such an attractive little boy that people had high expectations of him. And from a very, very early age, he tried to respond to that, to do his best, to be the person that people wanted him to be — in the sense of, to do his work well, to live up to the very high expectations and hopes and dreams that people had for him.

BARRIE DUNSMORE: Peter was treated at home sort of like a young boy at a British public school. Manners, etiquette, proper behavior, proper dress were all very, very much of the family code. His mother was the enforcer of that. And you could see that in many of his attitudes and behaviors. He was a very polite man. I think his proper dress

Peter

*The Jennings family in London, 1952*

and, generally speaking, proper behavior was a function of that upbringing.

KEN AULETTA: Peter's mother was a sparkplug. I mean, she was just a pistol. . . . His mother made sure he had good manners. She was a short lady, but she was an intimidating presence in that house, in the nicest way possible.

BARRIE DUNSMORE: Elizabeth was a very elegant lady. She was very attractive, and she was a very big part of Peter's life. I think that in her own quiet way, she was a strong value person that he would bounce ideas off. I think he wanted to please her, too. Not as much as he did the father image, but certainly she was an important force in his life.

SARAH JENNINGS: It's no accident that Peter and I grew up in a household that was tuned in to broadcasting because our father, Charles Jennings, is one of the original pioneers of public broadcasting in Canada. He left the University of Toronto to go into radio broadcasting in Toronto, which was just then getting underway. He gradually moved up in the CBC. So we grew up in a household where our father was either on the air, or, as he went on in his career, became director of programming and then a senior executive with the CBC. Consequently, our household was very much tuned in to it. For example, Dad would take us down to the CBC studios on a Saturday morning, while he worked. We'd ramble all over the building and be taken in hand by the announcers who were on duty that day. They were always very, very sweet to us, allowed us to sit in the control room, or took us to the cafeteria.

PETER JENNINGS: *I knew that my father had an interesting job because there were always interesting people around the house. And I think it somehow seeped in.*

SARAH JENNINGS: In Toronto in the postwar period, many of the more educated Europeans came to North America — to the United States as well, I'm sure, but many to Canada — as displaced persons. They brought their talents as musicians, and writers, and dancers, and performers. The CBC is sort of the cultural nucleus of artistic activity, so if you were a program planner, you were in contact with all these people. And many of these programming meetings would take place around our dining room table, you know, fairly lubricated with the best available liquid refreshment possible. Shows like *Wayne & Schuster,* which was a comedy team that eventually came to the States and worked on the *Ed Sullivan Show,* would have their start over our dining room table or in my father's office. Pete and I were always flies on the wall, listening in or serving drinks or passing food.

BARRIE DUNSMORE: Charles Jennings' prominence was at its highest during World War II when he was one of the major newscasters on the CBC. The other prominent newscaster of the day was Lorne Green of

*Bonanza* fame. However, Green came south. Charles Jennings stayed up in Canada.

SARAH JENNINGS: In the late '40s, my father was asked to go abroad for UNESCO. He agreed, and he went to the Middle East and he traveled to France, and so we were left at home with Mom. While he was gone, CBC programmers came to Mom and asked if Peter could be allowed to host a Saturday morning music program for children. This was to be a request program. Children would write in from all across the country. It would be broadcast on the national network of the CBC, which is to say it would run coast to coast.

Mom agreed and Peter indeed did start the job. When Dad came home, he was flabbergasted, and outraged. . . . How could they do this? But the program was already well entrenched and extremely popular, so he very, very reluctantly agreed that Peter could continue doing the show. . . but Peter wasn't allowed to take the salary, which I think was fifteen dollars a week.

PETER JENNINGS: *[My father] was pretty angry. Mostly, I think, because I was getting money for it. And he thought they, the CBC, had done something wrong by going behind his back. I mean, my father couldn't stand nepotism. . . . And he certainly did not believe that his young son should be spoiled by being paid for doing something from which he was getting a lot of pleasure.*

SARAH JENNINGS: Peter just loved what he was doing. I think from day one he had this great passion and enthusiasm for radio, for television, and for broadcasting — for communicating.

These great bags of mail would come into our household. Of course, it had to be responded to. I can remember my parents, on the weekend, sort of answering all these little children's letters on Peter's behalf. He'd probably be out playing baseball or doing something. And the utter boredom that would set in because the same song would be requested every single week, no matter what day of the week. That was "The Teddy Bears' Picnic," which was a famous song played at that time.

*As a boy, Peter was not an enthusiastic student. He struggled academically and later declared that it was out of "pure boredom" that he dropped out of high school. "I loved sports. I loved girls. I loved comic books," he said. "And for reasons I don't understand, I was pretty lazy."*

SARAH JENNINGS: Peter went to public school in Toronto. Our grandfather had gone to this private boys' boarding school, called Trinity College School, in Port Hope, which is about sixty miles out of Toronto. It was like an American prep school, I guess, where students board and get home on school breaks, and so on. Our grandfather had gone to that school, and our cousins, so, in due time, it became Peter's turn to go. He went at the age of eleven, which was, I think, very painful for him in some ways. I think he missed his home very much. He loved his family and his family loved him, but off he went. And again, this mischievous, naughty streak got him into regular trouble at school.

There was a wonderful old headmaster, Mr. Tottenham. . . . In those days, when you were naughty, you were caned. You got six of the best, which was typical of British boarding schools. Pete got quite a number of canings, from what I understand. Finally, Mr. Tottenham told my mother that Peter had come down one morning after one famous caning and said to Mr. Tottenham, "Look, you see: only one bruise." So, no matter what they did he wasn't going to be tamed, that's for sure. It wasn't that he wasn't inter-

39

ested in ideas, but he was bored by school. He was just bored. He was very high energy.

PETER JENNINGS: *I was bad in school. I was bone lazy. . . . It was of far greater interest to me to get out and play hockey or football than to study literature or, God forbid, math and chemistry.*

SARAH JENNINGS: Well, he was not thrown out of TCS, or asked to leave. What happened was, it was a rather expensive school to send your children to, and when Peter went into the senior school, the headmaster brought my parents in and said, "Look, I think we're wasting your money doing this." By then, my parents had moved from Toronto to Ottawa. Peter came back home, allegedly to do high school. The pattern repeated itself. He had a wonderful time and enjoyed sports and so on. But again, there just was no learning to be had. He wasn't going to do any formal schooling. Again, I remember my sweet mother going in and talking at length with the principal. . . . What would Peter do? Well, fortunately, they had some sort of contacts with friends in the Royal Bank of Canada. So, Peter dropped out of school and got a job as a bank teller. I still go to the bank today, and bump into

*Peter (center) at Trinity College School*

middle-aged ladies who remember Peter as a bank teller. We always felt he'd either be president of the bank or in jail because he couldn't count. Every day you had to balance your cash. That was a hassle for him.

PETER JENNINGS: *My parents were very disappointed with me in school, but not angry — maybe not angry enough, maybe not insistent enough that I apply myself. I am very conscious that I did not apply myself until I was getting a paycheck, first as a teller in a bank, and then in broadcasting.*

*My dad back then was feeling that broadcasting was getting bigger and more complicated and riskier. And I remember him saying to me once, I'm not sure that the family should have too many eggs in the one basket. And so I said, well, I owe him this at least, having screwed up in school. So I went to work for the Royal Bank of Canada. I did it for two and a half, three years.*

SARAH JENNINGS: In the meantime, he was always still exploring in his own mind how he was going to get into broadcasting. And he set about trying to find a job for himself. He did this without any help from his family, although I'm sure that people in the industry knew that he came from a broadcast family.

He secured a job in a small, private, commercial radio station in Brockville, which is a small town along the St. Lawrence Seaway in Ontario, right opposite New York State. . . . And he was launched.

BARRIE DUNSMORE: I think Peter's relationship with his father was very, very important in terms of the kind of person that Peter turned out to be. I think he spent a good deal of time trying to do things that he thought would please his father and make his father happy with him. I'm sure his father would have been ecstatic with the success that Peter had, and not just the success, but the extraordinary contribution that he made to television journalism. But I do know that his father was very much in his mind as he went about his work for many, many years.

KAREN BURNES: I loved his father. We used to go up to Canada, and they had that stone house, and we'd sit by the fire, and his father would talk on and on. He was an utterly charming man, very much like Peter. But, you know, it was a tough act to follow to be Charles Jennings' son in Canada.

TED KOPPEL: Peter was driven by a sense that he had to match, if not exceed, his father. Charles Jennings has been referred to as the Edward R. Murrow of Canada. I suppose enough time has elapsed and there are enough young people in the world today that you have to say that Edward R. Murrow was in many ways the founding father of American television news as we know it today — a great CBS correspondent and anchor. And Charles Jennings was the Canadian equivalent. So Peter clearly wanted to idolize his father, wanted to follow in his father's footsteps, and did in many strange ways.

*Peter at his second radio job, Brockville, Ontario, 1959*

*Charles Jennings, 1937*

TODD BREWSTER: Somebody recently described Peter's father as the Walter Cronkite of Canada. He was actually the earlier generation than Walter Cronkite, and he was on radio not on television, but he had that quality of being the voice of the medium. He was known throughout the country. People would come up to him, Peter said, as he would travel around Canada, and they'd say, "Oh, your father helped me cope with the Depression" or "Your father was the man who led us through this crisis or that one." So I always thought there was a quality to Peter's father that Peter inherited and that he brought forward. You could see it in 9/11; you could see it in the *Challenger* disaster; you could see it in a number of places where he actually served that same role for a lot of Americans.

Peter had this story which he would tell off and on about his father in which he said his father said, "Come out here and describe this cloud pattern." I think it was after Peter made the decision to be a journalist and his father was sort of saying, "Let's see you show your skills here." Peter said, "Well, there's white clouds and there's some blue sky and there's blah, blah." And his father said, "Now, take that cloud pattern, divide it like a pie into eight pieces and describe the eight pieces," in a way to teach Peter that there was description and then there was description — there was a way of understanding. Of course, his father was a radio man, so the words were infinitely more important even than they were when you got to television. There's nothing to look at in radio. But Peter had that quality, I thought, throughout all his work, where he tended to really be very careful about the way he would describe something. And every time I heard him say that I thought, that's the residue of that moment. There were moments like that for Peter where something happened, a little epiphany or something, which I think informed the rest of his life. And I think that was one of them.

PETER JENNINGS: *I think I still — to a very great measure — want to impress my father. I don't mean to sound plaintive. But I never met any one person who had better values.*

CHARLIE GIBSON: You could not spend a lot of time with Peter Jennings without hearing a great deal about his father. We all have, I think, a sense in life that we want to prove to our parents that we're worth a darn, and we spend a lot of our lives, even after they're dead, trying to do that. But it was magnified with Peter. I think he had built the image of his father as a Canadian broadcaster into this kind of huge monolithic image in his mind of how great his father was. And I think much of Peter's life was trying to live up to that. I'm sure his father would say, "Peter, you surpassed me years ago." But it's very difficult for a son to internalize that.

I remember being at his book signing party when *The Century* came out. Don Hewitt, the executive producer of *60 Minutes,* came over and gave Peter the book and asked him to sign it. Peter did, and then closed it and handed it to Don. Don said, "Thank you," and Peter said, "No, no, that was a very special inscription." Don sort of looked at him quizzically, and Peter said, "I signed it right next to my father's name. I don't do that very often." His dad was something of a god in Peter's mind, and he spent a lifetime trying to live up to it.

*The chance to work at his father's CBC finally came in 1960, when Peter's experience at the Brockville radio station led to a stint with CBC Radio in Montreal. A year later, he made the move to television, joining a new station in Ottawa, where his duties included hosting a dance show similar to* American Bandstand. *The next year,*

*CTV, Canada's first private television net-work and a fledgling competitor of his fa-ther's CBC, hired the twenty-four-year-old as co-anchor of its late-night national newscast. It was at that point that Peter Jennings caught the eye of ABC.*

SARAH JENNINGS: Peter was not permitted to fly to the CBC by our father because again, it was an issue of nepotism. Dad took the view that if he tried to do that it would look as if he was trying to get his son a job. But since Peter went off and got his own first job, he really established his *bona fides*, if you like. Therefore, he was then free to apply to the CBC, the Canadian Broadcasting Corporation. And indeed he did, and he was hired.

PETER JENNINGS: *One of my first jobs at CBC Radio in Montreal was working on the northern service of the CBC, broadcasting for the Eskimos and to the northern communities in the eastern and western Arctic at ungodly hours. I had to go to work at two o'clock in the morning.*

*I was basically trained at the Canadian Broadcasting Corporation, which is public, in-dependent, but financed by the government, and its mandate was to operate as a public*

*service. I don't think we ever would have asso-
ciated the words "journalism" and "entertain-
ment" when I was growing up. Not to say that
journalism shouldn't be entertaining, fun, exciting. But the mandate of the CBC was to
serve the public, not merely entertain the
pubic.*

SARAH JENNINGS: In Canada, we have a
dual system of broadcasting. When Peter
joined the CBC, the private television network was just coming into being and new li-
censes were being issued to commercial stations. They were looking for talent and,
obviously, Peter looked promising, so he was
hired by a television station called CJOH in
Ottawa, which was the local commercial station there.

At a local station like CJOH, everybody
had to do everything. Peter would be reading
the news one moment, and then they had a
program called *Club Thirteen,* also known as
"Saturday Date," which was sort of a
teenage dance program. Pete was always up
for everything. I mean, he did the Miss
Canada Contest. He would, you know, announce serious awards programs. But he was
always a good sport about these things and
had lots of fun. I still run into people around
Ottawa who were young, teenage ladies in

those audiences, who've never gotten over it.

Then, when they began to knit together the commercial network, Pete was hired, at the age of twenty-four, to be the first, in this case, co-anchor. Those were the days of Huntley and Brinkley, so it wasn't just one anchor. Peter had a partner in a man called Baden Langton. These two anchored and started the CTV national news in Canada.

BARRIE DUNSMORE: Peter and I were both working in Canada — he as the anchorman for the CTV network, based in Ottawa at

*Hosting the Miss Canada Pageant, 1965*

that point, and I as the Toronto correspondent for that newscast. This was in '63–64. It was probably a year or more before we actually met. I must say that I found him even more exciting in the flesh than I did on television. He had this life force that seemed to surround him — his enthusiasm, his boundless energy and curiosity. He was one of those people that was just a great sense of nirvana to be around.

We were both young — in our mid-twenties. That was to some extent the nature of television news in those days. There weren't a lot of people with a lot of skills on TV. In Canada, most of the stations had gone on the air in the mid- to late '50s, and this was only a matter of a few years after that. CTV had never had a network at all and never had a network news program. So, the notion of putting young people on it was really not so surprising at that time.

I think it might have been surprising to some people that Peter emerged as one of the co-anchors of the newscast. His background in journalism at that point was rather limited. He had worked at a local radio station but had not achieved any great prominence either as a broadcaster or as a journalist. So when he took that job, it was largely on the basis of the fact that he was a good performer. I think that was recognized by him and by others. But within a very short period of time, I think he demonstrated his journalistic acumen.

ELMER LOWER: Peter came to our attention early in 1964. Dean Rusk, who was secretary of state under John F. Kennedy, made a trip up to Ottawa, Canada, on some State Department business. John Scali was the ABC State Department correspondent at that time. So he went along to cover Dean Rusk. He was getting dressed for dinner one night, going out to cover something in the evening, and while he was waiting, he turned on the commercial CTV in Canada, which had just started at that time and had been on the air for maybe a few months. He saw these two guys doing the news, sort of like a Huntley-Brinkley. At that time Huntley and Brinkley were very top flight in the US. Scali came back and said, "You ought to take a look at these guys." So we got a videotape of Jennings and brought it back down to New York and took a look at it.

Well, the best thing he had going for him was that his father, Charles Jennings, was the Edward R. Murrow of Canada during World War II. If Charles Jennings didn't say it on the Canadian radio at ten o'clock at night,

Canadians didn't believe it. At any rate, Charles Jennings was a very famous journalist in Canada. And I thought, well, maybe his son will be as good.

He was about twenty-four years old. He looked pretty young. We were looking for anybody with any kind of promise at all at that time. It was hard to get people to work for ABC then because they never believed ABC would put up the money to compete with CBS and NBC. So we invited him to come down to Atlantic City to be our guest at the Democratic National Convention that nominated Lyndon Johnson for president and Hubert Humphrey for vice-president. He spent the convention with us. He wasn't on air, but he traveled around with all the crews and the political correspondents, and he was very, very pleased with that. He was excited about it.

And then he went on back to Canada. After that we made him an offer. But we didn't make him an offer as an anchorman, and I'm not going to tell you that I even saw anchor possibilities in him that early.

PETER JENNINGS: *I had only been to New York once before in my life. And as exciting and as awesome as it was, it was pretty intimidating for a guy who was living in a tiny city in*

Canada. So when I was first offered this job by Elmer Lower, who was then the president of ABC News, I was very excited. And then I thought, what if I screw up? What if I can't handle it?

And so I said "no." And about six months later I woke up and said, "Holy Jesus, that was a mistake." And I wrote Elmer Lower and I said, "Excuse me, could I reconsider?" And he wrote back and said "yes."

# 2
# BOY ANCHOR

*Peter Jennings came to ABC as a reporter, covering major American news events from the Vietnam War to the civil rights movement, a story that had a profound effect on him. He later recalled his early ignorance of the South's history and "peculiar ways": "I was a twenty-something-year-old without even a college education, suddenly thrust into the racial bitterness that dominated American life at the time," he said. "This Canadian was apt to pronounce the final battle of the Civil War 'a-PO-ma-tox' instead of 'Appomattox,' which I did once on the air."*

TED KOPPEL: We were both a couple of kids pretending to be a lot more self-confident than we were. I guess we met for the first time — really met, where we became friends — on the [1964] Goldwater campaign. In those days, we had three people covering

*I am one of those Canadians who went to the United States because it was irresistible.*

—Peter Jennings

each presidential candidate. There was a principal television correspondent. His name was John Rolfson. There was the secondary television correspondent. His name was Peter Jennings. And there was the radio correspondent. And his name was Ted Koppel.

So Peter and I traveled together throughout much of the Goldwater campaign, and indeed were together on the last maniacal day before Election Day when, as I recall, the Goldwater campaign began in Montana, flew to South Carolina, back to Pittsburgh, and from Pittsburgh out to California. I mean, it was one of the craziest days I've ever seen, and it was a day that was sort of emblematic of a candidate who knew he was losing. And then [in Arizona], on Election Day itself, the Goldwater campaign announced that the lid was on, which meant they weren't going to be making any announcements until after all the returns were in. And Peter and I took advantage of that day.

It was the first day in weeks and weeks and weeks that we had had an entire day off. Somehow Peter got hold of a rental Austin Healey, a little British sports car. There is a mountain, Camelback Mountain, with a winding road. We got a stopwatch, and one of us would stand at the top of the mountain waving a white T-shirt, and then the other guy would gun the Austin Healey and drive up to the top of the mountain as fast as he could. And then we would change places. So we did time trials, trying to beat each other racing up the mountain. And it was — as he and I looked back on that day — it was one of the most carefree days that I think either one of us had had in a long time or were to have for many, many years to come.

SARAH JENNINGS: It's quite true that when he came and took the first job, he lacked a really solid grounding that anyone who had gone through the American educational system would have, but he had the desire to learn, the desire to know, and he was not afraid to ask questions. I think that's one of Peter's most interesting qualities, and those of us who have traveled with him and been around him sometimes are quite astounded — I won't say appalled — at questions that he'll pose at people. You'll be trying to buy a toothbrush in the pharmacy and, before you know it, you'll have the life story of the pharmacist and how many children he has and so on. If you're traveling with him, it can be a little exhausting. But from the point of view of his own interests, that's how he learned.

*On the road in the mid-sixties*

ELMER LOWER: I was getting good reports from him. And the [news] desk seemed to like to send him down South where all those sheriffs chased him around during the race riots. He liked that. It was kind of exciting for him. But we did not, at that time, have any idea that he would be our future anchorman.

*Just six months later, at age twenty-six, Jennings was named anchor of ABC's nightly newscast, which was renamed Peter Jennings with the News. He was the youngest anchor in the history of American network television, a feat particularly remarkable because he was, after all, Canadian. ABC's evening news program was running a distant third behind CBS's and NBC's. "ABC was in bad shape at the time," Jennings later recalled. "They were willing to try anything, and, to demonstrate their point, they tried me."*

ELMER LOWER: Peter was doing fifteen minutes of news at dinner time. The other networks had doubled their news time to thirty minutes for both Cronkite and Huntley-Brinkley. Also, they had about double the lineup of affiliated stations that we had. We didn't have one affiliate in the whole state of Ohio carrying the evening news. Today it's almost unthinkable that these stations wouldn't carry the evening news. At any rate, that's what he was up against. People have often asked me, "Well, was he a success?" I said, "Why, sure, he was a success with what our condition was at that time."

Remember, just a year before he came, ABC didn't have any news camera crews. They bought the news coverage from Tele News. So whatever Tele News was covering, that's what you put on the air. When I joined ABC, I told them, "Well, I won't come unless you agree to establish TV crews around the world." Now, we didn't establish all of them like you have now, but we made a start.

TED KOPPEL: It was sort of a pathetic excuse for a news division. It was fifth in a three-man — or a three-network — race. There was CBS. There was NBC. And then you sort of looked around, and somewhere back there was ABC. We did a fifteen-minute, black-and-white film newscast every evening. The fact of the matter is that if ABC

*I don't care who watches my show so long as they watch it and get something out of it aside from the fact that my hair is combed and my teeth are straight. —Peter Jennings, 1965*

had been more of a network in 1963, they wouldn't have hired me. And if they had been more of a news division in 1964, they wouldn't have hired Peter. So it was really to both of our benefits that it was such a pathetic news division, because they wouldn't have hired a couple of kids like us.

PETER JENNINGS: *I mean, it was ludicrous. I look back now, and I wonder to myself what they must have been thinking. At the time, ABC was really into kids' programming. . . . We didn't have any news tradition here like*

*In the ABC studio with father, Charles*

*CBS and NBC. And I think somebody said, "Let's go kids across the board."*

SARAH JENNINGS: I think it took a lot of confidence for him to come down and, at such a young age, really think that he could make a run of it, against such sterling and established broadcasters as Walter Cronkite. The photograph of Dad and Peter on the set . . . showed our father, who was still an active broadcaster, and Peter. . . . Dad was giving him hints, trying to tell him, "Now, my boy, read it this way." . . . I think Peter had tremendous pride, not in the arrogant sense, but confidence, you know, that he could try to do this. And well, he did try.

ELMER LOWER: At first, Peter's being a Canadian might have hurt him a little bit in the United States — and the fact that he insisted for a number of years on using Canadian expressions. It was almost as if he wanted to emphasize the fact that he was Canadian. I think that might have been a detriment to him.

PETER JENNINGS: *I almost didn't recover from some of my earliest arrogance. My first inauguration, as Marines approached the White House, I said glibly that their anthem was "Anchors Aweigh," which was of course the Navy song. I insisted on saying "shedule" until my Jewish friends asked me what Schul I had gone to in Canada.*

ELMER LOWER: I think being too young, too pretty, too inexperienced, and earning too much money — I think all those things hurt him. But when we'd discuss it with him, he said, "You got what you bought. I mean, I can't change this. I can't change twenty-six years old to thirty-six years old."

JOHN ANDREWS: Not many people get to be anchormen. To be an anchorman, and a successful one, you need to have some quality that is very hard to define. But obviously it's visible before you actually become the anchorperson. I think that's what Peter had. I mean, why else was he chosen at the age of twenty-six? I think it was an ability to connect with the viewer — with something that conveys both authority and sympathy. You understand the viewer's concern, where the viewer's coming from, what the viewer wants to know, what it means to the viewer. Plus, at the same time, you need to be comfortable. I mean, some people are comfortable sitting in that chair and other people aren't. Some people just look good in front of the camera.

They come alive for the camera. And I think Peter had that ability. It's very, very hard to define. Top models have it as well. Some people, it happens.

TED KOPPEL: Peter was a presence, always, even in those early days when he may not have been that great a reporter. And when I say a presence, it wasn't just women who looked up when Peter walked into a room — and, by golly, they did look up. I mean, Peter was movie-star handsome, and he had an aura about him, a great smile, just a look about him that said — he didn't have to say — "Want to have a good time?" It just radiated from Peter. And it affected men in the same way that it affected women — in a slightly different way, but men liked being around Peter, too. He was fun to be around, and he was an exciting presence to be around. And somehow, you felt more alive when Peter Jennings was in the room. So what was it like in those days? It was just good to be with him.

HILARY BROWN: My first impression of Peter was on our first and last date, which was in New York City in the '60s. He took me to the studios to watch him perform. That was his idea of a date. And, of course,

he was clearly a very good performer, and I was very impressed.

He was cocky, charming, informed, dismissive, but he was also very entertaining, very interested in you, and what you think, what your opinions are, and very interested in the world around him. He was one of the most curious people I've ever met. It was a sort of boyish quality about him that's cute, this quality of curiosity.

KAREN BURNES: Peter was my father's best friend. . . . He was this sort of round-cheeked, cocky guy who wore red suspenders. I remember them because I'd never seen anybody wear red suspenders before. He had a bit of a swagger and this incredible boyish charm.

The thing that was so charming about him was that Peter knew even then that he wasn't ready for that job. He knew he wasn't experienced enough to do it. He knew he hadn't paid his dues, and he always believed in paying your dues. He was generous. He took my father and he said, "Here, share my office. It's too big just for me." And so my poor father got dragged out of his little correspondent's cubicle and put in this huge office with Peter. The two of them would sit there with their feet up on the desks and kind of chuckle at the world they found themselves in.

But that was sort of how he was right from the start. He had everything, and he wanted to share it.

TOM BROKAW: Listen, when you're in your twenties and there's suddenly a Canadian who's the anchor of the ABC network news, you pay attention. And then Peter came to California to cover the [1966] Pat Brown–Ronald Reagan race for governor. We had a mutual friend who introduced us and said, "You should spend the day together." Peter was working for ABC. I was working for NBC. Frank Sinatra had loaned a Lear Jet, which was still pretty new in those days, to the campaign, so Peter and I were in this Lear Jet with our camera crews all day long bouncing around the high desert — Santa Maria, California, and other places — and we had a great time. We got along very well, and it was the beginning of a long friendship.

ELMER LOWER: I remember being in Manila at a meeting of the Asian Broadcasting Union, and Charles Jennings, Peter's father, was there representing the Canadian Broadcasting [Corporation]. He and Mrs. Jennings gave a little cocktail party, to which I was invited, in this hotel where we were staying. It was very nice. And right there, on the table, was Peter Jennings' portrait. They carried it all the way to Manila to have it in their suite when they gave their cocktail party. They were very proud of him. And they should have been.

PETER JENNINGS: *We went to a lunch here in New York — Chet Huntley and Walter Cronkite and young Peter Jennings. And some man stood up in the audience and said, "You know, you guys are just like — you guys are*

Selling the new face of ABC

*just in show business." And Brinkley drew himself up to his haughtiest height and said, "Excuse me. The only concession I make to show business is on the way to the studio — I stop in the makeup room and I have these bags under my eyes painted up." And Cronkite piped in, "Yes, and Jennings stops in and has them painted on."*

ELMER LOWER: One of my problems in selling him to television critics — and at that time, it was very important that television critics give him a good review — they thought he was too young. They thought that he was inexperienced. They thought he was too pretty. They thought he had too many girls around. And they thought he was being paid too much money. Other than that, what's wrong? So I traveled the country. I did a lot of traveling at that time, always calling on newspapers, calling on people who covered television for newspapers trying to get them to say a good word about him. It was very difficult.

The ratings were going nowhere. And so we knew we were going to have to do something. I always thought that I didn't want to lose him. I thought, "Well, if we can give him some more experience, I think there's a possibility." I didn't know he was going to still succeed as an anchorman. There are too many "what ifs" in that business.

PETER JENNINGS: *It was a little ridiculous when you think about it. A twenty-six-year-old trying to compete with Cronkite, Huntley, and Brinkley. I was simply unqualified.*

TED KOPPEL: It was a difficult period for Peter. You have to recall that, you know, I said it was a pathetic news division, but in the late '50s or early '60s — I guess it would have been the early '60s — ABC hired a man by the name of Jim Hagerty to be the president of ABC News. Jim Hagerty had been Dwight Eisenhower's press secretary. He was a formidable presence. And he determined that the way to turn ABC News into a credible news organization was to hire a bunch of print journalists; they obviously knew about reporting, and television people did not. So you had a bunch of names that may or may not be familiar to people today — guys like John Scali, who was the chief diplomatic correspondent for the Associated Press; Bob Clarke, who was the chief congressional correspondent for United Press International; Bill Lawrence, who was a legendary White House correspondent for the *New York Times*. They were all brought over and hired by Jim Hagerty.

So you had these crusty old print veterans who were ostensibly reporting to this young whippersnapper of an anchor who was all of twenty-six years old, clearly didn't have a lot of experience, and clearly didn't know a great deal. Peter was smart enough and sensitive enough to realize that this wasn't going to work.

PETER JENNINGS: *I realized, enough already, I hate it. I went off to the Middle East at the end of the 1967 war and came back to my em-*

*ployers and said, that's enough, I want out of here. And they said, yes — very eagerly, I realized. I think it would have been only a matter of time before they'd have fired me.*

SARAH JENNINGS: I think the first go-round was not successful. It was just a ratings game, obviously. And he was very young and inexperienced. I think he came to terms with that fairly rapidly. When Pete makes a mistake, he doesn't try to hide it. He tries to just acknowledge it and deal with it. I think that's exactly what happened in that first go-round: he realized he wasn't good at this,

---

### A.B.C. Replacing Peter Jennings

Mr. Jennings . . . said, "I have not been chopped from the show. This is my decision. The company has granted my request. I only hope they will use me in the field as they did in the studio. I have agitated for more field work because the studio job on a full-time basis is just not rewarding enough in terms of the trade or the profession." —*New York Times*, November 14, 1967

---

and he better go off and, you know, learn his trade, learn his business.

*Over the next year, Jennings threw himself back into reporting, covering everything from the Paris peace talks during the Vietnam War to the communist government in Cuba to the political conventions in the United States. Back in the trenches, he flourished.*

LYNN SHERR: Peter and I met in 1968. I was a reporter for the Associated Press. He was a hotshot at ABC. We met at a demonstration in Central Park that we were both covering. I was dazzled, and not just by his personality. Coretta King had just spoken, and I was taking notes, being a print reporter, figuring out how I was going to do my story. I watched Peter. The second — not the minute, but the second — Mrs. King was done speaking, he picked up a phone and dictated a story to radio that perfectly captured the essence of what had just happened, a thirty-second spot. He didn't write it down. I didn't even think he had time to think about it clearly. He had it composed in his head, and he just did it. It was an incredible performance. He knew how to do that.

CHARLIE GIBSON: I first met Peter in 1968. I was working at a tiny, tiny little station in Lynchburg, Virginia, and I used to watch him do the evening news at the tender age of twelve or whatever he was. I went down to the Republican National Convention. I financed my own way because I wanted to go to a convention. The Railroad Association used to sponsor lounges with food and sandwiches, and I ate all their free sandwiches. It was the only way I could afford to be in Miami.

And there was dancing — bands and music — after the evening session of the convention had recessed, and Peter was in there one night, dancing. I thought, "Son of a gun, this guy is not only a consummate broadcaster, he's not only one of the handsomest individuals I've ever seen, but he's an incredibly good dancer." And every single woman in the room wanted to dance with him. I thought, "Darn, he's got it all." I went up and introduced myself as somebody who worked in this tiny little station in Lynchburg, Virginia, and he was very courtly and polite to me, but he really wanted to get back to the dance floor. I was too shy to tell him, of course, that what I wanted to do was work for the network news department.

DIANE SAWYER: I was a terrible weather girl at a local ABC affiliate in Louisville, Kentucky. He was coming to town, and we didn't have money to hire a car for him, and somebody had to get him to the airport. I can't remember what he was covering, but I got assigned the task to make sure he got to the airport because somebody who knew the streets had to get him there. I was so excited — it was like Elvis coming to town.

This James Bond thing that always kept cropping up was for real, and that trench coat wasn't an artifice with him. It wasn't a pretension with him — he was really out there. It was in his joints and in his bones. You could tell that.

He came to town, and I got him to the airport very, very early because I drove so fast, and he sat and talked to me for a long time and seemed really interested in local politics. He debriefed me on everything, and I thought, "Gee, this is amazing. Obviously I have stood out to him. I've really connected to him, and he's so passionately interested in me." I think it was only about a year or two later that I came to New York and I saw him and I said, "I'm the girl in Louisville who drove you to the airport," and he had no idea who I was. So, in the moment, Peter can give you this absolute concentration, and then bring you up humbly later when you learned he could do it with everybody, of all ages, all sizes.

ELMER LOWER: I knew he needed more experience, so it wasn't a hard decision to say, let's send Peter to Rome or let's send him to Beirut or somewhere to cover the Middle East. That decision wasn't a hard one to make because he did need more experience, which he got over the years. . . . He went much farther than I thought he'd go in 1964. Much farther.

CHARLIE GIBSON: When [the anchor job] didn't work, Peter realized, "I need to go out and learn my craft. I haven't failed so much as I'm just too inexperienced." And so he, without a formal education, decided — and it's an extraordinary thing for someone to think through — decided, "I will go out and get an education about the world on ABC's dime."

MICHAEL CLEMENTE: Peter's motivation as a journalist was tied into his lack of formal education. He had this gnawing insecurity about not having finished formal school. I think he spent the rest of his life making up for that fact.

TODD BREWSTER: This was something that nagged him. He felt that he was a fraud. I mean, he certainly represented in his manner somebody who was very educated and experienced. In fact, he *was* very educated and experienced, but just in a bit different way. He didn't have the degrees to mount on the wall. And that sometimes nagged at him.

HILARY BROWN: Peter never, ever tried to hide the fact that he was a high school dropout. He sort of bragged about it sometimes, even though I think he was very aware that others were highly educated. I guess his way of compensating was to read voraciously. He was like a sponge, and he was also a very quick study, so he could absorb information very quickly and keep it in his head. I think that he became what we call an autodidact. He taught himself enormously. I think probably it was a real asset for him that he had been a high school dropout.

SAM DONALDSON: As he himself said, he was superbly unqualified when, at age twenty-six, a Canadian citizen who knew very little about the United States, he was made anchor of the ABC Evening News. I think it's remarkable because when he was taken off — you know, in our business you

*Red Square,
Moscow*

*With the troops
in Vietnam*

*Saigon*

don't go from number one to number two and number three, you go from number one to zero — instead of leaving or sort of whining about how fate had dealt him such a bad blow, he became tenacious in going overseas and learning the beat, learning the story, learning the people.

Peter was a great broadcaster to begin with — handsome, good voice, presence — and he became a great journalist. Ironically, I think one of the things that helped make him a great journalist was the fact that he suffered that downward mobility early in his life and had to pull himself up.

PETER JENNINGS: *I was the youngest anchorman there had ever been in American television. I wasn't very qualified, mind you; I got the job because of how I looked and sounded rather than how intelligent I was. And one day, after a while, I woke to realize that my bosses were going to take it all away from me because they thought I had failed. Boy, did it hurt. Someone upstairs was making a judgment about how little value I represented to them. And I was about to be discarded. I felt like an outcast, assigned to the category of failure. . . . That moment of failure for me was also a golden opportunity. Because I was obliged to figure out who I was and what I really wanted to be. I learned that I had not been happy, sitting in a studio, pretending to be smarter and more important to the country than I was. And once I had dusted myself off, which didn't take that long, I went off to have the very best time of my life, discovering the world.*

# 3
## THE TALKING TRENCH COAT

*Following his unsuccessful stint as a young anchor, Jennings was determined to build his journalism credentials abroad. In 1970, he was sent to Rome and, in 1971, was relocated to Beirut, Lebanon, to establish ABC's Middle East bureau, which was the first American television news bureau in the Arab world. Friends and colleagues recall how much he enjoyed the often glamorous life of a foreign correspondent.*

BARRIE DUNSMORE: When we lived in Rome, he knew virtually everybody in the neighborhood. I'm talking about the people who sold the flowers, the waiters in the restaurant, and sometimes the people sweeping the streets. He got to know their names. He would ask questions about them and their families. He had this incredible capacity to focus in on somebody, maybe not for very long, but to listen to them and focus in

*For all my failure in school, I was very aware from the moment
I got into broadcasting that—as I still feel—I don't have
enough time to learn as much as I need and want to know.*
                                              *—Peter Jennings*

and make them think that he thought they were the most important person in the world at that point. And I think to some extent it was that ability — when translated into being in front of a television camera and communicating with millions of people, but communicating almost on a one-to-one basis — that was one of the secrets of his success.

PETER JENNINGS: *I was in Rome for a year and a bit, and my boss called me up one night and said, "We want to transfer you to Beirut" — because I had been going to Beirut a lot and to North Africa and to Egypt and to Syria and to Jordan and Israel and Cyprus, all those places. Beirut was pretty nice in those days. They said, "We want to open a news bureau in Beirut. We'd like you to do it." I said, "Excuse me, do you know where I'm living? Do you know where you're calling?" I said, "I live in Rome, right?" Bill Sheehan was the boss then, and he called back a second time. He said, "We'd really like you to go and open this bureau." I said, "You can understand that I travel all over the place, but I live in Rome. Have you seen my apartment? I live on the Piazza Santa Maria." Well, the third time I knew they were serious. I didn't have any choice. And so I moved to Beirut. And it was a glorious city and experience in every imaginable way.*

BILL BLAKEMORE: When Peter showed up in Beirut, so soon after having left his early stint as a young, very young, anchorman in the States, he clearly was on some kind of a mission, as we came to see it, of breaking open the story. . . . Peter was coming overseas to get experience. The Middle East brought him alive. He saw the opportunity of it. He loved the story.

*Egypt, c. 1974*

MIKE LEE: A lot of people thought Peter had a particular passion for the Middle East. I think that was because that was the first big assignment he landed, and he would have taken virtually anything to get out of America, where he was considered maybe a pretty boy. He wanted to get away from all that and prove himself. There was a lot of conflict going on at the time, and so it was a good assignment for him.

PETER JENNINGS: *I had, as my responsibility for all those years, everything east of the Mediterranean all the way to India . . . I had all of the Arab world, I had the territories that were occupied by Israel, I had Greece, and I had Cypress and occasionally Turkey. I had Iran and Afghanistan and Pakistan — I mean, I thought I had died and gone to heaven.*

BILL BLAKEMORE: You could see that he was already enjoying, for the first time in his life, I think, living and working amid people who had no idea who he was because the people in the Middle East didn't watch ABC News. And so Peter began to discover that he could do it without the influence of his father, without the fame of having been a young anchorman. Here he was in the Middle East, just being himself, which was a very intelligent, very curious, very energetic man, full of fun and love for people. Who was so curious when he got anywhere near a story that you just had to race to keep up with him. I'm sure that was the beginning of his real self-confidence as an individual journalist, in which he began to really feel his muscles.

BARRIE DUNSMORE: Being a foreign correspondent for an American television network in the 1960s was just about the best job in the world. . . . We were able to travel to some of the most interesting places. We flew first-class for the most part, at a time when flying first-class really meant something. We stayed in the best hotels. We did, however, go to some of the worst places in the world, where it was dangerous to be, where wars and other such things were happening. But between the times when things were dangerous, things were very, very good. I spent months of my life in a suite at the St. George Hotel in Beirut, as did Peter, before the office in Beirut was opened up.

One of the things about that time was that communications were very primitive in most parts of the world. We would often go off for weeks. I remember being off once for more than a month in Saudi Arabia, where I was completely and totally out of contact. I know Peter had similar experiences. We would go up and down the Nile on trips to find out about things in Egypt. We had time to read books about the places that we were visiting and working in. It was an entirely different world then from what we have today.

Peter absolutely thrived in this atmosphere of foreign correspondent of the 1960s, given the freedom that he had. He was able to do the things that he really and truly wanted to do, to find out about the Middle East, to find out about its traditions and its history, to meet as many people as he could, the famous people and the powerful people, but also the people on the streets.

BILL BLAKEMORE: I think one of the reasons he came to care about the Middle East so much is it was the first sizable story, with all kinds of danger and tragedy within it, that he could get his arms around journalistically. And he realized very soon that he had the privilege of coming to understand it in its complexity in a way that people back in the United States didn't. So I think he always felt a responsibility to try to help people back in the States understand the various points of view of the entire Middle East and not to accept any monolithic attitude towards it, which he understood could lead simply to hatred.

PETER JENNINGS: *There are nineteen countries in the Arab world, and I worked in them all. And I did a lot of stories in those days which said, "Hey, hold it, folks, Arabs are people. They don't just ride camels, they don't all live in tents. They drive Mercedeses . . ." And, of course, as we went through the '70s, we found that they had a considerable amount to do with our economic destiny.*

BILL BLAKEMORE: Every time we'd put the show on, every night, we were trying to hit home runs. Peter was always trying to hit home runs. It was his nature. He was bored with anything less. Of course back in the '70s in the Middle East he had access to people who were leaders. I remember one of the first people was King Hussein, who, after Nasser suddenly died in 1970, was the longest lasting Arab leader. And we flew down to Jordan and Peter charmed King Hussein.

CHARLES GLASS: The first time I saw Peter was in 1972 in Beirut. . . . I saw him standing in the rain in front of the building that housed the ABC office, wearing an old

Jordan Inter-Continental
Amman, The Hashemite Kingdom of
Jordan
Oct. 19, 1970

Dear Mom and Dad,

I'm afraid that my long and serious letter that I said I would write is being postponed, not by a reluctance to write it but simply by the chain of events which have kept us working like mad...
The highlight here in the last couple of weeks has been an hysterical evening with His Majesty. I was invited to one of his general's homes for dinner and then to our surprise, mine at least, the King showed up for dinner, too. The evening began soberly enough but ended with His Majesty and yours truly throwing pillows across the room at each other and then a long serious dissertation on what his troops had been through in the heat of the recent battle. A good deal of insight was gained into a fascinating and very determined little man.
Other than that we have been chasing the battles around the country, nipping

into Beirut for an occasional good meal, very occasional, and going to bed here when the curfew starts at nine every night...

I have done a great deal of work as I said I was going to do, a story a day at least, and there is some general satisfaction in New York I'm told about the quality of it...

God bless, keep well and happy both of you.

Pete

trench coat that I later learned had belonged to his father. He looked to me, first of all, like a movie star, and second of all, like the archetype foreign correspondent . . . jumping into a taxi, like he was going off on a story. It wasn't very long after that, that we met, and I started doing some work for him at ABC.

It was a very tough time for Peter when we first met. His father had just died. He had just married Annie Malouf, a Lebanese woman that he'd met in Beirut. And adjusting to the loss of his father for

*With Anouchka Malouf on their wedding day, 1973*

him was very difficult. We became close, I think, because it was a time when, unusually for him, he was very open. And self-reflective, which he tended not to be, as a rule. He had a slight shield, which enabled him to cover some of the worst stories in the world without being overaffected or overemotional about them.

In those days, before the war in Lebanon began in April of 1975, Beirut was the place that all the journalists went back to after covering wars in Egypt or Jordan or Israel. It was the peaceful base where you enjoyed yourself and had your R & R before going

91

back to some other place that was a bit more difficult.

There's no doubt that I and just about everybody else who got to know Peter in Beirut liked him enormously. He gave the most lavish and wonderful dinners at his and Annie's apartment overlooking the sea in Beirut. They had a beautiful flat in Ain al-Mreisse in West Beirut, right on the water, above a restaurant called the Spaghetteria. When Peter would get hungry, he'd call down to the Spaghetteria and they would bring up a wonderful Italian dinner, pasta and veal and Italian wines and so on. And whenever he came back from Iran he'd bring a lot of caviar, which he'd share with everybody who came over to the house.

BILL BLAKEMORE: Beirut in those days was the world's best kept secret: fourteen major religious groups, no one of them a majority, a very vibrant intellectual community, a lot of universities, a lot of businesses — and stories everywhere: down in Israel, over in Jordan, the Palestinian story, the Cyprus war. Peter loved it because within a very short plane flight of an hour or two in almost any direction there was yet another good story. All these stories, which were sometimes tragic because of the war, but were great news. The agony of the Middle East was beginning to come to the fore after the Vietnam War started to die down in those years.

I rarely knew Peter not to be having an awfully good time. His mind was constantly ranging somewhere else. He always wanted to be looking into something else, working on another project. But there was a great social life in those days in Beirut. People worked hard, they studied hard, and they played hard. You know, he was handsome as a movie star, wildly intelligent, and curious, and he made a great many friends there. It was all part of a very happy, youthful social life, in which people were at each other's houses becoming good friends when we weren't flying off to some other romantic story or war story in the neighborhood.

HILARY ANDREWS: I met Annie Malouf, and she and I became very good friends. We were invited over to the house, but Peter wasn't there. We heard so much about him — this wonderful, charming, gorgeous guy. I was having a birthday party very soon after that, and I said, "Look, bring him along to the birthday party." So he came, and he was wearing a kilt, which was very amusing for all of us girls because we were all wearing hot pants and little mini skirts. We thought it

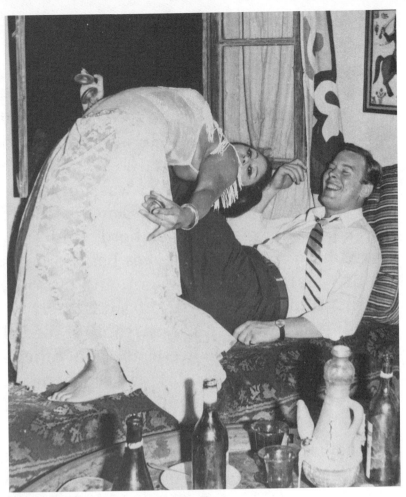

*Between stories in the Middle East*

was hilarious that Peter should come in a kilt.

He was very charming — sexy and charming. And he was a very hospitable guy. He loved to invite people over. But he was a very, very professional journalist as well. He worked incredibly hard. He was always off here, there, and everywhere. And in the meantime, Annie and I spent a lot of time together, waiting for our husbands to come home from wherever they were.

JOHN ANDREWS: I was teaching at the American University of Beirut. Peter was obviously a journalist. He'd established the ABC bureau in Beirut, and he came to a party that we were having — that my wife was having — and I said to him, "Peter, I'm fed up with teaching. I want to become a journalist. What should I do?" He said, "John, come and be my soundman. We're going to Pakistan next week." So he was my introduction into the world of journalism. One of the very first things he said to me was, "John, journalism is meant to be fun," and I've always remembered that. He liked to get into what people were doing, why they were doing it. He wasn't being glib or ridiculously light hearted, but it meant that he had a certain enthusiasm for the job. He liked to get into what people were doing, why they were doing it. He always had this *joie de vivre*.

HANAN ASHRAWI: I met Peter in 1968 in Beirut. I was an undergraduate at the American University of Beirut, and there was a whole group of reporters in Beirut, and I was in the General Union of Palestine students. I was also responsible for information.

At that time, the Middle East was undergoing a tremendous transformation as a result of the 1967 War. There were all sorts of changes, and it was the beginning of the resistance, the beginning of the underground *fedayeen* movement. Peter was intrigued by that. He was intrigued by the Palestinians because he said they were totally unknown to the West. He wanted to know who the Palestinians were. And he did a film on the new Palestinians. That's how we met. He wanted to see the young students, the new generation. He wanted to go beyond the label and the stereotype to understand Palestinian culture, Palestinian reality, Palestinian history. It was unusual to see in a reporter. But the whole region was being transformed by the Arab defeat of 1967, by the loss of Palestine. Peter had his antennas up. He was very sensitive to these transformations, to the fact that we were beginning to address new realities, and so he was constantly on a quest. He was out there following leads, following threads, but also trying to understand the depth and the significance of this transformation. He was there at a time of serious challenge, but at a time of tremendous promise. And he wanted to be there. He relished the excitement and the sense of discovery.

Peter was very glamorous to many people. He was really the heartthrob everywhere he went. Women would do a double-take. They found him absolutely irresistible. Every time he would come to see me or my classmates, the college girls would just go berserk over Peter. I think in a sense he knew that, but I don't know whether that made him conceited or that made him exploit his charm. No, he was absolutely charming. That's the word. He was charming. But he never exploited women, and this is very important. He always had relationships with women who were intelligent, who were his intellectual equals, or even sometimes superiors. He wanted to be intrigued by women's minds, wanted to be challenged. He was always looking for that sharp mind. Because he wanted to lock horns, to speak with an equal mind.

HILARY BROWN: Oh yes, Peter led a very glamorous life overseas. He certainly gave the perception of tossing off his stories between skin dives. He jetted around the world, and he knew everybody, and everybody came to know him. If you were in his wake, which I often was — I would be sent to a location where he had been — people would immediately ask, "Do you know Peter Jennings?"

I always thought he looked a bit like Errol Flynn. He was tall and he was well built and very athletic. And enormously charming. I mean, he could turn on the charm like a searchlight, and that was devastating to a lot of women.

I think Peter loved being a foreign correspondent. In fact, I suspect that maybe that's really what he loved the most — doing stories overseas, and bringing them back to the American viewer, making those stories come alive. He certainly looked the part. Of course, he had a beautiful trench coat and a very nice battered briefcase, which I think he kept with him until the very end because it was always there in his office — a very deep but very, very smashed up briefcase. I guess to him it symbolized those glory years abroad.

PETER JENNINGS: *For six years — six years — I never talked about anything but the Middle East. It's like taking drugs; you never get it out of your system.*

*Jennings' life as a foreign correspondent was exciting, but it could be grueling and*

*Interviewing Egyptian President Anwar Sadat in the Sinai, 1974*

*was often danger-ous. During these years he covered, among other tur-bulent events, the Indo-Pakistan War, constant conflict between Israel and its Arab neigh-bors, and the civil war in Lebanon.*

JOHN COOLEY: Peter's life overseas was like most of the foreign corre-spondents on that particular beat: it had its ups and downs. The glamour side of it was probably more perceived at the other end of the line on screen, rather than out where he was working, on or off camera. It was a big job, and it was a very exacting one. . . . We were having coffee in a hotel café in East Beirut, and somebody threw a hand grenade into the café. It was pretty close. None of us was hurt, but there was a lot of glass around, and a couple of people were thrown to the floor. Peter's first concern was whether any-body in the hotel or in his group or even out-side was hurt. He immediately got up and began to check that out, long before he tried to contact ABC or do a report on the whole incident.

BILL BLAKEMORE: When we came back from the Bangladesh War, we were marching with these guerrillas toward where the front line was, and one of the guerrillas came back towards us with a collaborator he'd captured whose hands were tied. He saw that there was this film crew, and he suddenly started getting very boastful, and said, "I'm going to execute this man." Peter turned around and the three of us turned around immediately, instinctively. We walked away and put our camera down to make sure that if the man were executed, it wouldn't be because we were there. That was Peter. He instinctively understood what was right in journalism. I've always been very proud of having been with Peter at that moment. He had a very highly developed journalistic ethical sense. And when he was faced with the actual test, he instantly did the right thing.

JOHN COOLEY: He was very, very strict about set-ups in TV combat situations. Example: One morning during the heavy fighting in Beirut in the civil war, I had the misfortune to go out with a Korean cameraman who carried chocolate bars and cigarettes to some of the guerrillas who were manning a barricade near our neighborhood. Whenever they saw him coming with his camera, they knew he had goodies for them, and they would set up their guns and start shooting. That was a perfectly calm morning, and in this particular episode, he provoked a major fire fight, in which I'm sure some people were killed. The Vatican mission was set on fire very close to us in that battle. I was scared out of my wits. And I was hiding behind some sandbags. When we got back to the bureau, Peter learned about the whole thing, and one of his first reactions was, "We gotta fire that cameraman." He was very, very concerned about set-ups, which was always a no-no in television combat coverage. Peter was strong on that subject.

JOHN ANDREWS: He wasn't a war freak. On the other hand, he wasn't war shy. I mean, he did report from Vietnam, and he did report quite a bit from the Beirut civil war. He didn't relish risking his neck. But he knew that to report the story, he would have to be involved, and so he was.

BARRIE DUNSMORE: I don't think that he was a traditional war correspondent in the old war-lover sense. He did it because it was part of the job. . . . There's no question that he was able to put aside his anxieties and go where the story demanded him being, but he didn't necessarily have to enjoy it.

HANAN ASHRAWI: To him, a situation in a state of flux or turmoil, a situation in the making, was a story that had to be told. And so he got as close as possible to the core of that story, which meant quite often he got close to situations that were quite dangerous. He didn't do it as a sort of cheap thrill. He did it because he wanted to get to the core of the story.

HILARY BROWN: I don't think Peter liked combat at all. In fact, he would be quite frank that he was scared sometimes. But he had to do it, and so he did do it, and of course he did it very well, right up to the end.

RUPEN VOSGIMORUKIAN: We were in Rawalpindi [Pakistan] in '73, working on a drug story. The fifth of October we finished work and came to the hotel. I went up to take my shower. Peter called and said, "Come down quick." I came and there was a twenty-five-people table. The sixth of October is my birthday. Peter had invited people from the hotel, people I don't know. There was cake, and people I don't know started to sing "Happy Birthday." He did those kinds of small things that he knew how to please people.

We were sitting and having fun — drinking. A guy comes up and says, "Mr. Rupen, there's a phone call." I run to the phone. It was New York; I think it was [executive producer of ABC Evening News] Av Westin. He says, "Rupen, I've been trying to reach you all day. Where's Peter?" I said, "He's next door." He said, "Well, you'd better get him quick. There's a war going on." The Sixth of October War. I said "Where?" He said, "All over the Middle East. Go to Beirut now, now, now!" So I went to Peter and I said, "Peter, we have to go to Beirut. There's a war going on." As happy as he was from the champagne and the vodka, it took him two seconds to sober up, took us three minutes to pack and get in the car, because we did not have a plane that went to Beirut from Rawalpindi. Pan Am used to fly from Karachi. So we drove to Karachi, and he knew the Pan Am director in Karachi, whom he called. He said, "You have a plane taking off in fifteen minutes; we'll be there in ten; don't let that plane take off." Finally we arrived at the airport, straight to the tarmac, in the plane, threw everything in, flew straight to Beirut. A car was waiting at the airport. Drove to Damascus.

We were driving in the middle of nowhere with nothing to hide under. There was a wall on our left. We didn't know there was an airport next to that wall. And suddenly there was an Israeli Air Force attack on that air base. The car we were in started to jump from the concussions. The driver didn't tell us that he had eight gallons of gasoline in the back of the car, so any shot would have blown us up to the air. Two seconds after the explosion of the bombs, which were falling, and flames striking down, Peter took his small tape recorder and started to record for radio. He goes, "Camera, camera." Of course, the camera was in the back. I got the camera, and he started to make the stand-uppers. Planes flying behind him, strafing. I think he did not realize sometimes the dangers. He had more worries about what he's going to say than the danger he was going through.

Fifteen years later, we went to Sarajevo. He was an anchorman then. And we were five or six in a tank going from one side to the other. That time they were shooting cats running on the street. For a minute, I saw

*With longtime cameraman Rupen Vosgimorukian, Saudi Arabia, 1974*

Peter with a helmet on his head and five people around him. "Peter, why do you have to do this? What do you have to prove? Why do you take these risks?" He did not answer. He would do that quite often; he would answer you three, four minutes later. Maybe because he was thinking about something else. He comes later to my ears and whispers, "To inform."

RUPEN VOSGIMORUKIAN: ABC was small then. We did not have as many crews and as many correspondents. So between me and him we practically covered all of Africa several times. We were supposed to be in the Middle East bureau in Beirut, but we used to travel nonstop. Peter was a workaholic. Back from trips . . . and he didn't want to lose a day. We would hop to another plane and go in another direction. Sometimes it was Europe, sometimes it was the Soviet Union, sometimes it was Greece. Borders had no limits for him. . . . Easy stories were very easy to do; and when the story was difficult, I could see the satisfaction he had in achieving what he did.

JOHN ANDREWS: We had a great time with Peter. We really did. We went to Karachi [Pakistan], where Zulfikar Ali Bhutto, who was still alive and hadn't been executed, gave an address to more than a million people. We went to Islamabad. We went up to Hunza, which was a kind of a Shangri-la in the wild mountains of the Karakoram Range. It was really quite something. And Peter was able to get links to people — to the American ambassador, to this person and that person. It was really very impressive.

He had a certain star quality about him. He was able to get to the very top people. Something about his mannerism, the way he used his voice, the way he used his charm. So although he wasn't the same kind of star that he later became, nonetheless he was a big deal as a foreign correspondent. And he really was a young guy. I was almost in awe of him. I'm sure a lot of my contemporaries were as well. He was someone you looked up to.

BILL BLAKEMORE: We were in Bangladesh. We'd been going in and out covering the Bangladesh War, each day going out with the Mukti Bahini guerrillas, and coming back to the Grand Hotel in Calcutta. One night we came back and we had a bunch of stuff to do. And Peter said to me, "Bill, you do the radio tonight. Just do a couple of spots." I said, "Fine." I was new to journalism, and I was an academic. I knew how to write a long, complicated, academic paper. So I sat down and started planning how I was going to tell this forty-five-second story. About a half an hour later, Peter came by. We had to go off and do some story. "Have you done the radio?" he asked. I said, "Well, I'm still working." He said, "What?" And he said, "Get up." And he sat in my chair in front of my little typewriter. He said, "Now, where did we go today?" I told him and he typed it out. He said, "Now, who did we see there?" I told him and he typed it out. "Why did we go there?" I told him and he typed that sentence. He ripped the paper out and said, "There's your spot. Go feed it. We've got to get to work, so let's go." He basically taught me the essence of journalism in about as long as it takes to type a forty-five-second radio spot. And it was a brilliant lesson.

RUPEN VOSGIMORUKIAN: Peter was one of the rare correspondents that I would sometimes throw the microphone to. We did not have the luxury of having soundmen then. Most of the stories were me and him. I remember a particular day when Syrian prisoners were released from Tel Aviv and they arrived in Damascus. Suddenly, hell broke loose, and there were people all over the airport. Next to the 747's wheels, the door opened and the Syrian prisoners started to come out. It was an unbelievable situation that no one knew would happen. I was up on the stairs on the plane, and Peter was down. I just threw him the mike with a long cable. He knew what for. He took the mike, and I think it was one of the most powerful standuppers he had ever done.

You didn't have to tell him. He knew what was coming. He knew the situation, and, by God, he knew how to ad-lib. As if he had lived in Damascus for six months, to be able to make that standupper with the feelings of

the local people, of the soldiers that are coming, what was their ego about.

Every day at dinner, when the work finished, we sat down and discussed what did
work, what did not work, and how can we do
next time something to make it better. I
learned everything from him.

BILL BLAKEMORE: We went to south India
and spent ten days driving around, doing
stories about this remote part of the world,
[which was] beginning to have environmen-
tal and overpopulation problems. I learned
so much watching him work there — about

the art of the standup, the on-camera, about how to make things come alive. He always made the point: "Don't stand like you're in front of a stage set. Touch the surroundings where you are. Bring it alive so that this two-dimensional medium we work in is one in which people can imagine being there and touching it." So he did one on-camera from the back of an elephant. Another one about overpopulation — he just gathered some Indian street kids around him and started snapping his fingers. And they started imitating him. He told the cameraman, "Start rolling." The kids were snapping their fingers. Peter turned to the camera and said, while snapping his fingers, "This is a game, but it's telling us something: every time you click your fingers, another child is born in India."

He had this instinctive way of using his very attractive presence, his rich, dramatic imagination, and his sense of how the camera could bring a story alive and make it possible for the audience to imagine being there.

RUPEN VOSGIMORUKIAN: The first time I found out he hates to fly we were going to — I don't remember. There were no computers then; there was his typewriter. He was sitting next to me, and I hear him typing on his typewriter, angrily. I said, "Peter, there is no paper." "Never mind!" "Why are you typing?" "So I can think about something else!" Later I found out he was doing this to not think about the plane, which was just taking off. He had to do something, to think about something else. I said, "If you're afraid of flights, you're in the wrong business." "Yeah, I know, don't remind me."

BILL BLAKEMORE: I can remember two or three times when we were flying around the Middle East and we'd have to get one or two martinis into him before he'd get on a plane in any kind of state at all. He just hated flying.

*The hard work paid off: Jennings earned respect as a skilled and savvy foreign corresondent and became an acknowledged expert on the Middle East. Though he was forced to fend off criticism that he was anti-Israeli and pro-Palestinian, Jennings said he was merely standing up for the quality he prized most in journalism: fairness.*

PETER JENNINGS: *Somebody in the superstructure understood that if we in the United States were going to understand the Middle East, we had to start covering something other than the world as seen from the Israeli point of view.*

HILARY BROWN: The Middle East, of course, has always been an enduring conflict and endlessly interesting, and probably endless. . . . And Peter was one of the first mainstream American journalists to see that there was actually another side to the Arab-Israeli dispute — that there was a Palestinian side. And yes, he was very interested in getting that across. But I would say he was always scrupulously objective. He made a tremendous point of that.

CHARLES GLASS: There was no question that Peter felt very strongly for Palestinian refugees in Lebanon and in the West Bank and Gaza, whom he met and whose children he befriended. I can remember going to villages in south Lebanon with him, and he'd suddenly disappear, and you'd find him playing soccer in some garden with a bunch of kids.

HANAN ASHRAWI: We were under occupation. I was in Beirut. I was a student, and I was forbidden to come home [to the West Bank] because my home was under Israeli occupation. So he used to go visit my parents and then he used to come back and tell me about them.

MIKE LEE: Some people later said that, well, he was too lopsided. He preferred the Arab view over the Israeli view. I really don't think that's the case. Peter did feel very strongly that all viewpoints needed a fair shake on the air, and he felt sometimes that one side wasn't getting that air time. Particularly the Palestinian cause.

He felt the story needed to be balanced. That people needed to make up their mind. And of course, the Palestinians were for many years considered underdogs in refugee camps in Lebanon. But if you watch carefully the coverage Peter led and helped engineer throughout the years, there was quite a bit of coverage of the difficulty the Israelis were facing as well.

BARRIE DUNSMORE: I think that the early accusations that Peter was pro-Palestinian came at a time when there was very, very little attention being paid to the Arab side generally, and certainly to the Palestinians. Anyone who was willing to talk about them and to try to explain their position was seen as carrying their baggage. I think, over a longer period of time, that it should have become evident that Peter's interest in that part of the world was not that he was pro-Palestinian; he was interested in telling the American people what was going on in that part of the world, and you could not tell the story unless you told the story of the Palestinians.

JOHN COOLEY: Peter was infinitely curious about the fate of obscure people, and also minorities who may not have been getting the best deal in the world. And that was illustrated by one of the very first projects I worked on with him, along with Barrie Dunsmore. We did one of the very early documentaries for ABC News, on the Palestinians and their problems. We interviewed Yasir Arafat way back then, as well as a lot of Palestinian intellectuals and other professionals who were not guerrillas or ragged refugees, which was the stereotype then of the Palestinians. The documentary was, I thought, a fine piece of work, and Peter guided it through. It was called "Palestine: New State of Mind." And I think it would still stand up very well today.

PETER JENNINGS: Having lost all faith in Arab governments, the United Nations, the superpowers, Palestinians are today more convinced than ever that their destiny is and must remain in their own hands. As yet, they pose no serious threat to the Israelis. But they will. Their emerging national consciousness is the most significant development in this region since the end of the war in 1967. Until they are satisfied there will be no peace in the Middle East.

JOHN COOLEY: Peter always tried to give both sides of any controversy a fair shake. The problem in the Middle East, of course, is that they don't have just two sides; they have three or more sides. Peter was always very, very devoted to showing every aspect that he could. If he were with us today, for example, doing a piece on the Middle East, on the evacuation of Gaza, he would show the woes of the Israeli settlers who don't want to leave their settlements. At the same time, he would give equal time to the Palestinian side of it. And probably some more time to the outside people who were trying to help resolve the whole issue. I have never in my life met anybody who was as fair-minded, as anxious to get all sides of a conflict, as he was.

PAUL FRIEDMAN: We were on the West Bank, and then we went into Amman, Jordan. He insisted that I spend some time with some Palestinians, who were talking about their feelings about Jerusalem. He said, "You know, this is not for any story or anything. But you need to understand that these people feel as strongly, and as emotionally, about Jerusalem as the Israelis, to whom you have had such easy access. Now you have a chance to talk to Palestinians about how they feel about this." That was what he was interested in. But to say that he was anti-Semitic or anti-Israel, that hurt him a lot. And it was just unfair.

BILL BLAKEMORE: Peter was at least as pro-Israeli as he was pro-Arab. Peter naturally had a bit of contrary, journalistic, skeptical instinct in him. When he heard one point of view, he said, "Well, that's interesting. And what about this?" And he'd sit and listen. But he was always working to be fair. I think history will bear him out on this. He covered all sides very thoroughly.

He may have become known as pro-Arab because he happened to be the first American network correspondent to establish a bureau in the Arab world. The Arab world is enormous, with a vast amount of cultural complexity and religious complexity. So some people may have mistaken Peter for

116

being pro-Arab, when he was at least as pro-Israeli. We saw this time and again, when he would go back and forth.

Peter was a very compassionate guy. He was a combination of compassion and discipline. When you'd see him sometimes tearing up when he was listening to somebody tell their story, whatever their religion, you could tell that he was listening to the person.

CHARLES GLASS: He wasn't pro-Arab or pro-Israeli. Or in fact, I should say, he was both pro-Arab and pro-Israeli. He loved Arabs and Israelis. He had close friends in the Arab world and in Israel. He covered the story very fairly and very objectively but also with great concern for the people on both sides of it, that they not suffer, and that [they] not make each other suffer.

Peter stands out as being pro-Arab because everyone else was so pro-Israeli. But in fact, all Peter was, was fair. He told it down the line. Arabs were kicked out of Israel in 1948. Everyone knows this. Even Israeli historians concede this now. Palestinians are still sitting in refugee camps in Gaza, the West Bank, Lebanon, and Jordan, and Syria. Why? These are questions that have to be addressed, and Peter, unusually for [an] American broadcast journalist, addressed these problems, and addressed them for a long time, and didn't let go of them just because he went to New York. He didn't lose contact with those stories or the people with whom he had become friends. They weren't just stories to be forgotten for him. These were real, flesh-and-blood people whose lives mattered to him, and he tried to make those lives matter to his audience.

YAEL LAVIE: As an ABC colleague, as a producer, but above all as an Israeli, I really admired Peter's agenda about the Middle East. He never gave up on it. That was the story he had passion for, almost as much as the people of the Middle East itself. And I think he was perceived many times as pro-Palestinian because, yes, that part of the story did appeal to him. His passion for the region, though, was genuine. As an Israeli, I can tell you that many times he was perceived as pro-Palestinian. As a producer, an Israeli producer, it was sometimes hard to get him interviews on the Israeli side because of that. You have to understand, when you live in a country that in the fifty years of its lifespan has seen five wars, has seen terror attack after terror attack on a daily basis — so much so that it becomes routine — and basically fights for its existence, surrounded by countries that are enemies, that passions run high. And Peter's sympathy to the Palestinian side, rightfully so though many times, was perceived as anti-Israeli. But that's also par for the course for the region. And I think above all, as an Israeli, I admired his passion for the story itself.

RUPEN VOSGIMORUKIAN: Peter would scratch, scratch, scratch to the bottom to get to the reality. And sometimes that scratching created a lot of problems. He would not be happy unless he knew the deep inside of the reality. And that's professionalism. Sometimes the reality did hurt a lot of people. After all, reality's reality.

For example, we were in Syria during the war in a hospital. One of my friends said, "Rupen, in that room they are operating on an Israeli pilot." Right away: "Peter, let's go." Went there, soldier operating. Surprisingly they let us in — the control was not as strong as it is today — and Peter said to the doctor, "How are you feeling to operate [on] an Israeli pilot?" The doctor did not answer. Two times he didn't answer. So Peter got a little bit angry [and] said, "You could at least answer my questions," and we left. Ten minutes later, the doctor came to us, took us to the window, and said, "You see the home over

119

there? It was bombed by an Israeli plane three days ago. My wife and two children died. It could have been him. But I'm a doctor." Peter reported that. A lot of correspondents would have had second thoughts before putting it on. It went on the air.

Pro-Arab, pro-Palestinian — I never felt that. When you report the Palestinian story, do you become pro-Palestinian? Excuse me. We reported twenty-three hours and a half, the other side of the story. If once a week Peter reported a Palestinian story, that doesn't mean he's pro-Palestinian. He didn't lie. He reported what was in front of us. He felt the obligation of reporting it. We used to go to Jerusalem and used to talk with Israeli families. And the same day Peter wanted to touch the same bases with the Palestinian families. What's wrong with it? Do you become pro-Palestinian when you do that? There is no story by itself, in one corner. To really complete your research, you have to report both sides — at least that's what I learned, in my small years of experience.

PAUL FRIEDMAN: It got really nasty. [People said] that he was anti-Semitic, or anti-Israel. It hurt him a great deal. I always thought that what you were seeing was a guy who was determined to make the point that

there are two sides in this extremely complicated, emotional story in a part of the world
where he had lived so much of his life, that
he felt it. He felt the pain of the Israelis, and
he felt the pain of the Palestinians. And then
he felt, too often, that we are getting only
one side because the Western press tended to
be sympathetic to Israel. Peter just thought it
was important to remind people, as simplistic as it sounds, that Palestinians bleed,
Palestinians die, and that's as bad as anyone
else bleeding or dying.

HANAN ASHRAWI: I don't know whether
Peter's attempt to be objective, to reach the
truth, to be understanding, to understand
the complexity of the reality . . . I don't know
whether this is the national Canadian attrib-
ute or whether it was Peter's own keen intellect. It was amazing. Peter had those skills,
those skills of asking the right question, of
seeing beyond and behind the platitude. Trying to explore really fully, not just the fact,
but the reality behind the fact and the truth.
He avoided the simplistic, superficial point
of the misleading generalizations of the traditional media, and he insisted on asking the
difficult questions and seeking the truth. It is
gratifying to find such depth and responsibility and humanity and intellect in journal-

ism — something that we rarely see, certainly.

I don't think he was pro-Arab or pro-Palestinian. I think Peter had the unique distinction of knowing more than his colleagues, of knowing more than the other correspondents who would come here and skim the surface and give you the standard argument. Peter's mind was never satisfied with a cliché. I've always described him as a person who would never accept reality to be two-dimensional; it had to be three-dimensional in its humanity. But it also was four-dimensional in the sense that he placed it in a historical context.

Western media, particularly American media, are satisfied with recycling, quite often regurgitating, the pro-Israeli version. Constantly. They were very dismissive of the Palestinian version of reality. Peter refused to play that game. He respected his audience. He respected his viewers. He wanted them to get not just both sides, but all sides of the question. That's why many pro-Zionist people felt that he wasn't Zionist enough. But Peter was an avid seeker of the truth. And he had the intellect and the courage to present it. He refused to be intimidated. That's why he's a tremendous loss — not to the Palestinians, not to the Arabs, not to the Zionists

— to the cause of peace and to all those who want to seek the truth and go beyond the headlines and go beyond the sound bites.

PETER JENNINGS: *Having lived in the Middle East as long as I did, I have become convinced that there is not one truth, there are not two, there are very often several.*

KEN AULETTA: He understood something that's fundamental to the life of journalism . . . which is that everyone thinks they know the truth, and they have it. And if you cover [the Middle East] honestly, as he did, you realize that there are competing truths and that people fervently believe that their truth is correct. And maybe it's partly correct. But the other side, or various sides, have some truth too. I think Peter went through life with that understanding.

*In 1972, Jennings was sent to the Munich Olympics as the sole newsman to supplement a team of ABC Sports reporters led by Jim McKay and Howard Cosell. When a group of Palestinian terrorists took Israeli athletes hostage in the Olympic Village, Jennings was the only reporter able to make his way onto the scene. Drawing on his vast knowledge of the Middle East, he chronicled the drama as it unfolded live and correctly identified the terrorists as belonging to the Palestinian organization Black September, a group few outside the region had ever heard of. His live reporting scoop was a major coup for ABC, whose news division still languished in third place behind CBS and NBC. It was also a turning point in the career of Peter Jennings.*

PETER JENNINGS: *Roone Arledge called and said, "Would you like some rest and relaxation from the Middle East story, and would you come to Munich and do all of our non-sports features?" It took me all of ten seconds to say "yes."*

DICK EBERSOL: Peter was handpicked by Roone Arledge, who was then the head of ABC Sports, years before he became head of ABC News. Roone thought Peter, from watching him as a foreign correspondent, was the guy to have, in case anything happened at those Games.

My particular memory of Peter at those games was the first week, which most people forget today. That first week of the Munich games was perhaps the most successful week of any Olympic games in history. It was peaceful, calm, a great party for the athletes.

Mark Spitz had won seven gold medals the first week of the games. Everything couldn't have been brighter. And Peter was chafing at the bit. There was so little going on from a news standpoint that Roone had assigned him, for three or four nights, to cover Leroy Neiman's painting of a big scene showing all the events of the Olympics. I don't think I have ever seen Peter that frustrated, then or after, because there was no news.

Roone had been amused, that first week of the Olympics, at just how frustrated Peter was. And actually, I think got a kick out of assigning Peter, with me as the producer, to cover a painter. . . . But that's just how soft the news was that time in Munich. And it's almost horrible to talk about it in those terms today because of what followed. But you have to see what went on beforehand to appreciate just how Peter started from ground zero with that story. I mean, boom! All of a sudden, there was a terrorist raid on the village. And there was Peter, right in the middle of it.

ROGER GOODMAN: I gave Peter a little walkie-talkie, and that's the walkie-talkie that he used to report on the hostage crisis. He was literally about thirty-five to forty feet away from the broadcast center. His communication was so primitive when you think about it today. . . . McKay asked him who he thought the terrorists were, and Peter said, from his experience, "I think it was the Black September group."

JIM MCKAY: Peter Jennings is inside the village. Let's go to Peter now . . .

PETER JENNINGS: There's a great deal of speculation one could indulge in, which would be risky. But if I were to guess at the moment at which of the commando organizations this group is to come from, I'd be most likely to narrow in on a group called Black September.

BILL BLAKEMORE: He was the first one who was able to call it, and he called it right. . . . Peter knew all about the ins and outs of the various factions of the Palestinian movement and many other movements in the Middle East at that time. . . . He understood what the components were because he remembered the attempts by the Palestinians with hijackings — four passenger airlines hijacked in 1970 — and he recognized in 1972 that this was the same movement.

DICK EBERSOL: I think what meant more to him than anything else was when that awful story unfolded, he was at the forefront of it. And he had in his ear, throughout it, Roone's voice. Because Roone was not only the boss of those Olympics, he was the producer. And he talked Peter through all those stories. And whenever we went on the air, they talked back and forth about how that story was developing, about Peter's feelings that it was Black September.

When he was the first to authoritatively say, "This is Black September," it was not a huge leap of faith for Roone to accept it. We bought into the fact that Peter really had the experience and the knowledge of the Middle East.

ROGER GOODMAN: It really was the beginning, in my opinion, of Peter's career. Peter was so articulate. Peter had so much knowledge of the Mideast. All our reporters were sports reporters; nobody had the knowledge and the experience that Peter did. And the picture that Peter painted for the world is the same style and technique that Peter painted for 9/11, or for the millennium, or for any of the other hundreds and hundreds of broadcasts that were done with him live.

DICK EBERSOL: One of the most important aspects of Peter's involvement in the Munich story was his willingness to get into the story, to be right in the village — to report, if it was only by radio phone. He didn't come running back to the studio to see how much "on-camera" time he could take. There were some ABC news correspondents who were in Germany at the time, as the story developed, who raced to Munich. And all they wanted to do was get into the studio and to be on camera, seated next to our anchor, Jim McKay. That wasn't Peter. He wanted to be in the center of the story. And I think a large part of the credibility that Peter had, not only with all of us who work behind the scenes but in the public's perception of him over the next thirty years that followed, was that this was a guy who was never afraid to get his hands dirty. He really, really worked a news story. He wasn't looking to be just "the face."

BARRIE DUNSMORE: It was a great professional break for him. I don't think there's any doubt about that. It was very big for ABC, and it was also good for Peter. Because this was an Olympic event, first of all, almost everybody would have been watching it anyway. And then, considering what was actually happening there, the entire country, if not the world, was focused on this event.

And because Peter and ABC were able to report this thing so effectively, it was obviously a major feather in the cap of the news division.

DICK EBERSOL: Prior to Munich, Peter had a real reputation as a foreign correspondent; there was no question about it. But his involvement with Roone in Munich in September of 1972 was a turning point in his career because that was a story that ABC News owned. They owned it. No other network could literally get on the air because ABC controlled the satellite time. And Peter's hours and hours on the air with many others, including Jim McKay, brought a credibility to ABC News, even though it was being produced by ABC Sports. And I am certain that what happened that day was largely responsible for why, four years later, Roone would be named the head of news at ABC and Peter, within a few years after that, would go on from being the chief foreign correspondent to being the anchor of ABC News. I think it all started on that awful day at Munich in September of 1972.

*I've been reminded in every story, in every part of the world, in every part of the country: truth is really hard to get at. It's about nuance. And part of the great thing about what we do . . . is going out and trying to understand the mix of opinion and philosophy, colored by age and gender and geography and economic circumstance. That makes what we do so absolutely, profoundly exciting.*

—Peter Jennings

# 4
# ROVING ANCHOR

*In 1977, Roone Arledge, then head of ABC Sports, was also named president of ABC News. The following year, he created a new look for ABC's last-place evening news program.* World News Tonight *debuted on July 10, 1978, with a groundbreaking triple anchor format — Frank Reynolds in Washington, Max Robinson in Chicago, and Peter Jennings in London, where he had already relocated to serve as chief foreign correspondent. One critic called the new approach, with its razzle-dazzle graphics that switched quickly from location to location, "a commercial for Dramamine." But the new aggressiveness of its reporters and the growing confidence of the anchors began to win over more and more viewers; within a year,* World News Tonight *was in a dead heat with* NBC Nightly News. *Arledge later said that the three anchors were his solution to not hav-*

*ing a single major star. But he clearly had seen the beginnings of one at the Olympic Village in Munich.*

DICK EBERSOL: I don't think you could say that it was obvious in September of '72 that Peter's career would re-rocket again. But what happened there was that a relationship was born between Peter, the bright young man of the news division, and the single biggest creative talent the entire ABC company had, Roone Arledge, who was then head of sports. So it was a natural that, years later, when Roone became the head of news, Peter was someone he gravitated to immediately because he knew how good Peter was, particularly under pressure. . . . I think there were other people at ABC News who were somewhat shocked in 1976 when Roone was made the head of news. Peter wasn't one of them. He knew what a great producer Roone was.

PETE SIMMONS: Peter told me he'd been summoned to New York to talk to Roone about this new concept of the three anchors. I said, "Do you really want to be an anchorman? I mean, you tried that once, and now you're having fun. You're doing what you really love and what you're really good at. Do you want to be an anchorman?" He gave me the old quote, I think it was Browning or whoever said it: "A man's reach should exceed his grasp." And he was off on a plane. The next thing I knew, he was Peter Jennings, anchorman.

It was a sacrifice, giving up the field. He really shone in the field. He was good at covering stories and finding stories and doing stories. He should have been an anchor, and it was destiny, I suppose, but it was a sacrifice as well.

PETER SHAW: We met in a kitchen in London. Peter had his head in the refrigerator; he was looking for pickles. He had rented the basement flat in our building, and the owner had told me that Peter was there and he was starting up a new broadcast that was going to emphasize foreign news, and he was looking for a writer. "You should go talk to him. I've told him about you." So I went down; we met. We were both correspondents. We hit it off, and we were together, working very happily, for the next twelve years.

JEFF GRALNICK: The triple anchor broadcast was different. It was more popular-culture. It had more graphics. It was different because it had no choice other than to be different — to see if it could survive.

*The triple anchor team (Max Robinson, left; Frank Reynolds, right), 1978*

MICHAEL CLEMENTE: I met him on the phone in 1979 when we started the triple anchor format. I was Frank Reynolds' writer, and Peter was the anchor in London. We used to have to call over there each day and have, sometimes, an uncomfortable conversation about what Frank would say versus what Peter would say, because Frank would come first, then Peter would come second, and then a correspondent. It was a little bit tortured.

134

PETER SHAW: His editorial contribution to the broadcast was immense. Not only in the knowledge that he brought to it but in his advocacy of a story that he felt needed to be put on the air. He would get into knock-down, drag-out verbal fights with the producers in New York to stand up for a story that he felt deserved to be on the broadcast. He elevated foreign news to the prominence that it deserved, if only perhaps for a while. And he made people understand that it's necessary to understand what's happening in the world outside the United States because it influences, if not dictates, what happens within the United States. And you must understand the "how" and particularly the "why" if you're going to deal with problems.

JEFF GRALNICK: Peter was a perfectionist. Peter wanted to know the answer to, "Why is this happening?" If you couldn't answer him, you were in trouble. If you were out covering a story, or you were arguing for the inclusion of a story, and you didn't automatically know the answers to all his questions, that story was in trouble. I mean, he was a perfectionist for facts. He was a perfectionist for language. He was a perfectionist for storytelling. And yeah, I mean, he made correspondents crazy. And he made producers crazy. But it was always to a good end.

LYNN SHERR: Peter, as the London anchor of *World News Tonight,* was a pain in the neck if you were a New York reporter, because it was a time and a space game. Everybody wanted his or her story on the air. Peter fought for the foreign news, which was his job as the anchor. If I was covering something in New York, I fought and screamed for my domestic story. So there were a lot of us who were not happy with him as the London anchor because he was taking care of his turf. And we had our own jobs, thank you very much, that we needed to worry about.

*Although he was called the London anchor, Jennings' beat was the world — and he wanted to be where the news was. If there was a major international story, he took the anchor desk on the road so he could continue to pursue his first love: reporting from the scene. His colleagues recall his tough work ethic. He was insatiably curious, interviewing everyone from taxi drivers to world leaders. He studied up on his subjects, reading incessantly. And he developed his particular reportorial style: straightforward storytelling focused on people.*

PETE SIMMONS: Peter Jennings was the consummate foreign correspondent. He looked the role; he knew his turf; he knew the geopolitics of all the areas. At that time, he was covering Europe, Africa, and the Middle East, as far away as India. So he had a big patch to cover. And he knew all the movers and shakers there, most of them by their first names. He knew how to contact them, and he knew their opposition. He roamed all over the world and we tried to keep up with him.

BILL BLAKEMORE: He was quite conscious of wanting, in an elegant and genteel way, to help educate the country about the various complexities of the world. Like all great journalists, what he did is, he took the complexity and made it clear without oversimplifying it. But it was that calm he had, walking into any foreign culture with a bit of elegance, a bit of grace, that made it possible and comfortable to follow along with him, even if you were only doing so by watching television, because he was in effect saying, "Come see what I found in this interesting culture."

PETER SHAW: I think he made people want to go and find out where places were, and where people were making trouble or making peace. I think he was inspirational in that sense, because he knew that if you don't know, you cannot understand.

TOM FENTON: As a friend, as a competitor, as a colleague, he was charming. He was suave. He had a certain air of distinction about him. He was the quintessential foreign correspondent, with or without the trench coat. He also had another quality which was rare in this business sometimes: he cared more about substance than he did about show.

PETE SIMMONS: He dressed like a European gentleman wherever he went. If he was in Mogadishu or somewhere, he might shed his tie, but he was always the straightforward personification of a gentleman correspondent, somebody who always respected his stories, always treated his subjects — even if he didn't like them — treated them with respect. And he just knew how to get the story and how to look the part and open doors. That was his job, and he really did it well.

JOHN COCHRAN: I first met Peter in the late '70s when I was working for NBC. I went overseas to be stationed in London. Peter was already an established foreign corre-

*Northern Ireland, 1981*

spondent, and we had some mutual friends who were going to be away from London for a year. They said, "Why don't you and Peter" — who was between marriages — "why don't you and Peter take our house for a year?" So we did. And the very first day we were housemates I get a call to go to Cairo on a story. And Peter says, "Well, do you have any good contacts in Cairo?" I said, "Peter, I've never even been to Cairo." So he says, "Hold it. Let me write something down." He writes down on a piece of paper three names and three telephone numbers, two of which I remember were the private lines of the prime minister and the foreign minister of Egypt. I said, "Well, Peter, this is very nice of you. But after all, I'm the competition." And, trying to make a joke of it, he said, "Oh, it doesn't matter. You probably won't ask the right questions anyway." But the fact is, he was always incredibly generous. I'll always think of Peter as the best of a vanishing breed: a gentleman correspondent.

PETER SHAW: Peter was one of the most natural people I've ever known. He made everything easy. He had a graciousness about him — doing the news, playing tennis, driving a car. When we'd finish the broadcast late at night in the early days in London, quite often Peter would drive me home in the white car that he had recently bought. He put on these leather driving gloves before we started out. It might have been a Ferrari riding around a race course or something, but it was the elegance with which he drove that car, the elegance with which he led his life.

HILARY BROWN: He was the chief correspondent, and I was the sort of junior correspondent. He was a merciless tease. At the time, I had been stupid enough to buy an E-type Jaguar, which he called "the jalopy," and it broke down pretty much every day. He'd stick his head out of the window and say, "How's the jalopy?" or, "Shall I go to the garage or will you?" or, you know, "I can give you fifty bucks for it and take it off your hands."

PETE SIMMONS: He was a hard man to keep up with physically and intellectually. He would give you a break if you couldn't keep up with him intellectually or physically, but God help the producer who couldn't keep up with him journalistically. He expected that.

For instance, if you went to Beirut or Tel Aviv or somewhere in the Middle East, Damascus or Baghdad, he worked twelve, thirteen, fourteen hours a day. Well, most people don't like working twelve, thirteen, fourteen hours a day. And then when Peter wasn't working twelve, thirteen, fourteen hours a day, he had his nose in a book, and the next day he'd start asking you questions: "Do you know about this?" and "Do you know about that?"

If you went on a story with him and you didn't know the story, you were, in the parlance of the times, dead meat. Peter had a favorite word for people who aspired to be journalists but didn't keep up with what they were supposed to know. That word was "fraud." And if he considered you a fraud, ha, well, you didn't work with him very much.

CHARLES GLASS: He was always reading. Whenever we would fly, say, from Beirut to Cairo, or Cairo to Algiers, or Algiers to Madagascar, wherever we were going, he had books. He'd always take books — not *a* book — *books* with him on every airplane. In the evenings, he wouldn't go get drunk in the bar with the rest of us. He would be up reading. It was partly because I think he enjoyed reading and partly because he liked talking about books and partly he was continuing that process of lifelong education.

PETER SHAW: Working with Peter was great fun. Because he was serious when he had to be serious, but he could really be mischievous when there was time to be mischievous. And he knew when to play and when to not.

JOHN COCHRAN: We both were covering an economic summit with all the world leaders in Tokyo. I was going out to dinner one night in Tokyo, and Peter said, "Stop by my room before you go." I did stop by, and I said, "I'm going to go to such and such a restaurant." He said, "Well, but that's a long way away. It'll take a lot of time." And I said, "So what? We don't have to be on the air till tomorrow." And he said, "Well, I've got all this studying to do." I looked over to this table, and there were these books — a huge pile — and pamphlets, and he intended to go through all of them. He was the only correspondent I knew who did that kind of research. It was an economic summit, and he wasn't going to get caught short; he was going through all this dry stuff. It was just amazing. And so he didn't go out to dinner. I saw him do the same thing on many other occasions when we'd be competing against each other — Poland, Iran. Peter did his homework. He really did.

PETE SIMMONS: He was so well-read. He was probably the most well-read man I've ever worked with. He was an expert on geography, on geopolitics, on history, on biography. He knew things that he'd just certainly flatten you with sometimes. Let's say you had a pretty good grip on Eastern Europe. Well, when you sat down with him and you had dinner with him, you didn't know anything because, you know, he was way ahead of you.

CHRIS ISHAM: At the end of the day, "these stories are about people," as he often said. "Stories are about people. And news is about people. People make news." Peter understood that what drives world events, and what drives news, is people. And he went out of his way to get to know people, to sit down with them, to have lunch with them, to have dinner with them, to try to understand what made them tick. Peter would spend hours with them, drinking coffee, which is what people do in the Middle East. He would want to know about their children. He would want to know about their parents. He would want to know what made them feel good, what made them feel bad. He developed an empathy with them. And that is one of the reasons that I think he had as good an understanding as he did of world events, because he understood the people that made them.

PETE SIMMONS: One good thing about Peter, whether it was Polish or Russian or Arabic, whatever it was, he would always learn a few nice phrases like "hello," "goodbye," "thank you" in that language, whatever country he was in. I'm sure if they ever sent him to Mars, he'd pick up a few words of Martian before he got there. Just so he'd be able to say hello in their language.

PETER OSNOS: I think the first major story we covered together was Pope John Paul [II]'s visit to Poland in 1979. Everybody present knew that they were watching a story of great political importance but tremendous, you know, joy. Basically, what you had was an entire country supposedly under the thumb of the Soviets turning out to welcome this amazingly heroic figure, this new pope. It was a great story to cover. But it was not one in which you could stumble in and know what was going on. You had to understand Catholicism in Poland. You had to understand the role of the party in that period in Eastern Europe and certainly in Poland. Peter was very good about those things.

PETE SIMMONS: I think what I remember about him most vividly was his absolute control of every story. He knew the people involved, he knew the ramifications, he knew the history of it. Whether it was in the Middle East or, or the most out-of-the-way place in Africa or anywhere in Eastern Europe — wherever you went with him, he knew the ground he was covering.

TOM FENTON: He loved the lifestyle. And

who wouldn't? It beats working. You ring up your bosses and you tell them there's something happening in Mozambique or in Cairo and off you go. And you got this great front-row seat to the events of the world.

*Despite his extensive travel and workaholic tendencies, Jennings led a rich personal life. In 1979, he was married for the third time, to fellow ABC correspondent Kati Marton. They had two children, Elizabeth and Christopher.*

PETER SHAW: Elizabeth had been born earlier that day. Peter came to the flat for something to eat. He telephoned his mother in Ottawa, and we have a photograph, which we can't find, of Peter with his feet up on the table talking to his mother on the telephone, telling her this wonderful news. And the grin on his face is one of those things that will be a treasure forever. It was absolutely ear to ear.

LYNN SHERR: Peter became a dad a little bit late in life. But boy, did he jump in with all four feet! You could not tear him away from those children when they were little. He practically wept — actually, I think he did from time to time — when he would have to

*Kati Marton, Christopher, Peter, and Elizabeth*

get on a plane and leave them when he was in London. He absolutely adored them.

*As he anchored more and more international events, Jennings grew deft at the complex art of weaving together a live broadcast, whether a planned extravaganza, such as the wedding of Prince Charles to Diana Spencer, or breaking news, such as the Iranian hostage crisis. He knew how to think on his feet and how to provide context for his American audience.*

PETER SHAW: Peter was a master of live broadcasting. He saw the camera as a friend. The camera was something that you spoke to as if you were trying to explain a story, tell something to your aunt, your sister, and neighbor. . . . He was a superb communicator on live television, when you only have one chance to get it right, especially when the news is breaking. . . . When Pope John Paul II was elected, we were on the colonnade of St. Peter's Square waiting for his name to be announced. The Vatican had provided us with one page biographies of all the eligible cardinals. When the name came up, I handed Peter this page with Wojtyła's name on it. A breeze promptly took it out of his hand and carried it across the piazza. And Peter carried on ad-libbing without missing a beat. There was a second copy of Wojtyła's biography in that press pack, totally by accident. The "Miracle of Pope John Paul," we called it. I handed that to him, and he picked up on all the details. No one would have ever known that he came very close to dead air, which is one of the worst things you can possibly do on television.

BARBARA WALTERS: Peter and I were partners in so many stories. The first big story we covered was in the Middle East, when

Anwar Sadat, the president of Egypt, left that country to go to Israel [in 1978]. Peter and I were at the airport, covering each moment of it. The Israeli bands were playing the Egyptian national anthem. I mean, that was unheard of. The Egyptian flags were waving, and there was the significance of seeing Anwar Sadat greeting his old enemies, Golda Meir and Moshe Dayan.

JEFF GRALNICK: When Sadat went to Israel, Peter was live from Jerusalem and Tel Aviv for hours and hours. It was just easy conversation. Peter wasn't saying, "Hey, look what I know!" But just basically, "Here's what I do know, and here's why it'll help you understand the event."

*Jennings' understanding was rooted in a close relationship with Sadat and the region, forged over years of reporting. Four years earlier, in 1974, Jennings had served as chief correspondent and co-producer of the award-winning "Sadat: Action Biography," which had involved four months of interviews with the Egyptian president.*

BILL BLAKEMORE: Peter got to know Anwar Sadat and got him to talk about what the paradoxes were of trying to be a great leader, and also at war with Israel, and Israel trying to sort out its own security so soon after World War II. Peter had this natural ability to be self-confident in the presence of the greatest world leaders, and they immediately recognized an equal in him — somebody who was at the top of his game.

PETER JENNINGS: Mr. President, quite frankly, a great many people in the West look at Sinai and say, this is nothing but sand. Is there in fact no way in which a compromise can be achieved, by which somewhere here in the Sinai Israel can have the security it requires and you can have the honor you demand?

ANWAR SADAT: This is very important. This is not the correct logic, you see. . . . [Whether] it is sand, mud or marshes or whatever it is, it is the motherland. I don't know if the older American cities can agree to the fact that anyone comes to the western desert—some of your deserts there— and grab by force a piece of this desert and starts to impose his conditions. This is the situation here. . . .

JENNINGS: How can you convince the Israelis, who are 17 kilometers from you—

granted, sitting on your territory—that once you get Sinai back you won't attack them?

SADAT: How can you convince me that on the other side that I shall not be attacked by them? This is the same thing.

BARBARA WALTERS: We then [in 1981] had the pain of covering Anwar Sadat's funeral, when he was assassinated by one of his own people. We had two different ways of looking at the funeral. I said, "The streets are empty; it's out of respect." Peter said, "Look again. Maybe it's not out of respect. Maybe it's out of the fact that there is a change, that there is a new regime, and that there are a lot of people who still were angry with Sadat for going to Israel." He had an insight and an understanding of the Middle East that few had.

I probably knew more about Anwar Sadat's personality. . . . What Peter brought to it was his knowledge of the Middle East. He understood the impact of the [Israel] visit. He knew how important it was, how controversial it was, how meaningful it was. And when Anwar Sadat was assassinated, Peter understood the ramifications. This was not just another assassination of a controversial leader. This had enormous impact, not just in the Middle East, but on the world.

CHARLES GLASS: Not many people will know this, but Peter made a historic contribution to the Middle East in this regard: He was the one who asked Anwar Sadat, when he was making a film about Sadat's life, the question, "What would you like your epitaph to read?" And Sadat thought about it all day and came back in the evening when they recorded the interview and said, "I would like my epitaph to read, 'He lived for peace and died for principles.' " That is what's on his tomb.

JENNINGS: As you're driving through the streets of Cairo or any other Egyptian town and the people are standing on the side of the street and cheering you, how do you really know they mean it?

SADAT: It's something you can feel by heart. By heart, I'm a man of the street, and I can feel it.

JENNINGS: Mr. President, what would you like people to write about you after you've gone?

SADAT: I should like them to write on my

tomb: He has lived for peace, and he has died for principles.

LYNN SHERR: He could work up enthusiasm for the littlest story or the most gigantic. The royal wedding — the wedding of Prince Charles and Diana Spencer — he knew everything. A lot of it was written down in front of him, but he'd lived in London for so many years, and he knew that information. My camera position was outside of Buckingham Palace at the Canada Gate. Well he, of course, loved that. So every time he'd throw it to me, it would be: "Lynn Sherr is at Canada Gate outside Buckingham Palace." My major job was to talk about the balcony appearances — you know, when everybody comes out on the balcony after an event. And I had memorized, by God, every single balcony appearance for the last ninety-two years of British history! And it turned out Peter knew everything that I knew! I would start to talk and he'd say, "Oh yes, but what about Y?" And I'd say, "Well, yeah, I'm getting to that." And he'd say, "Well, Lynn, I want to hear about that." He was amazing. He was there — for everything.

BARBARA WALTERS: He covered the whole parade route. He knew every horse, it seems to me, by the horse's first name. He knew where you turned left; he knew where you turned right. What he couldn't have cared less about was the wedding gown. That's what everyone wanted to hear. That was my area.

Sometimes he was a hog on television. "Peter," I would say, "It's my turn now," and he would look at me and wink, which meant, "Just shut up for a little while longer, I'll get to you."

But also — and this is very important — Peter knew when to talk and Peter knew when to be quiet. And Peter knew when to let us hear the service. Every sound, every piece of music. His silences were sometimes as important as what he said.

PETER JENNINGS: *I learned how to cover a funeral from my father, who used to say to me, be sure we hear the horse's hooves. . . . Stop for a while to let the people hear the gun carriage go by.*

*One of the biggest international stories of the '70s and '80s was the Iranian Revolution. Jennings was on the airplane with the Ayatollah Khomeini when the Iranian ruler returned to Tehran to take over its government.*

CHARLES GLASS: I was editing an obscure Middle East magazine in London back in 1979 during the Iranian Revolution, and I called Peter in Tehran and asked him if he would write me a letter from Tehran. He wrote:

We in the press corps called it the Ayatollah Special — the Air France 747 which carried him and us from Paris to Tehran. The Ayatollah said he sensed danger in the flight. With first light over the mountains of Iran, reporters craned their necks looking for unfriendly Iranian Air Force Phantoms. There were none, and an hour later I was recalling the birth of Bangladesh at the end of 1971, when Sheikh Mujibur Rahman had returned to his new nation and there was a sea of humanity to greet him. It was nothing compared to Iran's welcome for Khomeini.

One early morning, far from the frenzy, a senior mullah wonders if the young mullahs are becoming infected with too much power. He says, "They are becoming very politicized. We must be careful to see that the mosque doesn't overextend itself.". . .

The veil, or chador, is everywhere. Many young girls don't like it, but they

155

have worn it as a symbol of protest against the Shah. They worry, lest they cannot get rid of it again. . . .

It is all happening so fast. When Khomeini speaks, the people respond. Prime Minister Bakhtiar said all the people in the streets had nothing else to do. Now they have. The country, for better or for worse, and for now, is theirs.

It is at once some of the best journalism imaginable — not only well observed, but prescient. Just to read it is a reminder of what a great writer and wordsmith Peter was.

DICK EBERSOL: It was a great advantage for ABC News that Peter truly was an old-fashioned foreign correspondent. He was a young man, but he was an old-fashioned foreign correspondent who had lived in the Middle East, had lived in London, had a real sense of what was going on in that part of the world. And it was a great advantage for ABC News in the '70s and well into the '80s, as Peter became an anchor.

DON HEWITT: ABC wasn't even in the ball game until Roone Arledge and Peter Jennings put them in the game. Up to that point, it was all NBC and CBS. And then all of a sudden — wow! — they burst on the scene.

*It is a very big job. But it is a job. It is not being annointed. You sit down and ask yourself: Can I do it, with all its components? Am I emotionally ready? Am I qualified? I think I am.*

—Peter Jennings

# 5

# FLYING SOLO

*When Frank Reynolds, the Washington-based anchor of* World News Tonight, *succumbed to cancer and died in 1983, Peter Jennings was named sole anchor. With Dan Rather at CBS and Tom Brokaw at NBC, this signaled a generational shift in the evening news broadcasts and the beginning of what the media would deem the "Big Three" era. Jennings had spent the last fifteen years circumnavigating the globe, chasing stories. Now, with his return to the anchor desk in New York, he had to study up on America. It was not an entirely smooth reentry.*

MICHAEL CLEMENTE: The transition not only involved coming back to this country for the first time in many years, but it involved anchoring the entire show. It was a difficult time for Peter. It was a lot to take on all at once. I think it also dovetailed with his own knowledge of having anchored when he was in his mid-twenties, when it didn't completely work, and he went out in the field. How many times can you come back, take the chair on your own, and fail?

PETER JENNINGS: *My first instinct was to say no altogether. And Kati, my wife, was the one who convinced me this was a very important job, and you didn't just say no idly. We had a long, very difficult time in deciding to come.*

MICHAEL CLEMENTE: There was the pressure of anchoring the whole show during a time of big transition. I think our ratings had dropped a fair amount in the months that Frank was off sick. So it was a lot for Peter. He put as much pressure on himself as anyone. He wanted to succeed.

JEFF GRALNICK: I think — and Peter was candid about this — it scared the hell out of him. I mean, he was very frank: "Hey, I'm not Walter Cronkite." He was public about that. He had to feel his way into being one of the most powerful communicators on the planet.

PETER JENNINGS: *With me, Brokaw, and Rather, I recognize that there will be the factor of three pretty faces. That's an inevitable by-product of television. But if that is what it comes down to in terms of the approach we take — if our approach is that singular — then we will all have made a mistake.*

GRETCHEN BABAROVIC: Peter Jennings was first and foremost a journalist, and he loved it with every ounce of his soul. To transition from being in the field — "have trench coat, will travel" — was a real change for him. And he chafed at it.

MICHAEL CLEMENTE: So there was a lot of tension. And there was a considerable lack of knowledge about what had been going on in this country. Not his fault — he had been covering the rest of the world. . . . There was skepticism here in New York, and some around the country, about whether people would listen to a Canadian. Most people thought he was English. He had this accent. They didn't know he was born in Toronto. I think Peter was fine with it until he started to hear other people express doubts about whether Americans would listen to "a singing foreigner" giving them their news each day.

TED KOPPEL: He was never able to say

"about," it was always "aboot." He wasn't able to say "house," it was always "hoose." And I remember, for the first few years he insisted on calling a lieutenant a "leftenant." Americans, being justifiably proud of our culture, our own language, feel that it's up to foreigners to adjust to the United States. It took Peter a little while to do that, but eventually, he did.

PETER JENNINGS: *I was so instinctively resistant to saying Lootenant that they printed "LOO" on the teleprompter.*

GRETCHEN BABAROVIC: That first summer I came to work for him, he didn't come into the office until about eleven. He had the children, very small children. Christopher was literally in diapers. Lizzie was basically a toddler. And we worked in a little tiny space, where you could literally spit from one end of the room to the other.

Because he wasn't a household name at that point, Roone Arledge made him stay to do *Newsbrief* at nine o'clock. And he hated it. He would moan, and just really not want to be there. We had to stay till nine-thirty every night. And that was the beginning of it.

*Jennings' first hurdle was immense: the*

*1984 presidential campaign.*

WALTER CRONKITE: I watched this young Canadian come in, not having, I assume, gone through all those civics lessons and history lessons in high school that the rest of us had, grabbing hold of that story of politics in the great nation that is America when he had come from, we all thought, this farmland up there, of Canada. And he made a good impression on all of us. We saw him at press meetings, and he asked the questions that were right. He knew the story. He only was a little naïve about American politics, but he was grasping it very rapidly.

TOM BROKAW: I was doing *Nightly News* on my own for the first time in '83 — Peter was not yet in the anchor chair for ABC — and I went to Beirut for the war. Peter looked at me and said, "This is my territory." I laughed, and I knew that. He was really connected there, and Charlie Glass, from ABC, and the other ABC correspondents were well dug in. We did pretty well, but I knew what I was up against in that part of the world. So when Peter came back to cover our presidential election on the campaign trail, I said to Peter, "This is my territory." And it was all friendly.

TED KOPPEL: What created the sense of insecurity was when he realized that the general appetite for news from overseas was not as overwhelming, perhaps, as he had thought it was. He had to suddenly learn this new country, and this new country was the United States.

We had identical experiences. I came back and I was the floor correspondent at the conventions in '76. I still remember some magazine doing a profile of who all the floor correspondents would be. Next to my name they had written, "Might do better if the convention were being held in Hong Kong." Peter had the same experience. He was anchoring when he came back in 1984. He was fortunate to have as his co-anchor for the election coverage David Brinkley, who had forgotten more about American politics than Peter and I would ever know. So Peter had to start all over again, swapping, as he would put it — crashing and cramming, trying to get as much information about the American political process as he could. He applied the same voracious appetite for information that he had used overseas to learning about the United States.

HAL BRUNO: I was the political director for ABC at that time. So Peter and I were given oh, about a week, ten days just to go off by ourselves and start traveling and learning about American politics, bringing him up to date. We went to Iowa first, and then we went to New Hampshire, and we just roamed up and down, day after day, talking to the politicians, talking to the candidates.

He did have gaps, mainly because the American political system had changed while he was away. After 1972, when they brought in the McGovern-Fraser Reform Rules and they went to the primary system, having the primaries actually nominate the candidate, American politics was never the same. So Peter had to learn a whole new American political system. Plus, even though he had a breadth of knowledge, he didn't have a great depth of knowledge. He was painfully aware that he was lacking it, and he was determined to study. One of the first things he asked me was, "What book should I read?" I suggested a few books, but I said, "The most important thing is for you and me to get out and to talk to people who are involved in politics." And, of course, that brought out all the reporter instincts in him.

CHARLIE GIBSON: I was covering the House of Representatives. I remember Peter called me one day and said, "We need to have lunch." Fine. I thought it was a some-what social occasion, and since both of us are cheap, we wound up going to a soup cafeteria, and we sat at a Formica table in the back corner of the restaurant.

All of a sudden, I realized I was in an oral exam about the Congress. Not only that, I realized that Peter had probably prepped for this meeting for two or three days. His questions didn't come out of idle curiosity. He'd read up on this, and he was asking about the difference between an authorization and an appropriation bill; why some committees were 60 percent Democrat and some were 75 percent Democrat — the Democrats in those days holding the House — and why Tip O'Neill might have been doing certain things in terms of the way he was running the House. I felt like I was being grilled for a Ph.D.

We were there for two-and-a-half hours. We had long since finished our soup, and Peter had not long since finished his questions. They were all done off the top of his head. He wanted to know and he thought he ought to know to be a good anchor.

HAL BRUNO: He had that notebook going all the time. He'd never stop. I'd say, "Okay, Peter, let's call it a day." And Peter would

166

say, "Well, let's go on to this one other — there's one other meeting in this one township," and off we'd go. In those days he was not as recognizable as he quickly became as the anchor. People knew who he was, but it wasn't the same as being a superstar anchor. You could still be pretty comfortable in traveling, and he just relished talking to the average person.

JEFF GRALNICK: The first time Peter did a national convention was terrorizing for him. He was not shy about saying, "I don't know enough. I don't really understand the American political system. I don't really understand the American convention system. I don't really understand what's going on out there, and I've got to do this for four nights for the Democrats and four nights for the Republicans, and I'm not smart enough yet." But he found every smart person he could, and he just went to school on them. He would do long preparatory interviews before we ever got on the air. Just picking facts out of experts' brains and filing them away.

COKIE ROBERTS: David Brinkley was the most knowledgeable political reporter around at the point when Peter came to

*Covering the Republican convention with David Brinkley in 1984*

ABC. David and Peter would co-anchor the political election nights and the conventions. David had been covering conventions since 1948, so he knew a great deal. He was also from North Carolina, raised in the heartbeat of American politics. Peter was Canadian and he really didn't know very much at all. And David made it clear to Peter that he didn't know very much at all. So Peter set about learning.

PETER JENNINGS: *I had not covered an election campaign in sixteen years. So here I was going to co-anchor with David Brinkley in*

*1984, and he wasn't even sure I knew who the faces belonged to. And he was right.*

TED KOPPEL: We sort of have to remind people that David Brinkley was an icon. There was a time in the late '50s when everyone in America was walking around saying, "Good night, David. Good night, Chet," because Chet Huntley and David Brinkley were the co-anchors of NBC and they were huge, much bigger than any of the rest of us would ever be later on in the years that we became anchors. And then, of course, over at CBS, there was Walter Cronkite, who was huge.

So when Peter sat down and co-anchored with David Brinkley, he was co-anchoring with a legend. Brinkley, I guess by then, was in his late sixties and had been let go by NBC. And he came over to ABC, and Roone Arledge, who was then president of ABC News, was smart enough to realize that there was still some rubber left on those tires, so he created *This Week with David Brinkley* on Sundays. And then David became the co-anchor on the political coverage. He knew a ton about American politics, so he was able to counterbalance what Peter didn't know.

PETER JENNINGS: It is nine-thirty in the

East, eight-thirty in the West. The polls are beginning to close. We have not called the Senate race in Minnesota.

DAVID BRINKLEY: Peter, in Minnesota we did call the Senate race. Rudy Boschwitz, a Republican —

PETER JENNINGS: Yeah, I meant to say President, did I say Senator —

DAVID BRINKLEY: Right, the President we have not.

HAL BRUNO: On election night, things came fast and furious, and I'd be in the pit right in back of Peter. I'd be handing up cards, and as each state was called, he had his cards, with certain tidbits that he had written down. We would listen very carefully for a mistake of some type. There was one night when Peter had the winner carrying the wrong state. He had Mondale carrying Pennsylvania, as I recall. We immediately caught it and sent the card up and Peter, of course, adjusted immediately. He was a great believer in admitting on air, instantly, that you made a mistake if you misspoke. He had absolutely no inhibition saying, "Oops, I made a mistake. I meant to say this."

PETER JENNINGS (11:37 p.m.): ABC News now projects the state of Washington with its 10 electoral votes for Mr. Reagan, which gives Mr. Reagan 518 electoral votes, but also gives him every state in the country . . .

DAVID BRINKLEY (11:39 p.m.): We have now been able to project all of the 48 contiguous states and the only ones we have not been able to project are Alaska, which is where the polls are still open, and Hawaii, which we simply don't have yet.

JENNINGS: That was a very gracious correction, David. I did turn around and look at the map and Alaska is not on it, nor is Hawaii . . .

JENNINGS (11:42 p.m.): Speaking of states, I'd like to welcome Alaska and Hawaii back into the Union.

BRINKLEY: Oh, I'm sure they'll be happy to hear that.

HAL BRUNO: Here was David Brinkley, who was the icon, and here was Peter, who felt like the new kid on the block. And Peter was very self-conscious about his image, as it was being portrayed by some of the critics, which was that he was just a pretty face. David had this particular style and way of talking, and there was quite a bit of tension in the early stages. But I think what happened is we got thrown into a situation where we had to come on live and it was the first time that David saw the way Peter could handle a breaking story. I think that was the start of what later became mutual respect for each other.

LYNN SHERR: One of the great joys was seeing him on the floor of a political convention for the first time, not up in the anchor booth where they told him he belonged. He wanted to be out there on the floor with the rest of us. He just thought what we were doing was so cool — and, by the way, it was very cool — and he wanted a piece of the action. He wanted to touch the people. He wanted to hear what they had to say to him, not through an earpiece, not on a box. He wanted it face-to-face. He loved being out there on the floor so much, they had to drag him off of there and say, "Peter, get back in the booth. We need you to anchor the show, not to be out here interviewing people; let the floor correspondents do that."

SAM DONALDSON: He pulled himself up by his bootstraps. He had to learn the United States. When he started, he said "bean" and "shedule" and "Where is Iowa, anyway?" But he learned. He did. I think the important thing when you start out is not how little you know, it's how much you learn that distinguishes you. And from that measure, Peter Jennings was distinguished completely.

COKIE ROBERTS: Peter ended up falling in love with America. A lot of that had to do with his coverage of politics. You can't cover American politics, with all of its yeastiness and flavor, without having a love of this country.

*On January 25, 1986, the space shuttle* Challenger *disintegrated seventy-three seconds into its flight, dooming all seven of its crew members. Jennings reacted to the crisis with characteristic calm and dedication, remaining at his anchor desk for eleven straight hours. Americans responded, turning to television as their electronic hearth — a gathering place for warmth and comfort in a time of national crisis. Jennings' sure handling of the* Challenger *explosion showcased his ability to perform live under pressure.*

GRETCHEN BABAROVIC: It was the day of the State of the Union message. We were in New York, and we were to fly down to Washington that morning. It had snowed the night before. I met Peter on the plane, and the plane sat on the tarmac. It was late taking off because they hadn't cleared the runways. Peter was getting terribly nervous because he had to get to the White House for the traditional briefing before the State of the Union. The plane sat and sat, and Peter started to chew gum. He chewed, and he chewed, and he chewed. Finally, we managed to take off. As we landed, I said to him, "I will take the suitcases. You just go on to the White House, and I'll meet you at the bureau." But by the time I got to the bureau, Peter was already in the anchor chair because the word had come over to the White House and he had flown out of there.

LYNN SHERR: When the *Challenger* blew up, that awful, horrible day and we were all on the air for endless numbers of hours, Peter came on. He did not know a lot about the space shuttle at that point in his life. He was on the air, and I was on the air, and there were many, many other people on the air. I was astounded. Peter got it all right. And what he didn't get right he was smart enough to ask. He would turn to me, and he would ask a question. And he would listen to the answer. He would figure it out. He would come out with stuff that was dead on, spot on, even though he had never covered the space shuttle in his life.

I know, and everybody in this business knows, there were people feeding him material and there were people talking into his ear. He had research sheets in front of him, and he was not a dope; he had obviously followed some of this. But he was the one that

*Explaining* Challenger, *January 28, 1986*

put it all together. On what was one of many awful days we've shared as a nation on the air, Peter gave viewers an anchor, a sense of calm, a sense of understanding, not a false sense that everything was okay, but a real sense that "We are trying to get on top of this." It was just beautiful to watch and to participate in with him.

PETER JENNINGS ("ABC News Special Report," 10:00 p.m.): The flags are at half staff tonight here in the nation's capital and across the country. And this is why. [Picture of explosion] The picture is now etched in our minds but still horrifying. The disastrous end of the twenty-fifth shuttle mission. The sudden death of seven astronauts: five men and two women, including the first teacher in space. Americans once again reaching for the stars. And this time, the first time, not making it. . . .

This also appears to have been one of those incidents which gets so indelibly marked in people's imaginations that they remember where they were, as so many of us remember where we were on the day that John F. Kennedy was assassinated. . . .

We invested a large part of our national psyche in the space program. It is a catastrophe, it will surely set the program back, but America will stay in space, that's where America belongs. I'm Peter Jennings, thank you for joining us. . . . Goodnight.

GRETCHEN BABAROVIC: Peter sat there from eleven in the morning until eleven at night. He never left the chair. I don't believe he ate anything. I don't believe he even got up to go to the bathroom. He walked out of there at eleven that night, still wearing his galoshes. He couldn't stop talking. It was like a hydrant spewing water. Mike Clemente, who's another colleague, and I, walked him back to the hotel. And he must have talked for an hour after that. That was the beginning of it. I knew at that point that he was going to be so good. No one was ever going to be able to touch him.

JEFF GRALNICK: He had to be the voice that the country heard. He had to be the sane person in an insane world. That day, and then again on the show that night, and then again in the special we did that night, he began to do what Walter Cronkite did the day Jack Kennedy got shot. I mean, he became — the word I always used to describe Peter was "steady" — and he became a really steady force through that broadcast. And that grew. You saw it again when we were on the air for forty-odd hours at the first Gulf War. You could just see and understand the dependence the people on the other side of the glass had for the person sitting in his chair. And God, it's an awful responsibility. I think *Challenger* was Peter's turning point. That's where I saw the man.

PETER JENNINGS (1986): *When they hired me for this job, I don't think they had any idea whether I would succeed. I tend to feel the weight of social consciousness a good deal more than three years ago. When you've done the* Challenger *broadcast and seen what power this electronic beast has, it affects you. Hopefully, it makes you more modest.*

*The summer after the* Challenger *disaster, ratings for the CBS, NBC, and ABC evening newscasts were so close that, according to the* New York Times, *they had "transformed the normally spirited competition among the shows into something fiercer. 'It's trench warfare,' said Van Gordon Sauter, president of CBS News."*

*ABC's most powerful weapon was Peter Jennings.*

HAL BRUNO: The greatest experience you could have was going on air live with a breaking story with Peter Jennings as the anchor. And it was just plain fun. It was like being on a high wire without a net. But Peter had this ability to handle it. I remember when Ross Perot had dropped out of the presidential campaign and then suddenly, without warning, he dropped back in. We had all of five minutes to go on air and start reporting. Peter pulled up all of the information in his head that a few months ago we had paid attention to when Perot was a candidate. By that time he had acquired a refreshed knowledge of the history of American politics. And we went sailing for, I guess, it must have been an hour live, jumping around to different correspondents, but mainly Peter and I talking back and forth; and then David [Brinkley] came in and it was he and Peter talking back and forth. It was just a great journalistic experience to be on with Peter live with a breaking story.

Election night was always a great adventure. You just knew that Peter was going to hit it right. He would be very, very nervous before and very concerned. "Do we know

179

everything we need to know? Is there anything we've missed? Could this happen? Could that happen?" I'd say, "Peter, don't worry. We think we know where we're going." And once the light came on and we started broadcasting, he was just terrific.

ROGER GOODMAN: Peter had an incredible talent. We would run into a control room. We'd have no idea what the story is. Peter would sit down in his chair, he'd pulled something off the wires, he'd read it, and that was it. As we started getting remotes and voices and pictures coming in from around the world, Peter was sitting there. He'd see those pictures, he'd start telling that story, and his encyclopedia inside his head was drawing out that information.

Peter had an ability I've never seen before, and in forty years of television I've worked with a lot of people. During a breaking story you would have twenty or thirty different reporters, experts, commentators coming into the ABC headquarters and Peter would use those as his palette. He would interview those people and he wouldn't tell us where he's going, and we'd go from London to Russia to Chicago, never knowing.

And Peter had a little earpiece in his ear. And the producer and the director were talking to him, telling him where we think we should go, what we have, what interviews we have: "Peter, we have ten interviews coming in from Europe, we have about five domestic interviews, we have a doctor, we have a lawyer." We would tell him the information. He and [his researcher] Nancy Gabriner would be writing it down. And then Peter would say, "Let's now go to my colleague Jack McWethy at the Pentagon. Let's go to the Soviet Union and talk to the *Newsweek* correspondent." We'd never know where he was going.

Now Peter had certain little systems. And after doing this with him for twenty-two years, I'd look up and see him pulling on his earlobe and that meant, "I can't hear you, repeat." Or he'd fix his tie, which meant, "Tight shot now. I want to talk direct to camera." . . . He would do that while he was on camera and he was talking to the world, he'd be pulling on his earlobe and I'd be going "Uh-oh, I don't know where we're going," and we'd just sit and wait and follow and make it as seamless as possible.

We're sitting in the control room using computers; Peter's all alone. I have no idea how he did it. For twelve hours — be it Princess Diana, be it the space shuttle, be it any other major disaster we had — Peter always reminded me of a trapeze walker, with no net. There was nothing, it was Peter by himself. The only thing he would sometimes do to me is, he'd roll his forefingers around each other in a "speed-up" motion, which means, get off me, I need help. And then he would turn to wonderful Nancy, to try to extract some information. But that was very seldom that I ever saw Peter do that in twenty-two years.

Peter was exceptionally calm. We were rattled, we were screaming and yelling and trying to find out where we're going and, "Quickly, we need the pictures from California," "Quickly, where's the interview?" "We need the doctor from Chicago." And Peter was the orchestra leader. He was calm. He was quiet. I can't tell you how many times we'd go away to a taped interview and Peter would say, "I want you all to calm down, everything's okay, I've got control here."

MARC BURSTEIN: No one had better instincts in live coverage than Peter. What he thought was a good idea was just about always a good idea, and so it was very often just a question of how to implement those ideas. Peter's instincts were just spectacular. If he thought something was going to work on live television, it was pretty damn well certainly going to work.

JEFF GRALNICK: Peter and I had really serious fights while he was on the air because we disagreed about things. Nobody knew it. The viewer didn't know it. Nobody else knew it. I had a little microphone, Peter had the little earpiece, and we would argue back and forth. I would speak to him in short phrases, and he would nod or not nod, and in a way that only I understood. And then, if we ever got to a commercial, he would pick up the phone, and then we would have a more direct conversation. But it never stopped being professional. We were fighting for the best way to tell a story. And when Peter was out there, you knew you were going to be okay. You knew that if you screwed up, he was going to get you through, and that was a good thing. I mean, he was about as good at it as anybody ever was or anybody ever will be. Ever.

TED KOPPEL: Peter said about himself, "The more chaotic things get around me, the calmer I get." I think that's quite right. Those of us who work in television recognize that our principal value sometimes when we're on air, especially when we're on the air live, is not to let people know what's going on all around us. There may be a frantic voice in your ear telling you that you have such and such a guest who's threatening to walk out of the studio if you don't come to him right away; that we have just gotten such and such a piece of video that you absolutely have to work into your coverage. What you can't be doing at a time like that is saying, "Excuse me just a second. Can you hold on there? I'm sorry, what was that?" You have to incorporate all of that at the same time that you are maintaining a coherent flow of information and reaching back into your memory and your reservoir of experience to put events as they develop into some kind of proper context. That's a lot tougher than it looks. And nobody was better at that than Peter.

PAUL FRIEDMAN: Peter had an incredible ability to swing with whatever was thrown at him. And he could handle new pieces of information being thrown at him while he was on the air. And he could work those individual bits of information into a running story. He would make it part of the theme of what the story was, so that it made more sense. He did it on the fly. He did it without any, "Let me think about this for a while" because he wasn't allowed to. All three of the major anchormen have to do that, and they are — were — tremendously skilled at it. Peter was, by virtue of all the preparation he did on stories. Nothing was a total surprise to him; he always had something in his background he could draw on, something he had read that he could draw on, some other experience that he could draw on, so that it wasn't totally cold, even though it was breaking news. It was something that fit in some way for Peter, and that helped the audience put things in perspective and give some context.

CHARLIE GIBSON: I remember when Yitzhak Rabin died. I got called out of a Penn State–Northwestern football game to fly to Jerusalem to cover the funeral. I got on the plane — middle seat in coach — with probably three briefing books that were very thick. I read those briefing books cover-to-cover, and I thought I had a pretty good sense of knowledge of all this. And in the midst of the special, Peter began talking about the cemetery in which Rabin would be buried and the significance of the trees that surrounded the cemetery — how many there were, where they came from, what their religious significance was. I'm going through my briefing books — where did he get that? He just knew it.

ROGER GOODMAN: You know something unique about Peter: a phenomenal amount of information was going in Peter's ear. Sometimes it was factual. Sometimes we didn't have the accurate information yet. If he didn't feel confident in it, he wouldn't say it. If we said sixty people were killed, he would not repeat it on air until he had a piece of paper in front of him that proved it by two or three people.

COKIE ROBERTS: He would be on the air with all this information coming in — or worse, with no information coming in — and he would be able to keep the viewer engaged, keep the viewer feeling he or she was informed, and also pull back the veil a little bit from the mysteries of broadcasting. He didn't pretend that he was sitting up on that set all by himself and there was no one else there. He would say, "Wait a minute. I'm hearing in my ear," or, "Could you move the camera over this way, please?" which, of course, drove the director crazy. Or, you know, "I need the information on — Thank you, Nance," and get a piece of paper of what was going on. He made it clear that he was part of a team and that he was talking to the people in the studio as well as the people at home. He did it seamlessly. I think it relaxed people at home to see how he was just regular when he did those things.

PETER JENNINGS: *I have always found that the audience very much appreciates it when we say we don't know, but we are doing our best to find out.*

GEORGE STEPHANOPOULOS: I had a great privilege because I got to sit next to Peter on a lot of big events, like conventions, like election night, at times during 9/11 as the news was breaking. Peter would be really nervous before we would go on, yet when the camera went on, it all melted away. It's amazing. The hotter the pressure got, the more the news was coming in, the calmer he became. That was a great lesson, and it is terrific to be able to watch that up close.

I think one of Peter's great skills was bringing the audience in on the process. If he had three people talking to him at exactly the same time, and the pictures weren't matching what he was talking about, he would stop everything and say, "You know, we've got a little bit of a problem here, let me tell you what's going on," and then move on to the next story. And I think breaking through that wall was a big part of the connection he established with people.

JEFF GRALNICK: Peter was a pilot. The principal broadcaster on a major breaking story is in charge. Yeah, there's a producer in the control room, and there's a director in the control room, but we are basically setting a menu for him to pick from. He would take input in his ear. After a while, you learn when a broadcaster is talking but his mind is open to accepting information and you talk in the pauses. And Peter could take information in the pauses, digest it, give you an expression that only you understood as to whether it was okay or not okay to go that way. He brought command.

MARC BURSTEIN: He had this uncanny ability to be singularly focused on the one hand, and yet be absorbing all this information at the same exact time. Sometimes I'd be talking to him, in his ear, of course, making some suggestions, or just telling him we had this or that person available, we could go to this remote, that remote, or the other remote, and it would almost be like he wasn't hearing me. All I had to do was serve up a menu to him, and he knew almost instinctively where to go next, how to follow up, what the point was that was just being made, and how to make it all seem as if it was a scripted narrative.

*Inauguration Day 1997, with Nancy Gabriner*

GEORGE STEPHANOPOULOS: You've got Peter there with a computer, getting e-mails constantly. He's sitting right next to Nancy Gabriner, the world's best researcher, who's also feeding him information, minute by minute, second by second. He's got an executive producer and director, and who knows who else, in his ear. He's got six screens arrayed in front of him with journalists, with reporters on at multiple locations and he's usually got a couple people by his side. And it's his job to take all this information coming in from so many different sources, all at the same time, and tell a single coherent story. You know, he made it look easy. It's one of the hardest things to do in the world.

JEFF GRALNICK: Peter had what all special events broadcasters had: he had a great iron seat. I mean, he could sit for hours. He had a bladder that must have been larger than an elephant, because he could stay on the air for hours and never have to get up. It's something unique in the gene pool of anchor broadcasters.

MICHELE MAYER: The first night of the Iraq War, he came in and anchored in his pajama bottoms. We had all gone home, and Peter came running down the block like the trooper that he is. He had his suit jacket and his shirt on. He got right in that anchor chair and took over, and he was completely focused, but when he stood up, he was in his pajama bottoms.

VINCENT PERRY: Over the years, I sensed his rhythms, and I could get a sense of what he wanted to do, how he wanted to have the show flow. There were times when we'd have fifteen, twenty people standing by, and he would start to ask a question, and we were all saying, "Who's he going to? Who's he going to?" My hand is spread out all over the audio console, trying to figure out where he's going. And finally at the end of the question, he might say, "Sam?" "McWethy?" This person or that person. And I'd have to lunge to the fader to open up the right thing. There were a couple of times when he'd come up to the audio booth after the show, and he'd say, "You didn't miss one. You got them all." I said, "You weren't very helpful." "But," he said, "you didn't miss any of them. You got them all." Which was his way of saying, you know, "Good job."

BILL BLAKEMORE: Peter knew how to be the leader. I once watched him take over a situation where a giant tree had fallen over a porch. His mother happened to be there. She stood aside and watched him marshalling everybody to get this giant branch that had broken off the tree moved. She shook her head and said, "You've just got to be in charge." I've often thought of that since. Peter had that in him. He did just have to be in charge. That's why he was such a great anchorman.

Because when you're a field correspondent and you're out in the middle of some chaos somewhere and it comes time to get on the air, what you want most of all is to be well-anchored. Peter knew how to do that because he'd been in the field so much. So you knew when you were going to get on the air with Peter, trying to explain the chaos that you'd just been experiencing out in the field, that he'd make it possible for you because he had to be in charge of all of these different voices that he was trying to meld at once into something that made sense. He had that innate sense of control.

TED KOPPEL: By the time he was anchoring in the '80s and '90s and then at the beginning of this decade, he was just a master. What you had by the last fifteen, twenty years of Peter's career was a complete package: a man who was visually attractive, who had a lovely voice, who had a great presence, who had the background, who had the reservoir of knowledge, and who had the ability to process all of that information at the same time that all hell was breaking loose in his ear, around him, behind him, in the control room. Never to convey any sense of that panic, but to the contrary, conveying a sense of, "It's all right, it's going to be okay, I'm going to process the information, I'll let you know what's happening, I'll let you know what you need to know. Don't worry about it."

JOHN COCHRAN: I remember when he finally felt that he really was a good anchor. He'd been doing it for a while, for a couple of years, I guess, and he said, "The first year, when you anchor an evening news show, you just wonder, can I physically do it? Can I show up every night, you know, and just get through it, and carry the whole show?" And then he said, "You get into that second year and you start to gain your confidence, and it starts to become second nature to you. And by the third year," he said, "I really think I'm an anchor now. I'm okay at this. I'm gonna make it."

*I don't set out every day to educate people. I set out every day to inform people, as best I can, and to help them, as best I can, to understand that what we're reporting on that day has some relevance and means something in their individual lives . . . And if people keep coming back because they trust us to make that judgment on a daily basis, it's hugely gratifying.*
*—Peter Jennings*

# 6
## MAKING THE NEWS

*By 1990,* World News Tonight *consis-*
*tently led the ratings race. As Jennings*
*grew more comfortable in the anchor chair,*
*he expanded his editorial control over the*
*broadcast. His colleagues — from camera*
*crews and audio engineers to producers*
*and correspondents — describe how de-*
*manding he could be, particularly when it*
*came to the crafting of scripts; they had to*
*be clean and precise. But, while Jennings*
*could be controlling, he was also deeply*
*respected. Peter Jennings was a perfec-*
*tionist whose colleagues strove every day*
*to perform to his standard.*

JEFF GRALNICK: I always used to say about
astronauts that if you met an astronaut before they went up and then saw them after
they came back, they looked different, they
carried different, they had a sense of confidence because of where they'd been that

they didn't have going in. When Peter came to the chair, he didn't have that sense of confidence. But across the first five, six, seven years, he began to understand that he really was powerful and could exercise that power in a very good way in terms of the content that was going to make air that night. I mean, he understood the power. And he used it. And he used it properly.

PAUL FRIEDMAN: It always amazes me how often people out there in the audience assume that the anchor sits there in a chair and reads copy that has been prepared for him. In fact, all of the anchors, and Peter especially, are very much involved, every step of the way, in creating the broadcast. Peter was involved in choosing which stories we decided to do and in editing the scripts when the correspondents called in and in screening the pieces that we had a chance to screen before we actually put them on the air, then suggesting changes, and so on. There was always a very detailed process that he was involved in, word by word, scene by scene.

JON BANNER: Peter's editorial control was absolute. It was a wrestling match. He rewrote every single page that he read. He edited every script, made changes up until

*The "rim" at* World News Tonight, *where the broadcast is produced and written*

six-ten, six-fifteen. There would be times where he would yell over to one of the senior producers, "Why is this sentence still in the piece?" We'd say, "Oh, we'll change it," and then, of course, we ended up not changing it. He'd sometimes catch it on the air and one of us would have a little session with him after the broadcast. He was an exacting editor. He drove us all to do a much better job than we would have done if he hadn't been there. I think that if he hadn't had that senior editor position, the job would have meant nothing to him. That was a lot of what it was about, being able to structure and script things and control how the broadcast was coming together: the placement of pieces, how much other news was put on, what pages were in the broadcast, what pages were not in the broadcast. Those were all conversations we had from the time we walked in in the morning until the time we went off the air at night.

TOM NAGORSKI: Peter was intensely involved, almost round the clock. We all came in at the same rough time, just before the nine o'clock morning meeting where things all got started. Although the intense time of day was later, you had better be prepared at nine o'clock in the morning. I was first brought on the broadcast for overseas news, which was, of course, a huge passion of Peter's. His question was always, "What's the world look like?" Sometimes it was a phone call and sometimes it was an early-in-the-morning phone call. And more often it was just when he sauntered into the newsroom. And I'd have to have a very rapid-fire answer. Sometimes it was obvious what the world looked like. And sometimes it wasn't. And sometimes I had my own ideas and they were, you know, way off-base in terms of what Peter thought.

You know, it's a cliché, but he kept you on your toes.

PETER JENNINGS: *By the time we get the news on the air at night, we've actually done a heck of a lot of work in the course of a day, or very often weeks and months in advance, trying to relate developments, which are as relevant to people who live in Medford, Oregon, as live in Maine. That's sometimes very difficult because we broadcast to a very, very wide audience of people with very diverse interests.*

PAUL FRIEDMAN: Sometimes the correspondents were offended by how much Peter was involved and how much he pushed for his ideas on how to treat a story. I don't mean that in any political way; Peter respected the views of the people he worked with. But they had to make their points clearly.

I came to believe — totally — that Peter's pushing the correspondents, pushing them to write better, and pushing them to "see things better" was an effort to make them better and to make the program better. It wasn't any "I am the boss and therefore we shall do it this way," or, "I am the gorilla anchorman and I insist that it be done this way." He was trying to make the product as good as it could be, just as he was a perfectionist about himself and making himself as good as he could be. He tried to get that out of everyone else he worked with. That made him difficult, but it was worth it.

GRETCHEN BABAROVIC: Peter cared very, very much about the young people that came up. He had extraordinarily high standards when it came to the world of journalism. So he would always make the time to spend time with these young journalists. He took his job as senior editor very, very much to heart, but he would always find the time to carve out an hour to either talk to them or critique their clip reels or their transcripts or their writing. It was never a problem. It was never trouble. He wanted to do this. This was part and parcel of who he was.

DAN HARRIS: I was twenty-eight years old and I was terrified. What a lot of people don't know is that he edits every script. And he's a tough editor — an incredibly tough editor. So as a new correspondent you go through this process and it's terrifying. And here I was sitting across a desk from him, an American icon going over [my script] with a red pen — line by line. My proudest moment at ABC — and it happened to me once

— was he handed me a script with no changes. That was great.

[Another time] I was so scared, and just barely made air. But afterwards he sends me an e-mail saying, "Call me." So I called him, scared, and he said, "Great story. Next time wear lighter shirts." And that's Peter.

JON BANNER: Peter disarmed people and made them sort of like him but also sort of a little bit nervous and scared of him. The first time I met Peter was when I was a desk assistant. I was fresh out of college, and in those days desk assistants had to make the coffee for the entire staff. Peter was in very early one morning. I had just made the coffee, and I was sitting there at my desk, reading the paper and answering phones. He came out, got some coffee, and was walking back to his office. He looked over at me and said, "Lucky thing you want to be a journalist because your coffee stinks." Then he smiled, I smiled, and immediately there was a bond there. Peter was able to rib people the right way. He'd give that magical smile, and you knew that there was a connection there.

LAUREN LIPANI: I remember being in his office, and he had a correspondent in his office. He was tearing apart this person's script, and he told him, "You've missed the point." They rewrote the script, and that person left the office. And Peter turned to me and said, "He's going to be sensational one day." Peter was hard on people for a reason. He made them better. And I know people know that.

VINNIE MALHOTRA: Peter was a mentor to a lot of young people at ABC, from producers to correspondents. Everybody wanted to be around him. Everybody wanted to feel the power, feel the passion, feel inspired by just being around Peter Jennings. He was very hard on you, but he was always very good to you. He was a wonderful teacher, and he was a wonderful friend. Spending time with Peter Jennings was an education in itself.

One trip of mine with Peter stands out far and away more than any of the others, and that was the time we traveled to Jerusalem. We were just there to shoot a small portion of a piece and ended up having an entire day to ourselves in Jerusalem, at which point Peter Jennings said to me, "Have you ever been to Ramallah, on the West Bank?" I said, "I've seen it." He says, "No, I don't think you've really seen it." And we ended up spending an entire day traveling through the West Bank. Traveling through this area with Peter was traveling through this area with a history teacher. He'd point this out, he'd point that out. He'd explain why this is this and why that is that. He stopped in the streets. He spoke to people. The day ended with us arriving at Yasir Arafat's compound. Now mind you, we don't have any cameras. We're not there to do any story. But Peter, ever the reporter, ever the teacher, wanted me to meet Arafat. And we ended up going upstairs, sitting down, and having coffee with Yasir Arafat.

JOHN MCWETHY: I was sitting in a hotel room in Brussels, about to go into my first war zone. The phone rang, and it was Peter calling from New York. He knew that I was frightened, and over the course of about twenty minutes he calmed me down. One thing he said was, "I'm always terrified when I go into a war zone." That little bit of advice helped a lot. It's the kind of thoughtfulness that Peter could display in between times when I wanted to kill him.

TOM NAGORSKI: Peter was, in many ways, like a conductor. He was forever arranging and rearranging things. He rearranged our broadcast sometimes while we were on the air. He rearranged our travel plans occasionally while we were in the air. And he sometimes went so far as to try to rearrange your personal life.

We were on a charter flight to Moscow many years ago. We'd had a little wine, and Peter started asking me about my wedding, which was just a few weeks away. All of a sudden the nice conversation got very serious and agitated because Peter said, "Hold on, you're the Foreign Editor and you're getting married smack in the middle of the South African elections." I said, "You know, I planned this long ago. I can't change the date." He said, "Never mind the date. Let's work on the venue." And we had a little more wine, and pretty soon Peter had it all figured out, produced, planned, and I was almost convinced that we'd be married in Capetown.

VINNIE MALHOTRA: When Peter walked into the *World News Tonight* newsroom, everybody gets to attention. People sit up a little bit straighter. People got their scripts in order, and it's "go time." He's the commander-in-chief when he walks into that room. Everything goes through him. He brings out the best in you. He makes you work hard. He inspires everybody in the newsroom to be at the top of their game at all times. That's why the show was so successful. That's why he was such a great leader. You would do anything not to let him down.

JON BANNER: It had been sort of a lifelong dream to be executive producer of *World News Tonight* with Peter Jennings and so you got there and he was such a force. You spent your days trying to satisfy him, please him; you spent your days trying to argue with him and win your arguments. Everything about this job was the opportunity to work with Peter. There wasn't anybody who could make me feel as challenged and as successful as Peter did. He set the standard so high for all of us that we ended up performing beyond our wildest imagination. He had an incredible ability to push his staff, from correspondents to producer to senior producer to executive producer. He didn't give up. He didn't let you slide by. He really pushed and pushed and pushed.

MARTHA RADDATZ: Peter had a way of pushing you, pushing you, pushing you, and not always pleasantly, believe me. But at the end of that experience, you always learned something. You were always a better journalist. He asked you questions. He helped you learn. I don't know that people realize the back and forth that went on. People always talk about, "Well, Peter, you know, checked some scripts." Peter checked everything. At five-thirty in the afternoon, after he'd been doing so many more things than I'd been doing, he still would call me up about my script and say, "What does this mean?" and "Why did you use that?" and "What about that? Do you really believe that? I'm not sure I believe that." I'd have to defend it or I'd have to say, "You know, maybe you're right, Peter."

BOB WOODRUFF: Peter was hard on everybody. There are many different ways to motivate people. You can draw them out by being kind and nice and gentle, or you can push them by setting a standard that's so high you want to achieve his standard and you want to please Peter. That's the way he led. We didn't always want to hear from him. We didn't always want to have comments on our scripts. We all thought that our scripts were pretty good, our stories were well written. And Peter coming in and saying it was not well written wasn't something we wanted to hear. Not on that day, maybe even not that week, but a month later, two months later, we would look back at that story and realize that the way we originally had that story written probably wasn't as good as the way it ultimately came out. And that's because Peter Jennings put his mark on it.

SAM DONALDSON: Many correspondents felt Peter was very, very domineering. He was demanding. He was exacting. He would come in and he'd look at a script for the correspondent and he'd say, "I don't think that's quite right," or, "That's wrong," or, "He's moving in the wrong direction," or, "She really doesn't have an angle here that is worth the minute you're going to have." The correspondents would naturally bridle at this. I mean, "Yes, he's the big shot, but who am I? Am I not a craftsman here? They've hired me. They're paying me." And yet at the end of the day, more often than not, Peter improved things. The script was better. The story was told in a sharper way. The focus was more understandable. A detail without which the story might not have made a lot of sense was included thanks to Peter. So I think we all believed that even though it wasn't good to get that phone call that said, "Well, I just don't think this is right," it was a help to us and certainly to our viewers.

PAUL FRIEDMAN: There were some awful, awful fights around "the rim," which was the area where we worked—Peter and I, and the senior producers. There were some awful fights where a correspondent would come with a script and Peter would get involved in changing this word and that word. The correspondents felt quite often that he went overboard. "My word is as good as his word," they would say. It was my role to mediate a lot of that. It wasn't fun, a lot of days, but the product was better.

JEFF GRALNICK: He could be damn difficult. There were times when words were exchanged on the rim that are not fit for family television.

I've described broadcast production a lot like being in an emergency room. I mean, if you watch what goes on in an emergency room, something desperately important is happening, and everybody's trying to save it and shape it all at once. It's a lot of high-energy people, a lot of high-intellect people, a lot of highly paid people, a lot of people with distinct ideas about what's important and what's right on a given day.

And if they didn't fight, it wouldn't be a good thing.

BRIAN ROSS: I've never had a tougher editor in terms of scripts. That dreaded phone call would come and Stu Schutzman would say, "You'd better come over here and see Peter in his office." That was a very bad signal. It indicated Peter wanted to go over the script from beginning to end. You'd walk in and the script would be marked up and paragraph one should be paragraph eight and paragraph seven should be paragraph two. Peter had a lot of bugaboos about which words you do use, which words you don't use. He wanted stories told simply and clearly and directly and nothing too fancy. Break it down, make it understandable.

And now I've learned to write his way, and I always will. He changed me, made me a better writer and certainly a better broadcaster. I always will think of how he instructed me, guided me on how to write, how to deliver, how to give it punch and let it breathe. Peter wanted that single clear voice. He worked so hard and achieved so much in that elegant, simple style of writing that was a trademark of his program.

PAUL FRIEDMAN: He was absolutely compulsive about being as good as he could be — and wanting to hear it if he wasn't. No problem telling Peter, "You read that badly," or "You said that badly," or "You are missing something." He wanted that. Because he wanted to be as good as he could be.

PETER JENNINGS: *I don't think you could ever be too demanding of yourself. I think I am too demanding sometimes of others.*

STU SCHUTZMAN: Peter was a very clean writer. Not flowery. Very straightforward. Very easy to understand. He labored over every word, every phrase, every inflection when he narrated. He was a perfectionist. He would do it over and over again until he got it perfect. He made us all listen and read, and listen and read, to make sure that he got it right.

PETER JENNINGS: *I'm always looking for what is the absolute essence of a story. If you think of perfume having all sorts of ingredients, it has a very central essence. . . . I'm always trying to tell people the essence of a story as it may relate to their lives. You can't relate to everybody's life at exactly the same time. But if it's the war in Iraq, or if it's a struggle at home for a better economy, or a defense against ter-*

*rorism, there is, very often, an essential core to a story. And if I do that, everything else should build on it to some extent, add sophistication to it. But I always want people to leave having had the central truth of a story.*

JOHN COCHRAN: Peter didn't like pretentious writing. He wanted us to be able to write so that people got it the first time. It's not like a newspaper, where you can say, "What was that?" and go back and read that paragraph again. You've got to get it the first time it rolls by. Peter would call and say, "Can't you say that a little simpler? I know that's an impressive word you want to use there, but can't you find a simpler word?" He wanted to make it as easy as possible for the viewer out there. He thought he owed that to the viewer, who's had a hard day, probably sitting down in front of the television. The news can be unpleasant enough; let's don't make it hard by making our scripts so convoluted that they say, "What's that all about?"

GEORGE STEPHANOPOULOS: Peter taught me how to write for TV. I still have a long, long way to go, but I think what he really taught well is that when you're broadcasting, when you're dealing with a television story, less is an awful lot more. Be spare, be precise, take your time, and don't say too much. Let each word carry the weight of the story. It is a really, really important lesson.

TODD BREWSTER: It couldn't just be dutiful journalism. It had to have a certain spark to it. . . . Peter always would say — this may sound arrogant, but I don't think he meant it arrogantly and I don't think any of us took it that way — he'd say, "Well, this script needs a little bit more of *me* in it." What he really meant was: this needs a little bit more of a populist shine to it. That's a great quality in a popular journalist — we're not just here to talk to each other; we're here to try to spread the word. I think Peter felt that calling, that sense of mission. That meant not only telling us about the world we live in but telling it in a way that everyone could apprehend.

TOM YELLIN: One of the great things about Peter as a broadcaster is he knew when to be quiet. He knew when to not say anything. He knew when to step out of the way. And when we were working together, and he'd be in the editing room, he'd often say, "Take me out of there. I don't need to say that," and, "Get rid of my question." "Take out my narration. I wrote that, it's terrible, get rid of it." He had a producer's eye for the material, and his passion was to make it work. And if making it work meant no narration — "The material speaks for itself, there is a point here that's deeper, that comes through naturally without me stepping all over it" — he'd do it.

VINNIE MALHOTRA: He was, in the edit room, a menace at times. He used to always say that he could give any producer a run for their money, and he was right. You'd be crashing a piece very late in the day, and you've got Peter Jennings standing over your shoulder, watching your every edit. And he's pointing out things that he would do differently, or, "Do you really need to use that shot?" "Can you use this shot?" "Perhaps you can cut this down?" Just him being there was such a difficult thing, working under the gun with this intimidating presence standing over you.

In time, it made me a hundred times better as a producer, to the point where every time I would cut a piece, I would just feel Peter's presence over my shoulder. It got to the point where we'd screen a piece together and I would know before he would even say anything that he's not going to like this or I have to change this. Or I have to do that. The beautiful part was you knew the piece was truly successful when Peter would watch that piece and say, "Eh, it's okay," and walk away.

CONDOLEEZZA RICE: I first met Peter in, I think, 1986 when ABC News was looking for "young faces" to do some work on the Soviet Union. . . . I learned a lot from Peter. I learned how to communicate in a concise way. He had this way of phrasing things that was so elegant, and I always thought it was because he had great understanding of the issue. If you have great understanding of the issue, then it doesn't take one hundred words to communicate ten. And academics have a tendency to take one hundred words to communicate ten.

MICHAEL CLEMENTE: Writing for Peter could be frustrating. I had the title, "The Writer." I would give him "drafts" of pages — "pre-drafts" and "drafts." And he would always rewrite them. . . . No matter what I wrote or what he wrote, he'd rewrite it a second or third time. But he was usually right. He made a point about the fact that most of what was written — whether I wrote it or he wrote it or someone else did — were not words that you would speak but were words that you would write. He was all about speaking, and not reading pieces of paper. So a lot of times, he would simply talk about the stories and then he'd say, "That's it. Write that down. That's my page." And then he'd fiddle with the copy until he was about to say it. He'd have it on the teleprompter, but he would keep fiddling with it and ad-libbing because he wanted it to sound like a conversation, and not a pre-cooked narrative. . . . For television, it's probably the most effective writing style you can have. It certainly worked for him. And I think people at home understood that he wasn't trying to talk down to them. He was trying to converse with them.

TODD BREWSTER: You could look at a script and it could read beautifully on the page. Then you would watch Peter cut it up and you'd think, "Oh my God, what's he doing to it?" Then you'd listen to him read it, and it just took on a whole other brilliant quality. Because Peter would edit and write to his own voice and his own inflection. He would write to his own mind. He knew how he was going to deliver a script. He knew where the pauses were going to be. He knew where the inflection was going to be. . . . He had a quality, the way that he delivered it, that brought all kinds of extra meaning to it. He would have a certain inflection with certain words that suggested a certain pathos, a certain yearning, a certain gravity, a certain worry, a certain excitement, whatever it may be that came in the inflection of the word itself even more than the choice of the word. You couldn't hand that script to somebody else and have them deliver it the same way that he had edited it. You had to be Peter to deliver that script.

LYNN SHERR: Peter knew how to write for himself, which could drive you crazy because if he tried to change your script, you would say, "No, Peter, I don't talk that way. You talk that way, and for you it works; it wouldn't work for me." You cannot read one of Peter's scripts and make it sound the way he makes it sound. Many, many correspondents are interchangeable. They shouldn't be, but they are. You could take one of their scripts, give it to someone else, and it would sound just fine. You could not take a script that Peter Jennings wrote and make it sound good coming out of your mouth. He had such an individual way of communicating, and of expressing himself, and of getting it to the viewer, which is all that mattered. It was his way of doing things.

*Behind the scenes of* World News Tonight, *every evening was an adventure, because the business of news is covering what's new — even as it changes while the broadcast is airing. In addition, Jennings liked to keep his correspondents on edge to infuse the broadcast with fresh energy.*

MICHELE MAYER: My job is the stage manager in the TV3 studio, mainly responsible for *Newsbrief* and *World News Tonight*. My job on the floor is to keep everything under control. I cue Peter to which camera the director wants me to cue him, to make sure everything is good for him: The set is ready. His computer is functioning. He has the correct pen. It's a calligraphy pen. If you put anything else out in front of him, he would throw it right back at you. I learned to keep a stash of these pens in my locker, in my desk, in my drawer at home in case I had to go on the road with him at the last second. These pens were everywhere, the calligraphy pens.

I made sure that he had the air-conditioning on, the soda that he liked to drink. If we were doing a breaking news story, we had food for him. And Kleenex. At one point he was drinking tea with lemon, honey, and sugar. We had his Fresca. We had the floor under control. He needed to know who was on the entire crew — who were the audio people, who was on the teleprompter, who were his stage hands, who was his camera person. He liked to know everyone's name, and he made sure that he learned everyone's name on the floor. I left him a little note right next to his computer that listed the entire staff for that day.

One day I sent him a note saying I was going to be on jury duty. I liked to tell him who would be filling in for me while I was away. He sent back an e-mail: "Have a good time. And thanks, you do good work. Oops, I said it." So I have that on paper. It's on record, he said I did a good job.

DIANE SAWYER: One of the things that always amazed me the most was watching Peter get into the desk. He would wait very late, I gather, when he had that feeling that he had to come in. Most of us would come in breathless, but he would come in and slide right into the desk, and then he'd go, "Good evening. We begin tonight. . . ." No pause. One breath, one breath from running back in the back of the room and into the chair, "Good evening. We begin tonight." And it gave you a sense of what he felt about the day, which was: "I can't wait to tell you what I've got to tell you. You need to know this. I'm so excited for you to learn what I've learned today."

MICHELE MAYER: Whatever went on during the day downstairs on the second floor, when Peter came up to that studio at six-thirty, he was focused. He took every broadcast very seriously, did the best that he could every night at six-thirty, no matter what else was going on anywhere else in his life or on the second floor or with any of his other projects that he was working on. At six-thirty, that broadcast was the best it could be every night. He wanted the best performance from everyone who worked on a show, every night, regardless of anything.

JON BANNER: He was extraordinary in his ability to process information and talk at the same time. When you're getting a command in your ear while you're talking about a completely different subject and you're trying to jump ahead five minutes or jump back to something that we want to get back to — he was extraordinary in being able to process all that stuff. And he was flawless on the air at the same time. But he was very demanding.

If there was a mistake on the broadcast, he really let you have it. There was no room for error. His goal always was perfection.

PAUL FRIEDMAN: For many years, I was the guy at the other end of the earpiece that Peter wore. I was the one saying in his ear, "Peter, we have to go do this," or, "We are thirty seconds long, so let's cut items three, four, and six." This was either during commercials or while a piece was running. Sometimes, while he was on the air, I would have to say to him, "Peter, you gotta cut it," or, "Peter, you gotta go to so-and-so." He would handle these things with such calmness and such smoothness.

I think the audience was aware how smooth and calm he was in the worst of situations, the big events, but it was also every night. We were doing a live broadcast every night, and he was simply terrific at being able to make quick adjustments — cut a thing here or add a thing there. For a producer, what a pleasure to be in a bad spot, where a piece didn't run or there was a technical error, and to be able to say into Peter's ear, "Talk for ten seconds. I'll get something else," or, "Vamp for a little while, while I figure out what to do next." And then, as he got better and better, and more relaxed on the air, he started letting the audience in on this. He would say to the audience, "We are having a problem here," or, "We've got to fix something here," or, "Can you tell me what's going on?" It became a conversation between him and the audience, which I thought was absolutely natural and absolutely perfect.

MICHAEL CLEMENTE: He was so good at ad-libbing that one time, early on, he thought, "Forget this writing. Let's just ad-lib a whole show. I do much better when I just talk to the show." So in the afternoon, we all decided on the rim what the stories were going to be. We talked to the bullet points that he wanted to make, going into each one of the pieces. I had some little 4 x 6 cards, and I wrote the bullet points. Peter started off with "Good evening," and he ad-libbed his way into the first story. Then he said, "Okay, what are the bullet points for the lead-in for the second story?" He ad-libbed the entire show. It was fun. You wouldn't have known at home. But it was a little stressful. And even at the end of the broadcast, Peter acknowledged, "All right, maybe that's a little too much. Maybe we should write it down." But that's what it was like on any given day.

JON BANNER: One of the things he was famous for, which made us always very nervous in the control room, was that he would frequently start answering his e-mail when he went to commercial. People would get e-mails from him while the show was on the air, and they would be mystified as to how he could be broadcasting the news and answering their e-mails. Well, he did it. It made us extremely nervous in the control room that he was not paying attention, but he was, and as soon as we were counting down out of commercial, he'd be right there, back into the broadcast.

LINDA BIRD FRANCKE: He developed a terrifying habit of calling in the commercial breaks during the broadcast. You'd be watching the broadcast and they'd go to Alpo dog food or whatever it was and suddenly the phone would ring and it would be Peter. I'd say, "You can't talk now. You're about to go back." He'd say, "No, no, no. Tell me, do you want sausages for the cookout this weekend, or should we have hot dogs?" And I'd say, "Peter, you can't do this. You can't do this." I would be a total wreck. He'd hang up and go sailing right on with the broadcast. He said he loved to do it, because it whee-ed him up; it put him on a bit of an edge.

JOHN MCWETHY: When we were about to do something live, Peter would talk in generalities about what we might do, but he would never tell me the questions he was going to ask. I never had a clue. His response to me was, "You'll only rehearse it, McWethy." And he was probably right. Or he'd say, "I don't want you to become stale, McWethy." Stale?! I often was caught completely off guard. I had no idea what he was doing, and we would have sort of a stumbling conversation on the air. He loved it. I hated it. It drove me crazy. Nonetheless, he kept doing it.

JOHN COCHRAN: At six-twenty-nine, you'd be standing there chatting with Peter, and he'd say, "Well, I think what's important about this story maybe is what the president said about such and such." And I'd say, "Yeah, that's fine, that's fine." I'd get all geared up for that, and then of course the question would come down the pike and be something entirely different. He *never* asked those questions we'd already discussed. He wasn't trying to embarrass people; he just wanted you to be spontaneous. He just wanted you to have to think on your feet. He thought that was good for us, good for the show, and he's right.

BARBARA WALTERS: Peter had this habit that drove some of us crazy. Just before you went on the air, you sort of figured out what you were going to say, and then, two seconds before the camera was on you, Peter would ask you a question that you never expected. You'd stumble around trying to get the answers, and sometimes they were pretty good and sometimes they weren't, and when it was done, Peter would look at you, wink, and give you that dazzling smile. Those were the days I wanted to kill him.

GEORGE STEPHANOPOULOS: Peter would go around to everyone in the minutes and hours beforehand and get a general sense of what we wanted to talk about. But I think part of his skill as an anchor was never probing too far. He wanted to know just enough to know how to spark something but not so much that it would kill the spontaneity. That was one of his real talents. If he felt that you were getting a little scripted, a little stale, he'd let you know. "Just talk to me."

PETER JENNINGS: *One of the things I think about television is that it understands a phony at the drop of a pin.*

COKIE ROBERTS: Peter often asked people

questions right before they went on the air that would unnerve them. I think he and I had a slightly different relationship, maybe because I had come from public radio and still was on public radio, and he didn't think that he could tweak me quite as much. But what he would do that just drove all of us crazy was that you'd tell him something ahead of time, and then instead of asking you about that thing, he'd incorporate all that information into the question, leaving you to say, "Right, Peter." Stole your materials, but name me an anchor who doesn't.

DIANE SAWYER: He would do it with all of us before we went on the air, this thing where he'd turn and say, seconds before you had to talk, "You really want to wear that?" Or just before you had something to say, he would say, "We better double-check those facts." I think it was his way of keeping you fresh and new and not canned, because he thought the viewer could smell canned. I also think that he lived that way; he didn't live in perfect composure. That's part of what made him so exciting to watch on the air.

CHARLIE GIBSON: Peter would often indicate to you that he was going to ask you one thing, and then he would turn and ask you another. There was always a predicate to the question that says, "Listen, Mr. Congressional Reporter, I know this stuff as do you." To some extent, that was Peter making up for what he felt was his own inadequate knowledge about things. Peter wanted to say to you, "Don't underestimate me." . . . I love intellectual arrogance, and there was a little bit of that in what he would do with you in asking questions.

SAM DONALDSON: I'd stand on the White House lawn as White House correspondent, and Peter would say, "What did the president do and what did he say?" I'd tell him and he'd say, "What does that mean? Why did he say that?" Then he'd say, "Well, how is the opposition going to react to that?" Then, "What's he going to do about that?" In other words, Peter was not satisfied with the first layer of his story.

He would ask a question and expected an answer, and then he'd start boring in. One time I was on the White House lawn, and President Reagan had done something and I reported on it, and he said, "What would people overseas think about this?" My first reaction was to say to him, "Peter, I'm not overseas. I mean, you'll have to go to London or call in somebody from Moscow to find that out." And then I realized that what he was saying was, "Is the president prepared for a reaction from overseas? How is he going to deal with this?" And I finally concluded it was a good question and I ought to find out about it.

CONDOLEEZZA RICE: I will never forget the day that the Soviet coup had just happened. Peter said to me on the air, without any warning, "Do you think this coup is going to succeed?" I was a thirty-year-old analyst. I could see my career pass before my eyes. Somehow, from the back of my mind, I said, "You know, the Army isn't supporting this coup. I think the Army is going to split. And so maybe this isn't over yet," which was the best that I could do to couch it in a way that might not get me into trouble. Afterwards, Peter said to me, "You should have just said you don't think the coup is going to succeed." I said, "But suppose it does?" He said, "Sometimes you have to take chances, Condi. Sometimes you have to take chances." I always wish I had, because of course the coup didn't succeed. But that's the way he was. He was not someone who found the middle. Peter was someone who found the important edges, who was willing to make a call.

JOHN MCWETHY: Peter was so probing, so intense, so interested in the subject matter that he would often drive correspondents who had known him for decades absolutely crazy. What we had to admit, reluctantly, is he usually made the product better. So we would give him a hug, but at times we wanted to punch him too, because he was *so* persistent.

MICHAEL CLEMENTE: He could be very stressful to work with. It wasn't about "inside office politics." It was about getting the best story on the air and getting the best narrative. I think the tension and the competition made the broadcast better each day. Frustrating? Yes. Better broadcast? Usually. Fun? Not always. But it was work. And it was interesting. And we woke up each day, and we had no idea what was going to be on that night. It was that sort of in-house competition — writing and rewriting and tension — that made it better.

CHARLIE GIBSON: When we interviewed him on *Good Morning America,* Peter was impossible to deal with. For a guy who was used to doing things in prescribed time frames, all of that went out the window when he was on *Good Morning America*. He'd ask, "How much time do we have?" "Well, we've got four and a half minutes," "Okay, and what are we going to do? What clips do you have? So then I should give you a thirty-second answer on such and such." "Yes, Peter." Then he'd go way past thirty seconds.

For a guy who knew the business as well as he did, it was just impossible to get him to take a time cue. Now, part of that was based on the fact that he didn't want to go away. It's, "If I'm going to come in here this early in the morning and talk, darn it, you should

*With Charlie Gibson and Diane Sawyer on Inauguration Day, 2005*

give me as much time as I want." But it was based partially on his enthusiasm for whatever program he was working on. He wanted to get the information out. He wanted viewers to hear this. So he would go overtime. Then Diane would grouse at me because we had just taken a minute or a minute and a half out of whatever her segment was to be next. I'd say, "Peter, you went way over." "Yes, yes, I'll be better next time." And then, of course, next time he wasn't.

DIANE SAWYER: On the air, Charlie and I used to have bets. If we debriefed Peter on the air live, we would try to see who would be corrected first, and we would place a bet on it. For a long time Charlie would never be corrected, but I would always be corrected. Maybe I would have said "mayhem" instead of "chaos," and Peter would say, "No, mayhem is less than this, Diane. This is chaos." And I'd look over at Charlie.

On the day that Peter went into the Saddam Hussein trial, Charlie threw to Peter and said, "Peter, I understand that you're one of the few journalists inside." Peter said, "No, no, not few, three." He corrected Charlie, and I went, "Yes!" Even Charlie got it. It was this devotion to precision. Peter couldn't bear it if you missed by a quarter of an inch.

ELIZABETH VARGAS: The very first time I met Peter, he corrected my pronunciation on a Middle East publication. I think I was shaking. I was young and new, and he's Peter Jennings. Very quickly, the lesson I learned was, you better do your homework. And you better get it right.

BARRIE DUNSMORE: He was never satisfied with his work or my work or anybody else's work. He always felt that it could be better. He always thought that there could be more. Peter was a real nitpicker. I mean that literally, as well as figuratively. He would come up to me when we were about to go on the air or go out somewhere, and he would brush nonexistent dust or hair from my lapels and straighten my pocket hankie or my tie or something like that. I was always a little puzzled: Is he trying to tell me that I'm not perfect? Or is he trying to make me perfect?

LYNN SHERR: He was forever telling everyone what was wrong with their makeup, with their dress, with their hair. He was a perfectionist, and we all paid the price. Most of the time — I am really sorry to admit this — he was right. I will also tell you that occasionally when I get dressed in the morning I still think to myself, "Will Peter approve?"

DAVID GELBER: Oh, he was a pain in the ass. I mean, he was the most difficult man sometimes. Peter was very good for my physical condition because the gym was right across the street from my office, and when Peter would be annoying I would just go over and work out for half an hour. Some days I did three of these. But I never lost track of how deeply committed the guy was to the stories we were doing. He was not just filling air time; he wasn't just keeping the commercials from bumping together. He believed in his work as much or more than anybody that I've ever run into in this business.

CHARLIE GIBSON: You may not have liked Peter. He may have been difficult to work with at times. He may have been nettlesome. He may not have been appreciative enough of what you did. But you never begrudged him the job because you knew he could do it better than anybody.

*The people on the other side of the camera also appreciated Jennings' doggedness. While interview subjects admit that they were often intimidated at the prospect of facing Jennings' relentless questioning, they appreciated his skill and the level of preparation he brought to his work. Jen-*

*nings' interview style was dignified, force-ful, and polite.*

COLIN POWELL: When he gets a government official on camera, Peter will ask the tough questions, but he will do it in a way that is fair. I always felt that, in my interviews with Peter, he was always being fair, and he was always trying to get to the truth of the matter in order to help the American people understand.

JOHN ANDREWS: He was very, very good, always, at asking questions. He would ask his questions not in an aggressive way, but nonetheless, he was quite persistent. And he would charm people into giving him answers. He had this immense curiosity. So the questions were always good ones. One led to another and then he'd come back to something which he'd thought of earlier but hadn't asked. He taught me a lot. He taught me that it's very, very important when you're a journalist to actually like people and get them to like you. And I think that was one of the marks of Peter. He didn't come across as aggressive or as offensive. He got a rapport with the people he was interviewing.

TODD BREWSTER: Peter was unusual in the

world of cross-fire and attack journalism and the who-can-shout-louder method of getting at stories and telling them to the general public. His approach to interviewing was not to corner somebody; it was directly out of his Canadian WASP tradition of politeness: I ask you a question, and you give me the answer. He created an environment where people felt comfortable that they were being treated with a certain respect. And they therefore respectfully gave answers that I think were a response to Peter's level of sincerity. Sometimes that meant that Peter would use his language to go around a question or come in from the back door, rather than directly ask it, indicating that there's so much more to the subject, but that he was just going to drift around the edge and let you fill it in. It's not a technique that works with everybody, but it's a technique that works with many people.

COKIE ROBERTS: Peter was the voice of civilization on television. He could not have been more civil. That arched eyebrow occasionally would be the extent of the argument that he would have with you. He would just raise an eyebrow, or say, politely, "Well, wait a minute here. Let's talk about that some more." But certainly, not any notion of confrontation or rudeness. I don't understand today's television with people being rude to each other. Why on earth do you want that going on in your living room when you're telling your children to be polite to each other?

PETER JENNINGS: *Maybe it started with the Robert Bork nomination to the Supreme Court. Maybe it was the 1988 political campaign using the image of Willie Horton, or the Clarence Thomas hearings, Whitewater, the Clinton sex scandal, the Clinton impeachment, the 2000 election. Whatever it may have been, the public dialogue today is often rude and vulgar to the point where I think it is shameful. It is true that we have been through ugly cycles before. But today I think that it is made much worse by the constant need for the drama of conflict that many broadcasters seem to demand. Our national conversation is very often a shouting match — and too much of it is infected with venom.*

*I'm not naïve and I do not imagine a world in which we all get along. And I do not think we need to single out the right or the left, the talk radio ranters or the angry columnists. To some extent we are all culpable — including the staid center, which if only by its silence is not without responsibility. . . . Our modern com-*

*munications system and other technologies have increased the volume of public argument to an unholy racket. Our national conversation sometimes feels impoverished as a result. . . . Civility doesn't just promote decency; it also leads to a fairer exchange of ideas and a greater chance of finding workable solutions to the kinds of problems we face.*

KEITH SUMMA: Peter was a hard interviewer. He would ask hard questions and he would push and he wouldn't let go. He would tell people, "You're not answering the question. Now, answer the question." But what's amazing when you go back and look at all of his interviews, he was always composed and polite. He was never rude. He never played some of the games that are played in this business where you try and trick an interview subject. He didn't do that. He didn't need to. He was always very fair and decent with people in interviews. And in some cases, he let them dig their own graves.

TOM YELLIN: Peter and I had just started doing prime-time documentaries, and one of the things we wanted to do from the beginning was do stories that weren't being covered elsewhere. We had figured out, through one of our great reporters, that the United States was supporting the non-communists' resistance in Cambodia with lethal weapons, which was against American law. As a result, we were supporting the Khmer Rouge, which was against American morality. We thought that was a story that needed to be told.

Peter interviewed Under Secretary of State Richard Solomon. What's particularly striking about this interview is that Solomon made a horrendous mistake: he actually told the truth. And he was trying not to. And rather than point his finger at him, and say, "Oh, we caught you," Peter was just enormously polite with him. That was really, really effective on television. And that's Peter's personality. That's how he treated people. You know, he wasn't the greatest confrontational interviewer. He wasn't someone who was able to say, "Do you mean to tell me . . . ?" He couldn't do that. But he knew what the truth was. Holding people accountable to what's true, when he had really done his reporting and he had the information, was something he was enormously comfortable with. He did it in his own way — politely, but forceful. That was consistent with his on-air persona. It was dignified, it was forceful, and it was polite.

STU SCHUTZMAN: Peter knew so many world leaders on a personal level from all his travels over the years. And he was able to talk to them on their own level before the interview started. Once the interview started, he knew their subject cold, and he knew them cold, and he was able to follow up on questions. He wouldn't let them get away with an answer that he thought was less than truthful. He was always fair. He never tried to "trick" anybody, especially world leaders. He never tried to have a "gotcha" on them. And they sensed that, and most of the world leaders that he interviewed over the years were fairly forthright with him.

RUPEN VOSGIMORUKIAN: Other correspondents — I've worked with them. They think they have to corner whoever they're interviewing — a guy, a lady, a gentleman, a soldier — by putting difficult questions at the beginning, so that he will surrender and will say what they want. Peter never did that. On the contrary. Before every interview used to start, he used to go in a corner and speak with the person, try to know who he is, what he is. Then, for the first half of the tape, he will ask questions that the guy would like to answer. So when the moment came to hit the difficult question, the guy will be happy to answer because he has talked for the last fifteen minutes about what he wanted. Now it is Peter who's asking the question, so he'll say things after the first fifteen minutes he would not answer to any other correspondent.

STU SCHUTZMAN: The Saddam Hussein interview in 1991 was an amazing interview. It was done in one of Saddam's palaces in Baghdad. It was just before the Gulf War, before the invasion. It's a very tense atmosphere. You have to have your hands checked for poison before you could shake hands with Saddam. There are very nervous young guards armed to the teeth everywhere you looked. And Peter's first question to Saddam Hussein was, "So, Mr. President, when you go outside, out and about in Baghdad, how do you feel when you see your picture absolutely everywhere?" And it disarmed Saddam Hussein. He chuckled for a second, and he said, "Well, Peter, it's like getting up in the morning and shaving, just looking at yourself in the mirror." That set a different tone than either one had in mind for the interview. While it was long, it went quite well for the rest of the way.

COLIN POWELL: We need more Peters. We need more people who understand that their role as an anchorperson or as a media analyst, someone who presents themselves to the American people as a newscaster — not a shouter or a screamer, not a partisan on the left or a partisan on the right, whatever your personal views are — but as somebody who has an obligation to the American people, that this isn't the time to shout and scream. This is the time to talk to government officials, to talk to other people who have knowledge of an issue that's being discussed, of the crisis of the moment, and to help the American people understand. Not to sway them, but to educate them. And to do it in a way that is calming. To do it in a way that says: a professional is now helping you understand the problem, understand this crisis.

PETER JENNINGS: *Television interviews are often conducted as confrontations, with the questioner sometimes shouting down his subject until he reveals his "hidden" biases. . . . Much of today's journalism, I'm sad to say, seems to be grounded in the desire to hurt or expose or belittle. . . . It is always cheaper to shout an argument than to report a story. Reporting is not only expensive. It is unpredictable — that's the great thing about journalism, its unpredictability — but it very often introduces complexity that disrupts hard right or hard left points of view.*

AL SHARPTON: He definitely had a moral compass. I think that he saw himself as a reporter in the tradition of making sure the truth was told. I think that that's why he gave comfort to some that didn't ordinarily have comfort with mainstream media types, especially big network anchors. And probably discomfort to others who expected anchors to say and do things that were sort of by the script. You always got this feeling that Jennings had his own script and was going [to] his own place in the story. You never quite were at ease in the sense that you felt you had convinced him. The best you could do was perk his interest a little.

GEORGE STEPHANOPOULOS: [When I was at the White House] Peter was a little scary. Never knew what he was going to say. Never knew where he was going to come from. He had a healthy disrespect for politicians, even though he could also respect their skills, especially with President Clinton, but he was always skeptical of any candidate for office. And he communicated that, particularly if you were working for one of those candidates. He had zero time for spin. You could tell he wasn't listening, so you didn't bother trying.

BILL CLINTON: The truth is that it was always a little bit frightening because you knew that he would first ask hard questions and then ask harder follow-ups. He would never let anything go, and I liked that about him. He rose to the top of his profession based on dogged determination and an incredible curiosity, a lot of talent and hard work, and you knew that all of that was going to be bearing down on you every time he interviewed you. He would come prepared. He would be diligent and he would be insistent. You wouldn't be able to, you know, slink out of the deal. A lot of times as president . . . [there are] whole things you would just as soon not talk about. [You are] not ready to, or for all kinds of reasons. Peter would just keep putting the hammer down, and I liked that about him. Once in a while we had genuine disagreements, and sometimes we would have outright arguments, but I always liked him.

PETER JENNINGS: You love history, sir. Rate yourself as a president.

BILL CLINTON: I'm not going to do that. Anything I say is wrong. It's a lose–lose deal. I got, you know, my wife's in public service. I'm still trying to do things as a former president. And I have no business being the judge of my own presidency right now. . . .

JENNINGS: Fifty-eight historians, as I think you may know, did this for C-SPAN. And they were all across the political spectrum. And they came out, in general terms, that you were 21st. And on public persuasion and economic management, they gave you a fifth. Pretty good.

CLINTON: Pretty good.

JENNINGS: They gave you a forty-first on moral authority.

CLINTON: They're wrong about that.

JENNINGS: After Nixon.

CLINTON: They're wrong about that. You know why they're wrong about that? They're wrong about it.

JENNINGS: Why, sir?

CLINTON: Because we had $100 million spent against us and all these inspections. One person in my Administration was convicted of doing something that violated his job responsibilities, while we were in the White House. Twenty-nine in the Reagan–Bush years. I'll bet those historians didn't even know that. They have no idea what I was subject to and what a lot of people supported. No other president ever had to endure someone like Ken Starr indicting innocent people because they wouldn't lie, in a systematic way. No one ever had to try to save people from ethnic cleansing in the Balkans and the people in Haiti from a military dictator who was murdering them. And all of the other problems I dealt with, while everyday, an entire apparatus was devoted to destroying him. And still, not any example of where I ever disgraced this country, publicly. I made a terrible public–personal mistake. But I paid for it. Many times over. And in spite of it all, you don't have any example where I ever lied to the American people about my job, where I ever let the American people down. And I had more support from the world, and world leaders, and people around the world when I quit than when I started. And I will go to my grave being at peace about it. And I don't really care what they think.

JENNINGS: Oh, yes, you do, sir. Oh — excuse me, Mr. President, I can feel it across the room. You feel it very deeply.

CLINTON: No, I care. You don't want to go here. You don't want to go here. Not after what you people did and the way you, your network, what you did with Kenneth Starr. The way your people repeated every little sleazy thing he leaked. No one has any idea what that's like. That's where I failed. You wanna know where I failed? I really let it — it hurt me. I thought I lived in a country where people believed in the Constitution, the rule of law, freedom of speech. You never had to live in a time when people you knew and cared about were being indicted, carted off to jail, bankrupted, ruined, because they were Democrats and because they would not lie. So, I think we showed a lot of moral fiber to stand up to that. To stand up to these constant investigations, to this constant bodyguard of lies, this avalanche that was thrown at all of us. And, yes, I failed once. And I sure paid for it. And I'm sorry. I'm sorry for the American people. And I'm sorry for the embarrassment they performed. But they ought to think about the [way the] rest of the world reacted to it. When I — when I got a standing ovation at the United Nations, from the whole world, the American networks were showing my grand jury testimony. Those were decisions you made, not me. I personally believe that the standing ovation I got from the whole world at the United Nations, which was unprecedented for an American president, showed not only support for me, but opposition to the madness that had taken a hold of American politics.

COLIN POWELL: You knew that you were being interviewed by somebody who knew as much about your business as you did. I mean, Peter had been all over the world. He knew foreign policy. He also knew domestic policy, and he understood the mood of the country. He knew what people needed to know to understand the issues of the day. . . . He was going to get to the facts that the people needed to know, and you weren't going to spin him. . . . You should be tough with those of us who are in the government. We are answerable to the people. And the way we answer to the people is through free press. And the way we go about that is being accessible to correspondents and anchorpersons such as Peter. They have a responsibility to the American people to allow them to understand what's going on in the world. And nobody did it better than Peter.

BILL CLINTON: He often asked me questions where his own view was evident in the tone of his voice and the way he asked the questions. Like he couldn't pretend not to be a human being with feelings and convictions, especially on Bosnia. It was always clear where he thought we should be and

*With President Clinton aboard Air Force One*

what we should do, but that never stopped him from letting you get out a contrary view. . . . He couldn't help that his mind and heart were swayed in a certain way by problems he saw in the world, but if you didn't see it the same way, or you didn't do what he thought you should do, he still always let you answer the question in your own way, which is all you can ask of somebody.

CONDOLEEZZA RICE: In Peter's case, because he so loved international politics, I know he worked very hard on what questions he should ask. How could he break through the veneer? How could he not get just the talking-points answer from a certain leader? He worked very hard at that. He read. He talked to people. . . . You knew it was going to be a well-prepared interview, and you knew that the questions were going to be in balance and about the subject matter.

AL SHARPTON: We did a story about Gary, Indiana, and I talked about how we had lost the fervor in Black America that I felt we had in the '70s. I started talking a lot about my disappointment with black-on-black crime and a lot of our inward kinds of destructive behavior. And Peter leaned back in his chair, and he looks at me, and he says, "Are you

*Interviewing National Security Advisor Condoleezza Rice, Sharm El Sheikh, Egypt*

saying that you have come to see that maybe — you had to fight the demons in yourself, in your own community?" I think he made me come to terms with something that I probably didn't want to come to terms with personally. He had the courage to ask the question, but he . . . didn't do it in a condemning way. He did it in a way, like, "I kind of understand how you had to grow and develop, and I'm going to help you say this because I think it's important you say it, not only for you, but for the country." I will never forget that interview, out of all that I've done. It always strikes my mind because he was so honest, and so poignant, and so effective at how he told that story.

He kind of helped coach me into saying that some of what happened to the dreams was, we undermined the dreams ourselves . . . sometimes we were knocked down, but sometimes we stumbled on our own. And even though we were not responsible for being down, we were responsible for not getting up. It was, kind of, him coaching me through that interview that made me come to terms with that.

COLIN POWELL: When the cameras are off, and this is the case with almost every anchor or other media person that I've worked with in television, you kind of do a quick box score as to who won. Did I beat you? Or did you beat me? Did I best you? Or did you best me? And as one of my friends in the media business told me many years ago when I first started out at a senior level, he said, "We always win. As long as we can get you to tell us what you believe. That's all we're here for."

AL SHARPTON: With some reporters it's totally adversarial. With some you say, "I think I convinced him; I closed on that one." You never closed with Peter. You'd never hang up the phone, saying, "I think I closed on that one. Peter Jennings is going to go with this issue." He always would leave the door open, which I guess made him the great journalist he was, because he would always make you stay on your toes and really know what you were saying. . . . The close with Peter was always when you watched the news that night, and he would do it his way if he did it at all.

BARBARA WALTERS: He interviewed almost every world leader. He wasn't afraid sometimes to tease them. He would ask all of the serious questions and then do with the head of state what he did with us: ask the question that caught them off guard. I would watch sometimes and think, "There you go again, Peter! Even with Boris Yeltsin, there you go again."

DON HEWITT: Peter didn't seem to be one of those guys who wanted to call attention to himself. He wanted to call attention to what he was telling you. They're rare. There are a lot of reporters in television, and some of them are very good out in the field. But there's a special talent to being an anchor.

I hate that word, "anchor." I think it's the worst, and I invented it. We were in Chicago at the 1952 political convention, and we were sitting around the stockyards there talking. We had this new kid named Walter Cronkite, and said, "Well, it'll be like a relay team. You'll each hand the baton off, but Cronkite will run the anchor leg, the last leg of a relay." That's where "anchor" came from. There are anchors today who don't have the slightest idea why they're called anchors. They think it has something to do with boats. . . . I'm always amazed at how many anchor people have no idea that it's a relay term. And Peter was the ultimate. He was an anchorman in a class with Walter Cronkite. There's no higher compliment.

TOM BROKAW: Peter had anchorman élan. I didn't know how else to describe it. He just seemed to be born to fill that job. He did earn it — it wasn't birthright — but his broadcasting skills were matchless. You could see when he sat down in the chair how much he loved being there on a daily basis.

JON ALTER: The thing about Peter Jennings is that he was a complete television newsman. If he were a baseball player, he would be [the] guy who could swing from the left side of the plate, pitch, play the outfield, and do them all effortlessly.

TOM YELLIN: You know, being a great broadcaster is a talent. You either got it or you don't. It's like being able to play the violin, or being a great baseball player. And Peter has it, you know. He just had it.

*I get up every day thinking that something is going to happen in the world that I didn't know about yesterday and I have the opportunity to pass some of that on to the audience. I get up every day knowing that I can learn or understand something better—and that it is my job to do so. I think that's fabulously exciting. No wonder we're passionate. We'd be nuts if we didn't like that.*

*—Peter Jennings*

# 7
# WORLD NEWS TONIGHT

*Peter Jennings was an internationalist. He believed in reporting stories that mattered, many of which took place outside the United States' borders. Jennings was confident that his audience would continue to watch foreign news, presented in a meaningful and intelligent way, even when sensationalized domestic stories grabbed the headlines.*

JEFF GRALNICK: It wasn't *World News Tonight* by accident. It was *World News Tonight* because it covered the world. And that unique sensibility that Peter brought to his coverage of a foreign story, he brought to the anchor chair. When those of us who are U.S.-centric wanted to drop a story out of the broadcast in place of something else, but that story really was a part of the fabric of what was happening, Peter would lobby like hell for it.

SAM DONALDSON: He understood that if we in this country didn't know about the culture, the religion, the way of life, the way of political organizations of countries around the world, we couldn't deal with them effectively.

I think it's true that *World News Tonight* did a better job and a more comprehensive job when it came to foreign coverage. Peter cared about it. Peter pressed for it. Peter could get his way. If Peter said, "We need to do this story. There's a famine over here; there's genocide going on over there; there's a civil war raging here, and it could spread," then we did that story. . . . Peter was not insular. He understood that we are in this world and he wanted Americans to know about it.

PETER JENNINGS: *There are a lot of people in the world with whom the United States is in an adversarial relationship. I think it's really important that we understand how they think. It's very reassuring to know how we think, and what our standards are, but it's really important in order to either confront, deal with, challenge, even prevail over an adversary, to know how he or she thinks as well.*

JONATHAN ALTER: Peter carried the flag for

*With Soviet leader Mikhail Gorbachev, Moscow, 1991*

international reporting. Day in and day out he figured out a way to get stories that were not very visual onto his broadcast. They weren't "news you could use"; they didn't necessarily relate directly to Americans; but they were important. They might have been about Indonesia or Pakistan or places that people couldn't even find on a map. Why did viewers need to know that? Because, to be informed citizens, Peter thought you needed to know about the rest of the world and too few other people in our business think that way.

PAUL FRIEDMAN: Every day, Peter pushed to get the extra foreign news item in the show. "Nobody else is going to do that," he would say. "Let's do that." While we were on the air, we would cut things and add things. That's the way we did the program. Peter would always be pushing to use a foreign item. I would say, "No, no, no, that's boring" and we'd go back and forth during the commercial or sometimes while all the pieces were running on the air. Some days he would get his way, and sometimes I would get my way.

JON BANNER: His view of *World News Tonight* was that it was a serious broadcast that spent half an hour on stories that mattered and had impact. . . . And there were stories that you knew it wasn't even worth mentioning, because we just weren't going to do them. Peter didn't do them because he thought they were unworthy; he didn't do them because he thought there were so many more important things to discuss. He elevated the debate among all of us in his inner circle to the point that we ended up becoming much smarter about the stories that we ended up putting on the air.

PETER JENNINGS: *I think that all of us who*

*work in our newsrooms believe all the time that there are ethics and rules, very often unwritten, by which we should live. They have to do with responsibility. They have to do with being fair, and getting it right as often as you can, anyway. After all these years, I don't find it a burden. I find it an invigorating way to live, knowing that someone will come at us in the middle of a day with a particular story, and that I know, just instinctively, that I want to know the other side of the story.*

BOB WOODRUFF: One of the things I always appreciated about Peter was that he saw the world through a very complex lens. It has always been my feeling that this world is a much more complicated place than it often is portrayed in the media. He knew, as we've heard him say so many times, that there are always two sides to these coins. If you see one side, flip it over and take a look at the other. Whenever I went anywhere around the world, he reminded me that where you're going is not a simple story. You really have to probe layer by layer, level by level, to really understand what is going on.

TOM YELLIN: If you're trying to make a newscast or deliver information based only on what people have already told you they

want to know, then you're completely mis-
understanding the role of a journalist. That's
something that I learned from Peter. A journalist is supposed to figure out what matters
and then report on that. If you do that well,
then people are going to care about it. The
news by definition is something people don't
know. It's not something people do know. If
all you do is tell people what they already
know, over and over and over again, you're
not a journalist. Peter believed that with
deep, deep passion.

*Taping* Peter Jennings Reporting: *"Minefield: the
United States and the Muslim World"*

TOM NAGORSKI: One question Peter asked constantly, but particularly in our morning editorial meeting: "What are we going to do today that will distinguish us?" He despised predictability, mediocrity of any kind, laziness. He loved it when we were able to do something, even if it was just an angle or a phrase in a piece, that he felt, with the limited time we had, distinguished us.

About the worst thing you could do at our morning meetings was to come in and say, "Such and such is probably pretty interesting. It actually may be a pretty important story, but I can't imagine the audience is really going to care." Boy, did that drive Peter bananas. First he'd say, "What makes you think they're not going to care? Show me some surveys, some scientific proof that makes your point." And then he'd say, "You think they don't care? Let's make them care."

Peter disliked intensely any suggestion that the audience wasn't going to be interested in a story, particularly if we ourselves were expressing some interest in it. That might be the suffering of some community around the globe. It might be a fairly complicated political story that seemed impenetrable. It might be a story about the American West. Whatever it was, he felt it's a non-answer or a poor

261

substitute for journalism if you said, "I can't imagine the audience can care about that." His point was, really, we are supposedly intelligent people, let's tell the story in a way that will make them care. Peter trusted his gut, and I think he was right ninety-nine times out of a hundred about what the audience cared about.

JEANMARIE CONDON: When Peter became passionate about a story or curious about a story, he became very excited about the new things he was learning. We would sit down and he would say, "Why are we doing this? We should tell people why we're doing this. We have to tell them why they should care, why it's important." He said that over and over again. He'd want to share his enthusiasms with his audience, and he trusted them to be just as intelligent as he was, just as interested in the world, just as engaged with its problems, and just as capable of having their curiosity piqued by something as he was. He never thought his audience was stupid.

I've never met another journalist who had as much respect for his audience as Peter did. He never talked down to them and he never tried to make things seem simpler than they really were. He never thought that they couldn't handle the fact that the situation was complex. In fact, I would go so far as to say, the more complex the problem, the more he wanted to talk to his audience about it. Peter would get furious if you suggested

Dec. 19, 1988
Dear Roone:

I would like to go to the Middle East for at least a week early in the New Year. . . .

From Tel Aviv and Nablus, from Damascus, Amman, and maybe even from Beirut.

By the end of January or early February the first shock waves of the PLO's announcement will have made their mark, and a wide variety of people will be faced with making serious decisions about how they intend to pursue the future. Or the Past!

The theme of the trip should be "The Threat of Peace."

It will be time to hear from many people who have had their lives and their most ingrained beliefs turned upside down by recent events.

PJ

that you shouldn't do a story because the audience wouldn't care or just wouldn't get it. He would be furious about that.

JONATHAN ALTER: The rap on Peter was that he took himself a little bit too seriously. I thought that was a good thing because that meant he took the viewers seriously, too, and he thought the viewer could connect to the importance of some of these international stories that were a little bit hard to figure out. And if they couldn't and they changed the channel, Peter's attitude was, "I can live with that, and I'm going to use some of my prestige and my clout with the suits to make sure we still have this kind of reporting on *World News Tonight* and that *World News Tonight* is really *World News Tonight* and not just United States News Tonight."

I think of him in the newsroom and you're trying to do that rundown in a twenty-two-minute broadcast, and things are being cut left and right. What Peter did was, he put his own prestige on the line night after night to include international stories that would have otherwise gotten the ax. Basically, his message to the suits was, "Look, you can't fire me because your ratings will be lower if you replace me with somebody, so you are just going to have to suffer with the fact that I want to do some of this serious reporting that might not get the numbers that other kinds of reporting could get." And he made management accept that.

PETER JENNINGS: *If people want sports and fashion and cooking, and cooked-up personal conflict, there are plenty of places to find it. If they want news, we should resolve to give them that. The stories are out there. Curiosity is not dead.*

DAVID WESTIN: He would come in every morning full of ideas about what we should be covering, how we should be covering it, and, frankly, what we should not be covering. He was not shy about expressing those views and then pursuing them zealously throughout the day, right up to the time of the broadcast. We didn't always agree on everything, although, as Peter would say, we agreed on more things than people thought we did. But we knew what Peter stood for and that as our anchor he would keep us from drifting into currents that from time to time would seem pretty powerful but were not taking us to any good place.

KEN AULETTA: News presidents would come in, and he outranked them in experience and in knowledge. And they had to defer to him, not just because he was the 800-pound gorilla, which he was — which all anchors are with their big staffs and everything geared towards promoting the anchor — but because Peter Jennings, like Tom Brokaw and Dan Rather, had enormous experience. But they all had something else: they had clout. Any time a news president or a producer or a company president talked about Peter Jennings or what to do at the evening news — Maybe we should cut some more bureaus? Maybe we should cut more in this? — they also had to think, "What is Peter Jennings going to say? Is Peter going to go public?" If he goes public, I mean, he would instantly command major news coverage. So he was a kind of a counterwave pushing for more international coverage at ABC, keeping the bureaus open, keeping the news serious.

PETER JENNINGS (2004): *The U.S. is pretty much running the world now and in much of the media we are not telling you enough about how it is being run. . . . One would like to think that if the public rattled our cage more vigorously and made itself clear that it valued more reporting about the use of American power in the rest of the world, we would be more re-*

*sponsive. . . . Surely after 9/11 I do not need to make the point that events in distant places are having a profound impact on all of us. The television networks used to have news bureaus in most parts of the world. . . . We now have a handful of foreign correspondents. Unless you rattle the cage, is there any reason for the networks and the cables to believe that you really care? Those of us who do care could use your help.*

PETER OSNOS: It's so often the case that we're measured by our salaries or our ratings or the success of a given show. Peter did a lot of shows that defied the issue of the ratings. He earned, over a long career, the right to call the shots. At twenty-six, when he first went on the air, everybody looked at him and said, "He's a callow fellow." He went off and got decades of experience. Peter and I were in Vietnam. We were very young, and we were ignorant, but I think we had good instincts. We stayed on long enough until we stopped being ignorant, and hopefully we held onto our instincts. That's what Peter did. I think the work he did, the way he drove his colleagues to take on big subjects, and the passion and the devotion that he expressed to those things was something that he earned over time.

What made him so distinctive is that in a time and culture which is so driven by the ratings and the demographics, Peter had the stature and the experience to confound that. He did it because he thought it was right, and fortunately for him, he got the numbers and he got the demographics. But he couldn't have done it if he didn't have the experience, if he didn't have the depth, if he didn't have the curiosity, if he didn't have the respect of his colleagues.

PAUL FRIEDMAN: Oh, he cared a lot about ratings. When we were number one in the ratings, he used to say, "I don't like this. I don't like being number one because that means somebody is after us." Of course, he loved being number one. Who doesn't? Peter cared about being the best. And in our business, ratings often mean who is the best.

PETER JENNINGS: *I fear that one thing competition and financial constraints have done is not only to send us all chasing the same story, but very often forcing us to know in advance what we are going to get. It is competitive madness, which frustrates the viewer. I believe that as a consequence, we who work in the news divisions of the commercial networks have driven away that part of our audience, which for so long expected us to explore the world on their behalf, to seek out the unspoken issues and make them meaningful. And it is something of a vicious circle. We don't do as much exploring and interpreting as we might, so those who seek that leave us. So we do less and more people leave us. Surely someone will figure that out.*

DIANE SAWYER: In a day where there is an increasing blur of all sorts of lines between news into everything else, Peter had clarity. He had clarity about what he would cover on his broadcast. Sometimes you didn't agree with him. Sometimes you wanted to know some things that he wasn't going to tell you on his broadcast. But there was such integrity in knowing that he maintained his standards.

MICHAEL CLEMENTE: It was difficult at times because it's easy to give people what they want. If they want scantily dressed people dancing on the desk — sure, you can stop people from using their clicker by using any number of tricks. And in some cases, what Peter thought they needed to know was like taking medicine. But that was the right thing to do. It was *World News Tonight*. It wasn't *World Entertain-*

*ment Tonight*. That's where the tension was.

PAUL FRIEDMAN: I do believe that sometimes that judgment went too far in the direction of "purity." And, to some extent, it hurt our ability to get ratings. Obviously, it didn't hurt too much, because Peter was number one for many years. But there is a famous case where we were at a political convention and the story of Woody Allen and his marriage and his affairs broke all over the place. Peter absolutely refused to use that story. "We are here covering a convention. This is important business. We can't be wasting time on Woody Allen and what he is doing with various women." I agreed with him, and it was a mistake. The irony, as somebody later said to us, was, "You guys, there is no question about your commitment to quality and to 'important news.' If anything, that gives you the right to do the Woody Allen story that people are interested in. Then why not do it?" That was exactly right. We made a mistake in that case. A lot of it was this desire to be "purer than pure" about the news.

KEN AULETTA: Did Peter Jennings sometimes feel upset about what was happening to journalism, the business he grew up in and loved? You bet he did. . . . Suddenly the documentaries are about, you know, basically frivolous subjects that may grip attention — Brad and Angelina — but, my God, that's not a world he wanted to operate in. And when he saw it, it depressed him.

CYNTHIA MCFADDEN: As passionate as Peter was about the things that he liked, he was just as passionate about the stories he didn't like. I covered a bunch of them, from O. J. Simpson to Michael Jackson, Martha Stewart, Kobe Bryant. These were all stories that Peter found hard to swallow. His instructions were often very simple: be clear, be fair, and don't use adjectives. These stories were full of adjectives. He wanted the raw facts, as simply and as quickly as possible.

PAUL FRIEDMAN: Peter had extreme views about tabloid journalism. He hated the O. J. Simpson story. He hated the Michael Jackson story. He hated the "mother kills baby and found in the trunk of a car" story. "Let other people do that," he'd say. It was always a debate, because the conventional wisdom is that those kinds of stories were what interested people and what brought them to the program, and that they did wonderful things for your ratings. Peter felt strongly, "That's not me. That's not what I do." Frankly, I was never able to decide whether that hurt *World News Tonight* ratings, or whether people respected him and us for taking the higher road.

PETER JENNINGS (1995): *Where's the restraint? It isn't that I regret our coverage of the O. J. trial. I object to it having been so extensive in so many places, put on the air for fear of losing viewers that we crowd out much of the world in our somewhat crazed pursuit of the latest O. J. advantage. This is a hard question: How do we report in a restrained manner in such a competitive atmosphere? How do you hold back the piece of information that you know is merely alleged . . . when you know that the competition may go on the air with it? . . . Do we take that extra time to think of the ramifications of what we say?*

JEFF GRALNICK: I was at NBC and I was competing with *World News Tonight*. Brokaw recognized that the Simpson trial was culturally important. Here was one of America's greatest athletes, a member of the Hollywood establishment, who was being accused of murdering his white wife. Tom knew that this was going to be a story and that it was going to mobilize thought in the country. We sat and talked about how we needed to pay attention to this story in all of its parts. We agreed that we were going to devote as much time as that story needed each night. Other broadcasts elected not to. I don't know what was happening at ABC at that time, but we always viewed [what they didn't do] as a fatal error and as an opening. We leaped at it and it took NBC where it wanted to go, and it slowed ABC down.

CYNTHIA MCFADDEN: It's worth noting that when the O. J. Simpson trial was such a dominant force in the news, Peter was very proud to say that his broadcast did less of it than any of the other networks. And the ratings changed at just that point; NBC took over. Peter had been dominant. He had been in first place. And Peter was proud of the fact that, whether the ratings followed him or not, he was not going to "pander" to those kinds of stories.

TOM NAGORSKI: Peter was made well aware during the O. J. Simpson trial of a perception among the media critics and the establishment that we lost audience or lost ratings because that may have been a story that people *said* they didn't really care about or that was tawdry and yet seemed to keep watching. Peter's answer was never to say, "Okay, tomorrow I'm going to go do an O. J. Simpson story." His basic attitude towards stories like that was either, "We're just not going to do that," or, "If we're going to do it, we're not going to be record-keepers." He felt that a space on the evening news in that half-hour was valuable. It needed to have something extra and something different.

JON BANNER: He understood when stories were important, even if you had to drag him to get him there. But in the process of arguing with him about a story, he would find an angle that was interesting. He made you think smarter and produce pieces that were smarter on subjects that he thought were slightly tabloid. There were interesting angles to those stories that he found to be completely acceptable to the evening news format. There were Michael Jackson stories that he thought were interesting. There were semi-tabloid stories that, if you found an angle, he was very accepting of.

PETER JENNINGS: *I may surprise you by saying that not all of what you see as sensationalism should be easily dismissed. . . . Is it possi-*

ble that O. J. highlighted the continuing divide between the black and white in a society whose youthful idealism as regards the progress of race relations had long ago soured? [I] try not to serve sensationalism for its own sake, but to recognize that a story should be told for its significance, not merely its sizzle.

While America tuned in to the O. J. Simpson murder case, Jennings insisted on covering a very different subject: the war raging in Bosnia and Herzegovina. He would eventually devote three hour-long prime-time specials to the conflict. From 1992 to 1996, ABC dedicated more time to covering Bosnia than any other network, largely due to Jennings' commitment to the story.

PETER JENNINGS: *We're guilty in journalism of not paying attention to fires until they're roaring. And I am one of those people who believes that the more attention we pay to the first wisps of smoke, the more the contribution we'll make.*

GRETCHEN BABAROVIC: When Peter began to be interested in Bosnia, the mainstream media really wasn't paying much attention to it. It was out there, and you heard about it, but all of a sudden, he became engaged by the genocide that was going on over there, and it became very, very important to him, and therefore, we did the hours. We began to carry it on the nightly news. We did the children's programs. I've always felt that the attention of this country was brought to the forefront by his efforts.

JEFF GRALNICK: He argued with the network and with news management that we needed to do an hour prime-time live program on Bosnia. We built this map of the region that Peter walked around on for an hour. Basically, he did a wonderful geography and history lesson that made that place and its war and its ugliness totally understandable. Just one of those little lost programs we did that was probably one of the best we did.

DAVID GELBER: I remember when I first came to ABC, one of the executives took me out for lunch and showed me minute-by-minutes, which are ratings tests of what people supposedly want to see and what they don't want to see. His point was that people want to see stories that directly affect them — liposuction, how to buy a cheap airline ticket. Americans don't care that much about stories like Bosnia. I think they were trying to enlist me on their side against Peter's determination to get the Bosnia story on the air. But Peter wouldn't hear anything about that. He understood the historical significance of the Bosnia story.

PETER JENNINGS: *I wanted to go to Sarajevo because a great many people were being slaughtered in a manner which was altogether too reminiscent of World War II — a war from which we thought we were going to learn more, and after which the world said, "Never again."*

TOM BROKAW: Yeah, he owned Bosnia in a way that I admired and envied. He got in there early, he saw what it was, and he became an important element in that story. Peter Jennings inspired coverage of Bosnia.

DAVID GELBER: There was a death threat issued by Serbs on Peter's head because they weren't happy with what he had reported on Bosnia. When Peter said he wanted to go back to Bosnia, Roone Arledge, the president of ABC News, was appalled. This was his new star, the anchorman, the indispensable person in the ABC News division. They

*Sarajevo, 1994*

fought about Peter going back, but Peter was adamant. He was insistent that he was going to go back to Bosnia. Roone finally relented and said, "Okay, you can go back, but only for twenty-four hours." So Peter immediately started figuring out how we could extend that a little bit.

We had printed out an itinerary of what Peter was going to do once he got to Sarajevo, including a trip to the central open-air marketplace at twelve o'clock on Saturday. As it happened, we were in the marketplace earlier than that, and we did the shooting that we were supposed to do at twelve. When twelve o'clock came, we were about two or three minutes away from the marketplace. And suddenly, we saw, I remember, a gray hatchback carrying bodies, old women running faster than I've ever seen old women run with looks of absolute terror in their faces. A bomb had just hit the marketplace. We were the first crew to get there. It was a human butcher shop. It was the worst thing I've ever seen.

Peter was completely fearless. We knew there was a possibility of additional shells from the Serbs because they frequently shot more than one shell into the marketplace. And yet Peter had no reluctance in going and talking to people and getting the story. After that we went to the hospital, which was also a target. The Serbs would often wait until thirty minutes after an attack and then shell the hospital knowing that victims would be going there. Peter did a standup in front of a hospital, which is a very risky, gutsy thing to have done.

Of course the bomb landed in the marketplace at exactly the time that our printed itinerary said we would be there, so I understood later that Roone believed that the bomb was intended for Peter.

I'll never forget Peter in that marketplace. He didn't run for cover. He was right in the middle, right in the thick of it. I think if Roone Arledge had seen him he would have fainted. It was exactly what Roone was afraid of.

Peter was risking his life to tell one of the most powerful human rights stories, stories of civilians being targeted, terror stories. That was real terrorism, and Peter was determined to tell it, even though his management at ABC quivered at the thought of him going into a war zone and being targeted by people who wanted him dead. And they were right to be nervous.

PETER JENNINGS (*World News Tonight*): And now the voice of experience — not ours, we hasten to add. We spent much of a long weekend in Sarajevo talking to a lot of Sarajevans about their view of the future. Exactly twenty-four hours before that mortar shell did such horrible damage, we had been in the same marketplace with a friend, believing, as we had in the past, that it was one of those places where we were safe. So much for that wisdom. At one point, a little later, we went up to one of the very best vantage points in this once magical city, simply to have a look. It was there we met quite by accident the voice of experience, thirteen-year-old Eki Fočo.

JENNINGS: That shooting we hear — do you hear that every day?

EKI: Yes, every day. But that's nothing new for me, all day shooting on town. Today, I listen to radio and seven people die in Dobnia.

JENNINGS: So when you hear on the radio that seven people have been killed, what do you think?

EKI: I think this must stop because very much people are dying . . .

JENNINGS: Do you go to school now, Eki?

EKI: No, I don't go to school because of winter.

JENNINGS: Because it's too cold?

EKI: Yes. It's cold. They don't have firewood.

JENNINGS: No firewood? No heat in the school?

EKI: No.

JENNINGS: So what do you do all day?

EKI: I play football with my friends or basketball.

JENNINGS: Do you know anybody who got killed?

EKI: My best friend is dying in this war. I loved my friend Zet very much but he's dying. The one is shooting near his house in big part of Minsk. His head destroyed, you know. And I was lucky very much . . .

JENNINGS: What do you want to be when

you grow up?

EKI: I don't know. I don't think about that.

JENNINGS: What do your mother and father tell you what the future is going to be about?

EKI: They don't talk about that.

JENNINGS: How come?

EKI: They don't know what to say to me . . .

JENNINGS: Now, a lot of Bosnians who are your parents' age, they tell me that they don't like the President of the United States because he won't do anything to help the people in Sarajevo.

EKI: Yes, it's true. My father — like my father says, Bill Clinton just says, I will do that, I will do that, but he don't do anything.

JENNINGS: Do you think that the Bosnians — you people here in Sarajevo — you can fight this war by yourself?

EKI: It's very difficult, but you see we fight

with Serb very much time and I don't know how we can do that because we don't have very much means and shells and guns. But we have heart.

JENNINGS: You have heart?

EKI: Yes.

BILL CLINTON: He really understood the importance of America not walking away from the world after the end of the Cold War. . . . He was always insistently interested in Bosnia, the Middle East, and Africa, but especially in the Balkans. He thought America had to get in there and he tried to make sure that the American people understood what was going on and the implications of it without ever going too far into editorializing news stories. He was good about that. I liked that.

PETER JENNINGS ("While America Watched: The Bosnia Tragedy"): The story of the Bosnian tragedy suggests that as America seeks to redefine its place in a world without a Soviet Union, the fear of appeasement has given way to the fear of quagmire. Can a world power build its foreign policy on such a fear? In Bosnia, two presidents have tried. George Bush decided that America must stay aloof and the war would be left to burn itself out, and Bill Clinton came to pretty much the same conclusion. But the war didn't burn itself out and the public outrage that followed the more shocking scenes of massacre put great pressure on the White House to do something. By the time Bill Clinton was finally forced to act, the Bosnian tragedy had become infinitely more complicated and bloody. And while America watched, hundreds of thousands of people died in a particularly evil kind of war. The Bosnians paid a very high price, but so did those who stood by.

DAVID GELBER: He believed and said very openly that if those were Christians or Jews being massacred by the tens of thousands in Europe, the world wouldn't have stood by and let it happen. So why should they stand by and let it happen because they are Muslims? Peter understood that, and that was one of the truest facts about what happened in Bosnia. The world stood by and watched Muslims being slaughtered, and Peter felt that that needed to be brought to people's attention.

PETER JENNINGS ("The Peacekeepers:

How the UN Failed in Bosnia"): This is the country we used to call Yugoslavia. Here, in the last three years, the world has witnessed the cruelest aggression in Europe since Nazi Germany. The United Nations has failed to stop it. In the spring of 1992, the Bosnian government begged the United Nations to help protect its people against a brutal onslaught by the Serbian army. The United Nations refused. In Bosnia, town by town, the Serbs went killing and raping. Thousands of men and women were forced into concentration camps. Millions were made refugees. By the time UN peacekeepers arrived, there was no peace to keep.

DAVID GELBER: Peter didn't mince words. He said, "This is the biggest failure since the creation of the United Nations," that is to say, the failure of the UN peacekeeping effort in Bosnia. He was right. Sometimes television reporters want to find some mealy-mouthed, weasel-worded way of getting around what is an evident truth. Peter did not pull any punches. He was very direct.

PETER JENNINGS ("The Peacekeepers"): When the Serbs are shelling a civilian population, do you say, "Ah, that's a war crime"?

LT. GEN. SIR MICHAEL ROSE: Of course. Any shelling of a civilian population is a war crime.

JENNINGS: And do you therefore feel, when it's occurring, that you have got to do something about it, that your mandate requires you to do something about it?

ROSE: We always do do something about it.

JENNINGS: Well, you don't, really, do you?

ROSE: We always do something about it. If there is a deliberate shelling of a civilian population by one side or the other, then we will use force against them.

JENNINGS (voiceover): But that is not what the general did. The shelling of Gorazde continued. The United Nations did not call in airstrikes. And with no real threat to stop them, the Serbs unleashed an all out assault on the town.

DAVID GELBER: I've always seen Peter as

the guy who saved Bosnia, and there are a lot of Bosnians who would agree with that. He was the one, more than any other person, who forced Bosnia onto the national agenda, who made people care about this slaughter of innocents, this genocide in the heart of Europe.

DAVID WESTIN: Everyone recognizes that the American people, and therefore the American government, would not have been paying the attention to Bosnia that they did without Peter's really putting the spotlight on that subject. . . . He has taught us that there are these stories . . . If we open our eyes, and we are open to what's going on in the world, and we think about the impor-tance of events, we can find the next Bosnia, we can find the next East Jerusalem, we can find the next Baghdad, wherever it is. Peter set an example that will go on having an ef-fect on real events in the real world for years to come.

*Despite a slide in ratings, Jennings re-mained determined to cover complex in-ternational news stories, often in person. He was supported by David Westin, who had replaced Roone Arledge as president of ABC News in 1997. Though Jennings' primary role was that of* World News Tonight *anchor, based out of the ABC headquarters in New York City, he traveled extensively, following the news from Bosnia to Baghdad. His colleagues describe his almost manic energy on these trips abroad.*

PETER JENNINGS: *I like doing what I'm doing because it's always an adventure. I'm always going somewhere. . . . I don't think I've ever in all those years ever been bored for more than half an hour at a time.*

MICHAEL CLEMENTE: I don't think he saw himself as an anchor as much as a reporter who happened to be stuck behind a desk. If he had had his way, if the planes were fast enough, he would have been at the top story every day. And in a good part of the '70s and '80s and early '90s, we were there for most of the big stories. He wanted to be there, smelling it and tasting it and talking to the people. That's what you saw on the air. You saw this constant tension of liking to be in charge, liking to be the editor-at-large, but really rather being outside, without the coat and tie, without the desk, meeting people and talking to people up close.

PETER JENNINGS: *I spent twenty-five years overseas — and loved every minute of it. I, who had no formal education, was lucky to discover that if you are interested in other people, if you are interested in their culture, their contribution to a global society, their problems, and their language, travel is an education par excellence in and of itself. If you go, you become a wiser, more valuable citizen.*

TOM BROKAW: I don't think there was a "Eureka" moment when Peter and Dan and I in those chairs said, "We're going to change the DNA of being an anchor. We're going to take these broadcasts on the road." We cherished the ideals of being a reporter and the work of being a reporter, and at the end of the day, if you could also be an anchor that was a pretty good dividend.

TOM YELLIN: The hardest thing was to get Peter out of the anchor chair. Not for Peter; Peter loved to get out of the anchor chair. But it was just very difficult to take him out of there because it deprived *World News Tonight* of its primary reporter, and no one liked that at ABC. But Peter insisted on going and doing real reporting, not just showing up, doing a few standups, and talking to a few important people. So when we went to India and Pakistan, Peter interviewed some of the most important officials on both sides of that potential conflict, but he also insisted on getting out there, going up into the mountains, talking to the soldiers who were on the front line, seeing what life was really like, and reporting it from the ground up. That's something Peter always insisted on.

PAUL FRIEDMAN: I remember a time we were in Moscow covering one summit or another. They were all kind of boring. And we had a string of hours in which we didn't have to put on the broadcast. Peter said, of course, "Well, let's go do a story." "Well, what story would you like to do, Peter?" There was a map on the wall, and he said, "Let's play the map game." He closes his eyes, and puts his finger on the map. And he says, "Let's go there and find a story." So we get in a car, with Rupen, the cameraman who Peter loved so much. And we drive on one of those spokes — one of the highways out of Moscow — looking for a story. And within forty-five minutes, we come up on two.

Like so many successful journalists, he liked to find small stories that said something about bigger issues. So in this case, the first thing we come across, about fifteen minutes outside Moscow, is a man selling a pretty awful looking chicken that he had raised in his backyard. And people, we soon saw, were coming out of Moscow on these awful buses, looking for that kind of food raised by people in their backyards — because in Moscow there was no food. There was no meat. There was no chicken. So this man, selling this chicken from the backyard, became a little story, where we could say something about what was going on in the Soviet Union at that point. And we shot that story.

Then we drove a little longer and we come across a gas line. You know, cars lined up for a couple of miles waiting to get gas. So we set up the camera, and we watched for a while. And of course, what we saw eventually was that the woman in her white coat, who was running the gas station, would close down the pumps periodically. And then, when people got fed up sufficiently, they would get together and they would bribe her. And she would open up the gas pumps. Now, we got all this on film. And we had a nice little story about corruption and supplies in the Soviet Union. This was at a time when the Soviet Union could, quite literally, destroy us, but also had all this weakness.

You know, it was a third-world country. Peter's take was, "Let's get out and get a feel for what's going on and tell those kinds of stories."

JEANMARIE CONDON: He was so happy walking around the old city of Jerusalem, sleeves rolled up, notebook in his back pocket. For Peter, a place like Jerusalem wasn't just a war zone, and it wasn't just a place that you saw on the nightly news where people were beating up on each other or killing each other. It was a place where you sat in the garden of the American Colony Hotel and had bitter coffee and sat under the lemon trees. It was a living, breathing place. . . . Peter gave me a great gift because I was coming to love the place like he did. He just kept unfolding it for me. He was giving it to me, and he was getting pleasure from giving me that city that he loved.

DAVID WESTIN: He was almost childlike — his embrace of being in the field, meeting new people, seeing new sights, and finding new stories. He had a firm belief that you could take any good reporter and plunk him down in the middle of anywhere and he could just walk down the street and find ten great stories. Peter had that ability, with that notebook he kept tucked into the back waistband of his trousers. It was all part of a great, curious adventure for Peter that, fortunately, he would bring back to us.

PETER JENNINGS: *I'm sometimes referred to as a street-side writer by my colleagues because I sometimes do my best writing sitting on the sidewalk, long before I ever go back to the newsroom. I think it's the freshness of the experience, the freshness of the encounter with whomever I've met, and seen, and tried to understand, that may make some difference in the way I approach the news.*

MICHAEL CLEMENTE: Peter was trying to achieve something different, which was to include every voice that might have a piece of a story — not just the voice that was the loudest or the most noticeable. "Let's not just take what we are hearing from everyone else. Let's ask these other people around the corner. Let's ask those people behind the building. Let's ask those people who are not talking. Then we may have our story. Even though we are not going to have the full story, but we may have more of a story than anyone else. And not just for the sake of balance, but for the sake of understanding."

He never stopped. I mean, the only thing

that stopped him from gathering more information was the fact that he had to air at a certain point. At six-twenty-nine, he had to give up and say something.

DIANE SAWYER: Peter was monumentally curious, as everyone has said — a Ph.D. in curiosity. And you believed it. You believed that it wasn't ambition, that he would have done it no matter what else. He couldn't stop, he couldn't stop asking questions.

TED KOPPEL: Peter would use his natural curiosity to just vacuum information out of people. There is, in the final analysis, nothing more flattering than to have somebody sit there saying, "Tell me about you. Tell me what you know about this subject." Peter would do that and would pay whomever he was talking to the supreme compliment of being really interested. And he had a way of — you know how waiters carry that little folding thing that they put the credit card in in the back of their pants; they, sort of, tuck it in under their belt — Peter had a way of always carrying a reporter's notebook back there. He would whip it out and he would take notes. And, gee, it's awfully flattering when someone is sitting there taking notes about what you think and what you're say-

*Listening in the Middle East . . .*

*. . . and Haiti*

ing. The end result of that was Peter learned a lot. He was a good reporter. After all, a reporter has to be able to get people to talk. And Peter could do that.

LAUREN LIPANI: He asked so many questions because meeting new people for him was a chance to learn something new about someone and where they came from, where they lived. He might be in a taxi, late for an interview, or he might be exhausted at the end of the day, going back to his hotel, he's still looking out the window and he's peppering the driver with questions because he knows that driver is someone local and knows the city better than he does. He would just keep asking questions: "What's this? Where's that? What is the population of the people who live here? Who are they? Where do they come from?" So many questions. Other people might take it for a time to sit back, catch your breath, take a nap, but not Peter. He was always looking out the window.

GRETCHEN BABAROVIC: He had more energy than ten men put together. We used to call him the Energizer Bunny. Sometimes things would get short shrift. Sometimes you'd wonder where he'd find the energy.

But he never stopped. Whatever engaged him, he seemed to want to do it instantly.

MICHAEL CLEMENTE: We called him "the flea" because he would just jump around, from story to story, person to person, item to item, car to car, whatever it was.

TOM NAGORSKI: When we were on the road, Peter didn't just leave the competition in the dust; he very often left his own colleagues in the dust. My notes from those trips make for exhausting reading. Here's one excerpt from March 2000: "Clinton visit to India: Broadcast from New Delhi three a.m.; flight to Kuwait seven a.m.; flight to Amman; drive to refugee camp in West Bank near Bethlehem for arrival of Pope John Paul." Essentially, we did that because Peter couldn't stand the idea of missing either the Clinton visit to India or the Pope's trip to the Middle East.

MICHAEL CLEMENTE: Traveling on the road with Peter was invigorating, and exhausting. It was invigorating because they were usually new places, and they were usually big stories. And it was exhausting because we would never stop. We went to Manila one time for the sort of "pretend election" that President Marcos was putting on at the time. We did *World News Tonight* on Friday [in New York]. Then we went to JFK and flew straight to Manila. We spent the weekend working. I think we slept for one night, which may have been four or five hours. We did the broadcast Monday night live, which was at seven-thirty a.m. on Tuesday. Then we went back to the hotel. Peter said, "What are we going to do now?" I was collapsed in a big chair. I said, "I think we need to go to sleep for a little while and recharge." The next thing I knew, I woke up in the chair. I had been asleep there for a couple of hours. Peter was gone. He was out, getting the next day's show. I phoned around, and I found him. That's what it was like. It was exhausting, but it was always an adventure. We would fit in a little fun. We would fit in a lot of work. And we would find out a lot of things that other people hadn't found out. And that's what you saw on the air.

JON BANNER: He was up earlier than anybody else, he went to sleep later than anybody else, and he spent every waking minute finding out something new about the story he was covering. He knew enough to keep asking questions. . . . He had an ability to find stories, and to go where the action was that was instinctive. He just knew where to show up.

MICHAEL CLEMENTE: An earthquake happens in Mexico City. The phone rings, at ten o'clock at night. We get on a charter and fly to Dallas and make a connection into the heart of Mexico City. He puts a reporter's notebook in the back of his pants. We hire a driver, right out of the airport, and we start combing the city, shooting, videotaping. From the moment we hit the ground, he is talking to people. He would spend as much time as he could each day in the field, soaking up as much information as he could. With an hour or an hour-and-a-half to go before airtime, then he would sit down and say, "All right. What are we going to say?" As a producer, I would think, "This is not going to happen. We are not going to be able to make air with this mess." And collectively, we'd pull it together. It wasn't a magical trick each day. But somehow, he had cooking in his head all day a narrative, or a storyline, or his takeaways on what was new and different. And it didn't matter if we wrote it all down — it mattered to the control room and it mattered to the producers because it was quite disorderly — but to him, he had it in his head, and he ad-libbed it.

TOM NAGORSKI: We went to Cuba once. Peter took his son along. I like to be very organized before I go on a trip. I like to game out what we're going to do. I had my whole agenda, and there weren't that many checks on the list because the Cubans at the time were still pretty restrictive about what we could and couldn't do. Rather than just line up a slew of interviews, Peter said, "Why don't we just go for a drive?" I said, "What do you mean go for a drive?" And so we set out for a truly memorable ride in a big old clunky Jeep into the Cuban countryside.

Our three-, four-hour drive stretched to an entire day because we'd come to some poor little village and Peter would say, "There's a line for bread over there. Let's go talk to those people and see what that's like." We passed some sugarcane fields. We all knew that the sugar harvest was a critical thing for the Cuban economy. I just thought, "Well, we'll go take some pictures of the sugarcane fields." Peter said, "Let's find some of the farmers out here." So we hiked through this muddy sugarcane field and found a few guys out there and talked to them. Peter loved what we used to call the point-and-shoot. He loved to just look at a map and say, "Okay, we'll go down here, get out wherever, come what may." For those of us who tended to crave organization on a trip like this, it could be very tough because things changed all the time. But for the end product, which is what mattered, it was wonderful. Had we stuck to my plan, I probably wouldn't remember a lot of the things I'm telling you about. But because we followed Peter's instincts — and his instincts were always good and interesting — we had truly memorable times on the road.

PAUL FRIEDMAN: Whenever we would go out on a story he carried a reporter's notebook around with him — a small spiral notebook that he used to put in the back of his pants, inside the belt. He would take incredibly detailed notes. So if you went anywhere in the world, he would go back to his file of spiral notebooks and you'd hit the ground running because he could say, "Well, there is this guy I talked to last time. Here is his telephone number and we'll call him." All reporters do that, but Peter did it in incredible detail.

I remember going to Cuba with Peter on a story. We needed a sugarcane field for a standup, talking about the economy. Peter looked in one of his notebooks and he looked around and said, "If you go down that road about a mile, there'll be a church on the left. Hang a left at that church, drive a little while after that, and there will be a sugarcane field." Sure enough, there it was.

RUPEN VOSGIMORUKIAN: In Tehran, there was a traffic jam so he got down from the car and started to run traffic. Who would do that? And he managed, without speaking a word of Farsi, to let the cars go. Stopped another one. Road was empty. He came back to the truck, he said, "Let's go."

PETER JENNINGS: *I do have this notion — and I don't think it's appreciated by everybody — that if we are privileged to be in this business — and it is a privilege — and we are paid as well as most of us are, then we should be working our tails off for the privilege, if not for the money.*

TOM BROKAW: Our job was hard at a lot of different levels, physically hard. You had to get on the airplane, get off the airplane, race across a strange city, start covering the story, framing it in your mind, get back to maybe a hotel room, hope the telephone worked, get on the air somehow, try to get it right. It's now three o'clock in the morning and you've been up for thirty-six hours; you get four hours of sleep, and you start all over again.

And out of the corner of your eye, you're watching Jennings over there doing it and hoping that you're doing it as well as he is. He is keeping his eye on you. There was also a psychic difficulty about it. These were big stakes that we were dealing with: Are we getting it right? Are we going too far? Are we being fair?

A lot of people weighed in. They weren't always happy with what we had to say, so we had to have a mental toughness to deal with that, too. And then, when you had these high-profile positions, you were the captain of the team so you had to look out for your other teammates and make sure that they were doing okay and getting their first shot and getting the rest that they needed or the psychic help that they may have required along the way. It was hard work, but it was so rewarding. It was just so damn much fun.

JON BANNER: On all trips, he carried around a notebook in his back pocket. He tucks it in between his pants and his shirt. It hangs out the back, and he's constantly scribbling down notes. Constantly. When you look "reporter" up in the dictionary, Peter's picture ought to be there.

*Peter Jennings' last major foreign reporting was on the Iraq War.*

TOM NAGORSKI: Among all his abilities as a journalist and as a reporter, Peter had great foresight. Journalists are often said to be writers of the first draft of history. There are many examples of Peter seeing days or weeks down the road in terms of the way the news, and to some extent little pieces of history, would actually play out.

JON BANNER: In the run-up to the Iraq War we were criticized for raising questions about troop levels, about weapons of mass destruction, and about all those things that were the big basis for war. Peter pushed us to do those stories. He pushed us to ask those questions because he was a student of the Middle East. We were quite heavily criticized at the time, but he turned out to be absolutely correct.

PETER JENNINGS (2004): *I ask whether in general we [the news media] did enough in the run-up to the war to foster public debate about the administration's stated intentions and the possible consequences. On my own broadcast we tried — and ironically, we were castigated for it by some who accused us of not supporting the administration. Even, on occasion, of not being patriotic enough.*

BRIAN ROSS: In the lead-up to the Iraq War, Peter, more than any other person — certainly at ABC, but maybe in journalism — was so skeptical of the claims made about weapons of mass destruction. And he kept us honest because we were hearing from the same sources everybody else was hearing from that Saddam Hussein had these weapons, he's just hiding them, and so on. Peter was so skeptical of that, and he required us to be very stringent in assessing the facts.

Peter was a skeptic about conventional wisdom, but mostly he was a skeptic about big government and Washington. He was very suspicious of their motives and the politics behind why they were doing certain things. Again and again, he kept us honest and on the right track and he served our viewers very, very well.

KEN AULETTA: I remember talking to him once after the run-up to the Iraq War in 2003 and the immediate aftermath, when people were questioning whether he and ABC were patriotic. He said, "Look, I'm doing what I always did. I'm asking questions. That's what I do. I can't stop asking questions just because of the emotional moment. That's my job. Are there weapons of mass destruction? I don't know. I've got to see them. And my job is to ask the questions about whether they're really there or not, and to analyze, not to assert that France is a terrible country because they're not supporting us, but to ask why are they not supporting the United States' position. That's not supporting France. It's doing what journalists do — We ask questions."

VINNIE MALHOTRA: I remember specifically a trip that we took to Kuwait. We flew to Doha, Qatar, to interview General Tommy Franks, who was the commander at that time. It was a tough interview. It was clear that Peter wanted to get some answers for the American public. He asked this amazing question: he asked Tommy Franks how he was going to win the peace.

PETER JENNINGS: You have argued from almost the outset in this process for more men. And you've had to fight for it on occasion. Do you have enough men now to win?

GENERAL TOMMY FRANKS, COMMANDER,

U.S. CENTRAL COMMAND: Peter, let me, let me, let me challenge the first, let me challenge your question for a second.

JENNINGS: Okay, okay.

FRANKS: There actually isn't truth in the speculation that I have been arguing for more men. What, what I've done and, in fact, what the Secretary has also done, what the President of the United States has done, is take a look at military options available over time and want to be sure that the military options available are credible, that they can accomplish the objective, and that's a little different than, than a suggestion that, that one or the other has argued for more troops or less troops or more time or less time.

JENNINGS: Okay. Let me remove the question. Let me ask you the question that Americans want to know: Do you have enough men to win the war? And do you have enough men to win the peace?

VINNIE MALHOTRA: Right there was a quintessential Peter Jennings question, which showed that Peter was seeing through the forest. Peter was looking at how this was going to play out after the ground war was completed. It was a classic example of Peter having forethought on a story, or seeing the story in a way that perhaps other people hadn't yet thought.

TOM NAGORSKI: I took the general to be a little bit perplexed by this focus on what would come after, which is understandable in a way; he was there to fight a war, and to get Saddam Hussein out of power. It almost seemed to some that Peter was badgering General Franks on a point that didn't seem so relevant on the verge of war. "Okay, we have a war to fight, why are you worrying so much about whether we have the troops to win the peace?" I don't think many people would argue with the fact that it was, in retrospect, certainly a pretty appropriate question to be asking at the time. And that was typical Peter. That's a question he felt was very important. And he pressed it and pressed it hard.

PETER JENNINGS (2004): *It is always difficult when the country goes to war, when American lives are at stake, to be as aggressive reporting the potential dangers. It does not help that in the fog of war, we are at times overwhelmed by information, mis-information, and dis-*

*information. We might well be in Iraq anyway if the public had been more fully informed. But a public informed and consulted is more likely to make the longer term sacrifices that such an ambitious military and foreign policy demands.*

TOM NAGORSKI: Once war broke out in Iraq it was a no-brainer that Peter would want to go. The only discussion we had was: is it safe? Peter was much braver than most of us, but he wasn't a fool about it. And because safety was such an issue, did that mean that he was going to sit in a compound, or sit with the U.S. military somewhere and not really do anything valuable? That was a nonstarter with him. There were, and still are sometimes, reporters who go to Baghdad and park it in a room and read the wires and very rarely venture out. That just wasn't Peter's thing.

JON BANNER: He was aware of the danger, but he also knew that this was a defining moment for the country, and a terribly important story. He knew that he had to go cover it, and he was relentless in covering it. I remember for his first trip for *World News*, there was a huge bombing outside a hotel. I called him and I said, "Where are you? We may do a special report on the bombing.

*In the aftermath of a car bomb, Baghdad, March 2004*

He's like, "I'm on my way there." And he rushed over to the site of a terrorist attack. You know, it's not exactly a safe thing to do. It's the middle of the night; nobody travels in Iraq in the middle of the night. And he was doing live reports there.

Peter had acknowledged before the trip, "Look, I'm not going to go racing off everywhere every time something happens. I want to go there, I want to report, I want to get access to certain stories, but I don't want to be completely irresponsible about my life or the lives of the people I'm with," meaning his cameraman and producers. But when something big happened, there was no question: he was out the door before we were on the air with a special report, before anybody else was on their way out to the story. He was — fssssht! — gone.

MARC BURSTEIN: There was a question of who would be allowed in the courtroom the first time we were going to see Saddam Hussein since his capture. We heard Peter would be in the courtroom, then that Peter would not be in the courtroom; Western journalists would or would not be allowed in. Then it became Peter in particular: he had permission; his permission was denied; then he had it again; and it was taken away. All through the night, I knew Peter was not going to be denied being in that courtroom.

I woke up the next morning early, and the first thing I heard was that Peter was not going to be in the courtroom; they had emphatically said that no journalists would be allowed in. I didn't believe it for a minute. Tom Nagorski, his producer on the ground there, and I had worked out in advance that we would have an open phone line from just outside the courthouse into the control room. It was just about seven a.m. I went up to the control room. We had heard for a few minutes that Peter was missing. There was

312

no doubt if he had gone missing, we assumed that meant he was in that courtroom. Sure enough, about fifteen minutes past seven, *Good Morning America* was on the air. All of a sudden that phone line had been opened and I heard Peter's voice, "This is Jennings in Baghdad. Are you there?" We were there, and in less than three seconds, he was on the air.

We interrupted *Good Morning America* with the special report. He described what had just taken place inside that courtroom in such painstaking detail, in such a compelling manner. He must have gone for ten or fifteen minutes nonstop. Had there been three or four cameras in there, had you been in that courtroom personally, I don't think you could have learned more about what was going on than listening to Peter. It was riveting. At this point it was probably about seven-thirty in the morning, and I can guarantee you, no one who was listening to his description of what went on in that courtroom changed the channel or left for work until Peter Jennings was finished.

ANNOUNCER: This is an "ABC News Special Report."

CHARLIE GIBSON: Good morning. I'm

Charles Gibson from ABC News at our Times Square studios in New York. But the focus this morning is on Baghdad. Saddam Hussein, not seen for seven months since his capture, this morning in court . . . The only network anchorman in the court, Peter Jennings, who is joining us now by cell phone from outside the courtroom. And we're hoping the cell phone connection can work. But, Peter, can you give me a description of the proceedings as they went on?

PETER JENNINGS: Yeah, I can, indeed, Charlie. Saddam Hussein walked into a courtroom where only about sixteen of us were and a single judge and a court reporter, sat down in a chair two or three feet from the judge, was asked his name and said, "I am Saddam Hussein. I am the president of Iraq." . . . He came in very slowly and looking very uncertain, more uncertain, I think, than Saddam Hussein can be imagined to look, walking into a room over which he controlled for so many years. He looked rather anxiously and uncertainly around the room at the half a dozen of us who were there to witness this, at the judge and at the four or five television cameras from Iraq and the rest of the world. And then as he sat down, he looked particularly nervous. He was well-groomed, wearing a dark suit and a white shirt, but no tie. His hair was certainly shorter and far better combed than the last time we saw it. His beard has been trimmed. Grey with white on the end. But I thought he looked anxious and uncertain at the very beginning.

TOM NAGORSKI: It was a great coup. While everyone else in the world was waiting for an official word of what had happened in that courtroom, Peter was on his phone, having taken immaculate notes as he always did, telling the world what had happened and doing it with all the touches and the color that he could bring. It was one of many days that I spent with him on the road, when he had the enthusiasm of an intern's first few days or weeks in the newsroom. He was very excited, very energized. Who wouldn't have been? He loved it.

STU SCHUTZMAN: Peter got much more access to the American military than most of our reporters. The last time we went, we were embedded at the main U.S. military base in Iraq. We got to see the inner workings of the base, the decision-making process. Peter got very close to the general in charge and his staff. He went out on raids with them. He went out on patrol with them. So from the top to the bottom, he really got to know and show how the U.S. was working in Iraq.

TOM NAGORSKI: Peter was hugely effective right up until the last trip he took for the elections because he ventured out everywhere. He was tireless. If you go back and look at the tapes of his last trip, it's unbelievable. Forget the cancer for a moment, if you can, and just think: here is a sixty-six-year-old man getting up at the crack of dawn in an incredibly tense environment, on the biggest story of our time, flying all over the country with the U.S. military, getting in line with Iraqis going to vote on a day when it's widely predicted that those Iraqis are going to be the targets of terrorism. It's a tour de force of reporting. . . . As I look back on it, all of Peter's enormous strengths as a reporter and journalist were on display: his stamina, his tenacity, his encyclopedic knowledge of both the story and the history, and what most of us appreciated most — at least I did — his unquenchable desire to know more. . . . If you took everything else out of his career and threw it aside, his trips to Iraq in the last few years stand as great landmarks of their own. And then you take in the fact that he was so ill during his last trips, and it's all the more extraordinary.

PETER JENNINGS: *I've been a reporter for all of my adult life. And when I go someplace strange for the first time, or even for the fifteenth time, I want to understand why something is happening. So I assume that people in our audience want to understand why something is happening, not just hear that it's happened. So whether it is health care, or whether it is the war in Iraq, or whether it is this unending, complicated challenge of the war against terrorism . . . I want to help our audience understand better what is happening.*

*We're not the only source of news and information for people in America. So, I think we have to make ourselves valuable, make ourselves distinctive. And one of the ways I find that we are distinctive, and one of the ways I think we are more valuable is giving some people some sense of context that the world is acting in the way that it is at any given moment. . . . With the war in Iraq, and the war against terrorism generally, America has been rather confused about who are friends, and who are enemies. The president says if you are not with us you're against us. But the world is really more complicated than that. . . . Nothing is black and white.*

*ABC has always encouraged me to follow my instincts while making it a point to temper my enthusiasm when they thought I was going overboard.*

—Peter Jennings

# 8
## ENTHUSIASMS

*Jennings often fought for extended coverage of topics that he felt couldn't be adequately explored during the thirty minutes of* World News Tonight. *He hosted town meetings and children's programs, and he created a documentary series, Peter Jennings Reporting — primetime ABC News specials dedicated to a single issue, from the pharmaceutical industry to U.S. policy toward Cambodia to Christianity, all subjects that had seen little network coverage at that time.*

TOM YELLIN: Peter had a particular passion for these documentaries. He wanted to use the leverage and the clout that he had created over an entire career, wandering the world, doing some extraordinary reporting, to do one more thing, and that was to tell people stories they couldn't find anywhere else. He shouldn't have done it because he should've enjoyed his life more. He had the opportunity to take off weekends, and not work at night, and not come in early, and not do all these other interviews, but he couldn't help himself. He just felt that this is what he had to do.

KEITH SUMMA: Peter's one of the few people I know who not only had the desire to do documentaries about stories that sometimes didn't fit television but would want to jump into a complex public policy issue that didn't lend itself to television.

MICHAEL CLEMENTE: I think it was part of his understanding that the media are all very limiting. If you have a newspaper, there is a limit to the number of pages. In broadcasting, the limits are even greater, but that doesn't mean you have to be confined to what's going on in Washington and on Wall Street and in the major stories of the day.

DAVID WESTIN: Peter loved doing hard things on TV. I mean, that was just an opportunity for him — not even a challenge, but an opportunity. If it was hard, that's probably what we ought to be doing, is the way he often came to it.

GRETCHEN BABAROVIC: The nightly news was his platform, but the documentaries were his substance. In those hours, he could explore as he wanted to explore the things that he was so interested in. It brings to mind the AIDS issues. He was ahead of the curve on AIDS. He picked it up just as it was beginning to gather momentum, when the public really didn't understand and really didn't know about AIDS. We were allowed to do it for public broadcasting. And it was such an education for the public at large. It really, really was.

CHRIS ISHAM: My sister died of AIDS in 1997. Peter had taken an interest in her and had gotten to know her very well. He spent a lot of time with her and understood a lot about this disease. He had done quite a bit of work on AIDS but had felt that this was something that needed national resources focused on it. So I personally saw close-up how Peter became engaged in a major issue — on a national level, on an international level, and on a very personal level.

It meant an enormous amount to me. It meant a lot to my sister, when she was alive. It meant a lot to her kids — and it continues to. It meant a lot to the entire family that he was so committed to seeing that this issue received the kind of national attention that it deserved.

> PETER JENNINGS: This broadcast is about AIDS, which means it's about public health and private agony. It's about prejudice and fear, and the awkwardness, for most of us, of having to talk about very intimate matters far sooner than we might want to. But growing up in the age of AIDS leaves us no choice. This is about sex, and death, and there are so many questions which need to be answered.

CHRIS ISHAM: There is no question that Peter put AIDS on the national agenda, both through his own work on his own broadcast, *World News Tonight,* and through his work through other outlets. He was committed to making sure that the world focused on this issue.

KEITH SUMMA: In 1994 we had done some really aggressive reporting at ABC with other reporters and aired a bunch of different stories that infuriated the tobacco industry. In fact, Philip Morris sued ABC for ten billion dollars. As a result of that, there were a lot of people at ABC who basically made us back off the story.

Peter didn't like that. Peter never liked backing off a story. So he called all of us who were involved in that reporting together to sit down and said, "You have to prove to us that this reporting is sound." I remember having a breakfast meeting at his house with him, and he wanted to go over all the facts. When he was convinced that what we had done was sound, he said, "We need to continue reporting on this story." That's when he wanted to do a documentary about tobacco, which became "Never Say Die: How the Tobacco Industry Keeps on Winning."

PETER JENNINGS: This hour is about cigarettes and the people who make them, which means it is about the only product that you can buy virtually anywhere which, when used as directed, kills more than 400,000 Americans every year.

It actually only costs pennies to make one of these, and every year the five major cigarette makers make several billion dollars in profits. Tonight we're going to show you how the tobacco companies continue to prosper despite the damage these things do and despite the increased pressure the companies are under from lawsuits and proposed government regulation.

TOM YELLIN: Peter took on the tobacco story for three reasons. First, I think he understood personally from his own experience as a smoker, and then as an ex-smoker, that smoking is enormously addictive and potentially very, very destructive. Secondly, I think he felt that smoking is the number one public health problem in this country, and that government, journalism, and industry were not dealing with it. The third reason he took it on was more personal: He felt, as the leader of ABC News, that ABC News had done some very courageous and very extraordinary reporting on the tobacco story, had been sued by a tobacco company, and had settled the lawsuit, even though, in his opinion, that was a mistake. So he felt it was important to continue reporting on this crucially important story, in spite of the attempts by the tobacco industry, which he felt were partially successful, to intimidate ABC.

When questions were first raised about the reporting ABC News had done about tobacco, which Peter was not involved in, but I was, he came to me and said, "What did you do? Did you screw it up?" I said, "No, Peter, we didn't." He said, "Okay, prove it to me." All of the people involved in reporting that story came together, and we had to prove to Peter that we hadn't screwed it up. He was tough. He was as tough as any lawyer or any investigator. He asked every possible question that he could think of, and then he thought about it some more, and then he asked us some more questions. Once we could prove to Peter, to his own satisfaction, that our original reporting was accurate and that our original reporting was strong and supportable, he said, "We're not backing off this story. I don't care what the corporation has done; we've got to keep going." And it's because of that that he started reporting on tobacco.

I think it's a measure of the stature that Peter had inside ABC News and inside the ABC network that, once he decided — once we decided — that we needed to do more reporting on tobacco, no one questioned us. It was not hard to get those programs on the air. We were not told, "No, you can't go there. That's not allowed." That didn't happen at all. I think a lesser reporter might have had a much harder time. In fact, I believe that if Peter had been the original reporter on the tobacco stories, there's absolutely no way in the world that Cap Cities or ABC would have settled that lawsuit, because the damage it would have done to Peter would've been too great.

PETER JENNINGS: This is one of the classic cigarette commercials from the 1960s. It was meant to convey the message that smoking made life better. And it was very effective.

TV AD: Come to where the flavor is. Come to Marlboro country.

JENNINGS: But in 1967 the government ordered that television stations should also run public service messages, including this one, that advertised the dangers of smoking. They were also very effective, and people began to smoke less.

TV AD: Cigarettes. . . . They're killers.

JENNINGS: So what did the tobacco companies do? They agreed to a total ban on televised cigarette advertising which meant, of course, stations didn't have to run those pesky messages that said smoking could kill you. And one year later, cigarette sales in America were up.

No one should underestimate the tobacco industry's determination to win. This hour is about an industry that never says die.

KEITH SUMMA: After the documentary, Peter called me into his office and he said, "Look, this is a very important story. I want you to do nothing but cover the tobacco story full-time," which in network television is kind of a rare thing.

In 1997, as a result of Peter's commitment, we did scores of stories about the tobacco industry and the tobacco issue, which aired on *World News Tonight*. It was unlike any other competitors in this business and probably exceeded what a lot of newspapers did. He insisted on aggressive, smart reporting.

SARAH JENNINGS: I don't think Peter took tobacco on because he was going to proselytize. I don't think that Peter was ever a proselytizer, or took on an issue because it was his cause. I think he saw a very, very important story in that tobacco program, where the American public was seriously misled, if not lied to. He was bound and determined that these facts would come out, and indeed I think that's what the tobacco show did.

TOM YELLIN: When it came to tobacco, I think one of Peter's great strengths as a journalist is that he wasn't sentimental. He really believed that the truth held its own virtue. And the truth about tobacco is devastating.

I think Peter felt a profound responsibility in his role as one of the most important broadcast journalists in America to take that on. So what you see with the tobacco story was Peter exercising his full responsibility to use that to try to make a difference in the real world — to try to cover stories that will actually have an impact, not just cover things that are kind of interesting or cover things that he has a curiosity about or that other people think might be something that someone might watch to get a rating. He knew that if he did it well, something was actually going to change in the real world. Peter believed that tobacco was something that needed to be addressed, that government isn't doing it, that the public health community hasn't done it properly, and that journalists haven't done it properly. So he felt that as a leader among journalists, it was his responsibility to take it on.

KEITH SUMMA: He recognized it was probably the most important public health story in the country. So he really insisted that we report on that aggressively. That meant that we had to know more than anybody else about it. That meant we had to be ahead of everybody else on the story. When he threw himself into a story like he did the tobacco story, that meant we had to own that story.

MATTHEW MYERS: Peter Jennings recognized both the magnitude of the tobacco story and the individual tragedy. He moved beyond the statistics to the individual people. He understood that while smoking causes more deaths in the United States than any other single cause, it was people's mothers and fathers and sisters and brothers. He made it a human story.

Most importantly, perhaps, he recognized that unless you covered tobacco over and over again to tell the story, you weren't really reaching the broad public. As a direct result, I think Peter Jennings has done more to increase awareness of the hazards of tobacco than any other journalist in the world. I think his work will probably do more to reduce the incidence of lung cancer than any other journalist's work.

MICHAEL CLEMENTE: What about religion? No one, at least in television, had had a regular religion reporter. That was one of several issues that Peter decided to accent. I think he felt that we could put a spotlight on any number of issues that were outside of the norm, and make them important to people.

PETER JENNINGS: *I think what comes as a surprise to people just descending on America for the first time is the degree and intensity of religion in public life, as it has always been in this society. . . . There are a lot of people in the country who believe very strongly that the country is in moral danger and that religion is another way to have bearings, moral bearings. I'm not surprised by that. I find it fascinating.*

JON BANNER: One of Peter's passions was religion. He forced the news division to hire a religion reporter and started to cover religion stories. He started really to care about faith in all of our lives. He found it remarkable, given how important religion is to the public, that we weren't covering it more often.

TOM NAGORSKI: He felt very strongly about religion. He felt that it was under-covered. For a period he said, "Why aren't we doing that story about the evangelicals? Why aren't we doing the story about the Christian Right more than just a political Washington story? Do we feel we understand evangelicals in this country? Do we have an evangelical in this newsroom, at this table? Do we know somebody who we really feel understands that community?" And for a while I think news management didn't appease Peter, but they felt, okay, we'll cover it a little bit more. That led to the assigning of a full-time religion beat, a producer and correspondent who would do nothing else. That was an example of Peter's different kind of tenacity — not just the daily crunch of news but a philosophical desire to bully something through.

PETER JENNINGS (1995): *In the overwhelming majority of newsrooms in America there is an appalling ignorance of religion and faith.*

JEANMARIE CONDON: He had lived in the Middle East. He'd lived in Beirut at a time when religious factions were tearing each other apart, destroying a city that had once been called the Paris of the Middle East. He watched that happen. So he had seen firsthand the ways in which religion moves through history and changes people's lives and changes the course of history.

He thought that religion was severely undercovered by the American media and by the media in general. He thought journalists didn't take it seriously enough.

PETER JENNINGS: *I was fascinated. From*

331

the time I first joined ABC and went off to the South to cover the civil rights movement — and thereafter in so many parts of the world — I have seen people motivated, and often driven by, faith. In almost every corner of the world, I have seen, as any foreign correspondent who was paying attention would, how people's faith has sustained them in times of great worldly stress.

I had seen how Catholicism was an element of survival for millions of people in the darkest days of Communism. . . . I have reported on the new freedom for the Russian Orthodox Church in Russia, seen first hand what a profoundly destructive force religion has been in the former Yugoslavia, and earlier in Northern Ireland. Most of all, I had the good fortune to spend seven years in the Middle East, where the Bible is quite literally a guide book, and where I lived every day with the great impact that Judaism and Islam have had on one of the great news stories of all time. When I came back to my current job, and began to wander around this country again, I was very struck by how in the midst of such plenty, so many Americans were hungry for something more than our vaunted consumer society could provide for them. And very slowly I began to realize the most obvious fact: that people's faith and re-

*ligious beliefs were connected in so many ways to everything that was going on around me.*

PEGGY WEHMEYER: I get a phone call one day at home. The voice on the other end sounded very familiar. He said, "Hello, is this Peggy Wehmeyer?" I said, "Yes it is." He said, "This is Peter Jennings." And I wanted to say, "Yeah, right, and I'm Barbara Walters," but he went on and said, "I have two questions for you. One: Is it true that you cover religion? And two: Are you willing to make a major life change?"

So he flew me to New York. It was supposed to be just an afternoon interview. My husband was at home taking care of the kids, cooking macaroni and cheese. I was supposed to get back that night. And then Peter looked at me and said, "Hey, do you like ice hockey?" I said "Sure!" I had never actually been to an ice hockey game. . . . And after that evening, talking about religion and watching my first ice hockey game, his driver dropped me off at the hotel, and Peter said, "Well, do you want this job?" I said, "Well, I think so."

I like to say that Peter was my rabbi. He didn't just initiate the religion beat, but he protected it.

BILL BLAKEMORE: He had this desire to bring religion into the realm of things so it could be talked about more openly. That was a natural, deep journalistic instinct. He'd see something that people were afraid to talk about and he'd say, "Why should we be afraid to talk about that?" He was the embodiment of the idea that there is nothing that can't be talked about with a little bit of tact and sensitivity and sensibility. And he was always trying to push those frontiers.

PEGGY WEHMEYER: Peter understood the role of religion in people's lives — for good and for bad. In the United States, he saw the culture wars coming. When I met him in New York, he said, "So often, we go as reporters to cover some big catastrophe like a plane crash or anything incredible in the news and, as good journalists, the first thing that we ask people is, 'How do you make sense of what just happened to you?' or 'What did you do when the plane crashed?' And the person would say, 'Well, the first thing I did was pray to God.'" Peter said, "People always respond about their faith, and then we edit it out." He said, "I would keep saying, 'Why are we editing this out? This is how people are making sense of life. This is part of the story.'"

PETER JENNINGS: *There is a fundamental difference in the way we, as secular journalists, see the truth and the definition of the truth accepted by many people of religious faith. People of faith believe that what they believe is true. We secular journalists are trained to believe that it is our obligation to put what we encounter to a rational test that we can comprehend. Someone pointed out that Saint Thomas, doubting Thomas, could well be journalism's patron saint.*

JEANMARIE CONDON: Peter knew that there were certain stories that were so complicated that you couldn't talk about them in a two-minute piece on the nightly news and really get at everything you wanted to say about them, or everything that was important to know about them. So he used his considerable clout to get the network to allow him to put on the air, several times a year, one- and two-hour documentaries about these topics, topics that, for the most part, were things that he felt that people were ignoring and that people needed to know about.

We had run across some very interesting historical research on Jesus. One day I said to Peter, "Why don't we do a documentary about Jesus?" never thinking that he would say yes. And he said, "Oh, yeah, let's do it." I thought, they are never going to do a documentary about Jesus. Peter went to our bosses, and he said, "I'm doing a documentary about Jesus."

PAUL FREIDMAN: Although Peter and I had a shared interest in doing more coverage of religion, and had sought a correspondent to do religion, and tried to put more stories about religion on the air than anybody else was doing, when I heard about Peter's interest in doing a long-form documentary treatment about the life of Jesus, I thought to myself, "There he goes again. You know, one of his enthusiasms." Nobody else would do this on commercial television, but good for him. It was one of the ways he used — but did not abuse — the power he gained as an anchorman.

TOM NAGORSKI: I wasn't in on the meetings, but I cannot imagine that when Peter first broached doing hour-long, two-hour-long documentaries for ABC News about Jesus and St. Paul — I think he probably threw some people when he first raised it. The fact of the matter is, those are some of the most distinguished — and mind you, very well watched — pieces of reportage that

ABC News — and I think it's safe to say Peter himself — ever did.

DAVID WESTIN: Long before he came to me with the idea of doing "The Search for Jesus," he and I had talked about the need for us to find ways of covering religion and faith. Now, I had thought, "Okay, we'll do more reporting on the Southern Baptists, or we'll do more reporting on conservative Jews, or we'll do more reporting on the Catholic Church." It never occurred to me to take his penchant for being a reporter and say, "Well, what would a reporter do if he were reporting on the subject of Jesus?" At the time, it was a revolutionary idea. I did embrace it very quickly because it was clever and it was the right thing to do. But more than that, when Peter came with a real passion for something, most of the time, you needed to listen to him.

Now, it was a challenge. When I went to the network and the company and said, "Oh, by the way, we'd like to do, not one hour, but two hours, in search of Jesus. We're going to do reporting on a man that lived two thousand years ago, and may even raise some questions about the received wisdom of some organized religions about exactly where he was born, exactly where he lived, and what happened," that was tricky. It took a little doing on Peter's behalf and on my own. I'd like to say, I got that done. I think Peter's insistence on it really made a difference. This was long before things like *The Da Vinci Code,* and all of the other programs that have come along behind. In retrospect, it looks obvious, but at the time that Peter came up with it and pushed so hard for it, it was far from obvious.

TOM YELLIN: No one warmly embraced it in the corridors of power at ABC. What they said was, "I find that really interesting, but no one's going to watch." That's the kind of thing that drove Peter crazy. You couldn't say that to Peter because he believed that if you found something interesting, and he found it interesting, that's two people, so there have got to be millions more. He applied that principle to the religious programs. The search for the historical truth about Jesus touches a nerve in everyone, even if you're not Christian, because it deals with deep questions about who we are and where we came from and where we're headed and how we got here. Everyone wrestles with these and Peter instinctively understood that.

One of the things Peter loved as a journalist is to go cover the story that everyone else was ignoring. Here was the thing that's an essential question at the essence of the human experience, and no one was doing it. For a journalist, that's the ultimate opportunity. I think that's how Peter viewed it.

JEANMARIE CONDON: These shows allowed him to go back to the region, not just to cover wars and hijackings, but to get out into the desert and to climb around archaeological digs, talking about the Dead Sea caves and the Dead Sea Scrolls. He loved that. He had fun with it. . . . In the Middle East, nothing gets destroyed. Everything is built on top of something else. Peter liked to dig down through the layers. . . . I remember we were leaving one of these archaeological sites and he grabbed my cell phone and he called his wife, Kayce [who he'd married in 1997]. He said, "Darling, guess where I've been? I've just been walking around all day in the first century."

When Peter would read some of the stuff we'd written, where we'd really got into why we were doing it and what was important about it, he would have a hard time actually reading it without his voice cracking, without breaking down a little. I remember there was the conclusion of one act of our "Search for Jesus" show, he tried it five or six times.

*From* Peter Jennings Reporting, *"The Search for Jesus"*

Every time he read it, looking at the pictures, hearing the music, he would start to cry. Finally, we just had to stop and use one of the takes where it was the least obvious. Today, if you listen to the show as it aired, you can still hear his voice cracking.

PETER JENNINGS: It is the man who inspired such astounding faith, such beautiful stories, whom we were looking for. What really happened in this tiny corner of the world during the brief time that Jesus lived here?

We kept looking and asking because something about being in this place, walking the same hills and roads that he did, standing at the sites people have venerated for centuries . . . it all gives you the strange feeling that maybe you can find the answers . . . if only you just look around the next corner, or the next one . . . or the next one.

TOM YELLIN: Peter was not immune to the commercial pressures of broadcast journalism. When everyone was telling him that no one was going to watch this program about Jesus — it would be incredibly interesting, but no one was going to watch it — he was very, very nervous. What that meant was that the first fifteen or twenty minutes of the program had to be perfect. We did a version that we thought was great. Peter saw it, and he said, "Oh yeah, that's pretty good. Let's change it." We did another version. Same thing. Did another version. By the time we got to the twenty-fifth version — I'm not exaggerating — I thought we'd done it. We did ten more versions. There were thirty-five versions of the first act. That was a clear expression of Peter's anxiety, which was brought on by all these voices in his ear who were telling him, "No one's gonna watch this; no one's gonna watch it."

The first program we did about Jesus got huge numbers. Millions and millions of people watched it, many more than anyone thought.

PETER JENNINGS: The gospel stories describe Jesus impressing his followers by performing supernatural feats: walking on water, turning water into wine, and feeding thousands of people with just a few loaves of bread and a couple of fish. But most scholars we talked to think these stories were invented by the gospel writers as advertisements for Christianity in its early years. Christianity, after all, was competing for followers with Judaism and with Greek and Roman pagan religions.

DAVID WESTIN: He was asking very basic questions, ones that cut very close to the bone, or very close to the heart, for millions of Americans. For those who believe in Jesus as the Savior, does it really matter whether he was born in Bethlehem or not? Is that really of the essence? He was asking some very tough questions, and there was criticism. I'll tell you just personally, I showed it to my mother in advance, and she was disgusted. She was offended by what was done because we were asking some of those questions and she didn't think it was appropriate, as a matter of faith. . . . Faith is not just an intellectual matter in this country. It's an emotional matter. It affects people very, very deeply, the way family does, and loved ones do. And this captured that.

At the same time, Peter was doing something on the screen — or not on the screen — that he did when he was at his very best, which is that he was taking a subject we thought we knew about — whether we'd been raised in Sunday school, whether we'd memorized [First] Corinthians 13, or however we learned about it — taking a fresh look at it, and making us at least think, "Wait a moment, maybe there's a different way to look at this. Maybe it's something different from what I thought it was." That was one of Peter's great strengths: to take things that we thought we knew, and to make us pause a moment, take a fresh look at them, and say, "My goodness, maybe, maybe it's different."

PEGGY WEHMEYER: Often I found that people in the media either had a disinterest or a disdain — sometimes a contempt — for religion or people who followed religion. Peter was just the opposite. Peter had an insatiable curiosity about religion. I can't tell you exactly why. People always ask me, "Why do you think Peter was so interested? Was it because he was religious?" I think Peter was a never-ending seeker, and he wasn't at all put off by religious movements or religious people. He was very secure; he wasn't threatened by them.

Religion is a very personal thing. I don't know exactly what Peter believed, although we talked about faith a lot. We talked about different religions and the role of religion. The thing that impressed me most about Peter was that he wasn't closed-minded to religion. He wasn't contemptuous toward people who believed things that he might have found different or odd. I think the most interesting thing about Peter was that he was always pursuing and curious and interested about why people believed what they believed, and how did they believe it, and he wanted to know more about it.

PETER JENNINGS: *Don't be confused at all that somehow my interest in religion, faith, and spirituality is somehow driven by any sense of faith or spirituality of my own. It is a fabulous story. It intersects with people's lives. . . . This is a good and irresistible story, and it is — my God, what else are we looking for in life? — it is relevant.*

TIMOTHY JOHNSON: He could've chosen many other areas to explore, but there was something that kept drawing him back to deeply religious, spiritual questions. I honestly don't know what his belief system finally might've been, but I know that he was constantly thinking and searching. . . . I think he was smart enough and wise enough to know that the big questions of life are always worth asking and thinking about.

JEANMARIE CONDON: When Peter got on fire with a topic, he would not let it go. He would grill anyone and everybody about what they thought about it. And even when the cameras were turned off, he kept going. You'd be standing on an airport line and Peter would turn to the person behind him and start grilling. I mean, imagine you're standing on line in the airport and this guy turns around and it's Peter Jennings. He's in your face, and for some reason he's saying to you, "What do you think Jesus really looked like?"

*Peter Jennings took particular pleasure in doing specials for and with young people. These were interactive events, in which Jennings interviewed the children and teenagers in the audience, allowing them to voice their questions, concerns, fears, and frustrations. Some, such as "War in the Gulf: Answering Children's Questions" (1991), "Growing Up in the Age of AIDS" (1992), and "Prejudice: Answering Children's Questions" (1992), tackled specific issues. Others, such as his two programs featuring President Bill Clinton, were conducted in the style of free-ranging town hall meetings. Their intent was always the same: to educate — without lecturing.*

PETER JENNINGS ("Kids, Parents, and Straight Talk on Drugs"): Now, this program is not going to be just another lecture on the dangers of illegal drugs. And anything kids hear here tonight they can hear in five minutes in any school hallway in America. But perhaps we who are their parents will learn something from them. Because in so many ways, they are the experts in a world where fourteen-year-olds have every imaginable drug, including cigarettes and alcohol, at their fingertips.

JONATHAN ALTER: Sometimes Peter would go into an explicit teacher mode, and he would actually do specials where he would teach kids and interact with kids. He always seemed very natural in doing that. And I think a lot of people learned about a lot of things — geography and history and politics — they wouldn't have known otherwise.

Television was supposed to be an educational medium when it was founded. Over time, news, which had not been expected to make money, started to make money, and then it *had* to make money. And now we're in a world where everyone assumes its purpose is to make money. But the original purpose of television news was educational. In that sense, Peter was a throwback to the ideas upon which television news was founded: to give people a window on the world and to enhance their understanding of complex national and international events.

PETER JENNINGS ("War in the Gulf: Answering Children's Questions"): Good morning, everybody, but good morning especially, boys and girls. For the next ninety minutes, this program is specifically for you. We'd like to talk to you this morning about the war in the Persian Gulf. We'd like to try to answer your questions. We'd also like to hear what you think about the war.

JENNINGS: Hi, Alison, how are you this morning? Do you have a question?

ALISON: Yes. Can Saddam Hussein bomb us?

JENNINGS: Can Saddam Hussein bomb us? In the United States?

ALISON: Yes.

JENNINGS: No. No way. Do all you kids understand that? Saddam Hussein can do a lot of bad things, but he cannot bomb us in the United States. His missiles can't get here and his aircraft can't get here. Why couldn't he get here to the United States? Want to take a guess?

SECOND CHILD IN AUDIENCE: It's too far a trip.

JENNINGS: It's too far a trip. It's almost 7,000 miles from New York to Iraq. It's almost 10,000 miles from California to Iraq. And he doesn't have an airplane and he doesn't have a missile that can get this far. So the first thing kids need to understand is . . . that we in this country are safe from his missiles and from his bombs.

STU SCHUTZMAN: He never talked down to kids. He had some ground rules with kids:

he would come halfway down to their level, but they would have to come halfway up to his. And it worked. He got a lot out of kids. I think he had the same approach with our regular adult audience. He never talked down to people, but he did try to inform them in as clear and concise a way as possible.

GRETCHEN BABAROVIC: Peter was like the Pied Piper with children. Whether he saw them in the studio, or whether he was doing the hour-long children's specials, he would squat down, and he'd look at them in the eye, and he'd engage them in a dialogue. He'd ask them questions, just like he'd do on a grown-up interview. It was quite amazing. Kids just loved him.

PETER JENNINGS ("Prejudice: Answering Children's Questions"): Good morning, and welcome. . . . We're going to spend this morning talking about prejudice, as in to prejudge other people because of what we see on the surface. I can't help but notice that some of you kids here have got green collars on today. Want to tell me about that, Mary Ellen?

MARY ELLEN: Well, the people with blue

and green eyes, we have to wear a green collar, and so — to separate us from the people with brown eyes.

JENNINGS: Why do they want to separate you?

MARY ELLEN: I don't know.

JENNINGS: Victor, here in the front row, why did they separate the brown eyes and the blue eyes?

VICTOR: I think they did that because they just wanted to show you how black people were treated back then, where we — when somebody looked and they made a funny face at us and other things.

JENNINGS: Oh, really. Tracy, down here in the front, how'd it make you feel to wear a green collar this morning?

TRACY: Well, it makes you feel different from everybody else, and everybody stares at you because you're different and everything.

JENNINGS: And how did it make you feel?

TRACY: Well, bad. You feel — you feel like everybody hates you for something you can't help.

*In 1993 and 1994, Jennings enlisted President Bill Clinton for two televised town meetings with children.*

BILL CLINTON: Peter was fabulous with kids. He could get children out of their natural reluctance. . . . I was surprised when we did the first town hall meeting, the way he got these kids to talk. One of them was a girl with cerebral palsy. I will never forget this. He called on her and she said that her twin sister also had cerebral palsy and couldn't speak and couldn't move as well as she, but was just as smart. The child said [to me], "I want you to help my sister go to school because the law says she can go to school," and Peter Jennings said, "Yeah, you are the president. Do that." It was hilarious.

GEORGE STEPHANOPOULOS: President Clinton [and Peter are] both big guys, and they're both great talkers. I think they knew that about each other, and frankly, I think they knew how to get under each other's skin. You could see that time and time again. You know when you play tennis with someone who's a little bit better than you and it brings your game up? It was fun to watch them in that first town meeting with children. Here was something that they both thought that they were the best at in the world. And they brought each other's game up. I think that also created a bond between the two of them.

PETER JENNINGS: *Kids have given me — my own very much included — have given me a window on the world . . . because kids sometimes ask the questions that we are too embarrassed to ask.*

DAVID WESTIN: I like to think that Peter was the real Peter, the unvarnished Peter, when he talked with children, in part because he didn't have to be that conscious of who he was and what he represented. He didn't have to be conscious of it because the children he was talking to weren't. I think that that was something of a relief and a release to Peter and he took great joy in it.

*Jennings' most spectacular and elaborate special celebrated the millennium on December 31, 1999. The program, broadcast from New York City's Times Square, beginning at four-fifty a.m Eastern standard time, transported viewers to the dawning of the year 2000 around the planet. Jennings stayed on the air live for twenty-three straight hours, as an estimated 175 million people tuned in.*

DAVID WESTIN: Everyone — not just the Walt Disney Company, but everyone — was scurrying to find the biggest idea for 2000. There was a big imperative from the company, starting more than a year before, saying, "What can we do for 2000?"

What you have in the millennium is the dawning of the sun in twenty-four time periods around the world. So why don't we cover it in twenty-four hours and just bring it to the American people — the celebration, or however it was being observed — as the clock turned to midnight in each time period? This idea would not have worked without Peter at all, because Peter is the person who could cover the world. He could cover all these different locations with all these different cultures and different geopolitical situations, and he could weave that all together.

Peter understood the idea immediately and embraced it immediately. Not everyone did. There were a number of people inside the news division and inside the company who were deeply skeptical of this idea. Some people declined to participate because they thought it just was not going to work. But Peter was enthusiastic from the beginning.

MARC BURSTEIN: He prepared, and he studied, and he did his research, and he knew he had to learn even more. He took it very seriously. He knew it was an enormous challenge. There were moments leading up to it when I'm sure, truth be told, at any given moment, many of us involved in that broadcast thought, "Is this going to be a huge mistake? Or is this going to be the greatest thing we've ever done?"

DAVID WESTIN: About two days before December 31, 1999, we were going through rehearsals and planning and things. I went down to Peter's office. He was alone in his office, and he had this big stack of 4 x 6 index cards, which he was basically memorizing. He was going through them, memorizing essentially every fact about the world for two thousand years. Now, that sounds like an exaggeration, but it's not a very big exaggeration. That's what he was trying to do. I remember sitting down and saying, "Peter, relax. You are meant for this. You know this. Whatever happens during this twenty-four hours, there is not one viewer who is going to walk away from this and think, 'Peter Jennings doesn't know things. Peter Jennings isn't smart.' That's not the risk. So put the index cards away and relax."

BARBARA WALTERS: He would make us do the kind of homework that he did, and I'm pretty compulsive about doing homework. My anchor place was the Eiffel Tower; what could be better? So, I'm thinking about the sparkles and the lights and how many are there going to be in the Eiffel Tower, and what's on the Champs Élysée? Then Peter said to me, "Do you know anything about the student revolution in Paris?" I said, "What student revolution?" So suddenly, the day before I'm on the air, I am cramming everything I could possibly know about the student revolution in Paris. I can't let Peter down; I can't look foolish. You know what? He never asked me one question about the student revolution in Paris. But that was Peter. He wanted to know everything, and he wanted to make sure that we did, too.

CHARLIE GIBSON: He was cramming and studying and whatever, trying to come up with facts that he could throw out in virtually every time zone. Of course, he didn't need to do that. Peter never let himself be complacent. Now, you can say that that was because he was insecure, or you can say it was just that he was nervous and worried all the time about what he would do on the air. But once he got on, all those 4 x 6 cards that he'd memorized were essentially irrelevant. What he did was quickly realize the tone of all of this — that it was a uniting experience that we were going through, and that with his deftness he could simply make this work in ways that didn't require the interjection of whatever various facts he had learned. It was just thematically bringing it together. And that's what he did so well.

ROGER GOODMAN: About a week before the millennium, he said, "Roger, the world is big, and twenty-four hours is a long time. I'm going to use you as a crutch. Every time I get lost, I'm going to say, 'Roger, where are we going?' And I want you to give me thirty or forty seconds so I can figure out what I'm talking about." Over the twenty-four hours, we stayed there, we never left him. Nor did he leave us. It was one of the most incredible feats that I've ever seen in my entire career. He could go from event to event, from city to city around the world, effortlessly, seamlessly. He told the story to 175 million people. And if you look at the tapes you'll see a number of times, "Roger, where are we going?" I'll never understand how he did it.

PETER JENNINGS: Good morning and welcome to the very edge of the twenty-first century. Good morning, you hearty souls, I should say. We begin, as you can imagine, with a tremendous sense of awe from our studio overlooking Times Square here — awe at what is behind us as well as what is ahead of us. We're going to begin this morning, in just a second, by going to Tonga and Kiribati out in the Pacific.

ROGER GOODMAN: We had two hundred cameras, and each of those cameras told a story. When Peter saw a picture — be it from the Eiffel Tower, or people dancing in the Kiribati Islands, or London, or the United States — he just told the story. During those twenty-four hours, Peter told the story of the entire world. All I'd have to do is hit the little key in Peter's ear, and say, "Peter, take a look at this little girl." That's all I would say to him. And he would sit there and he'd look at that little girl in Australia, and he'd tell a story. He would tell a story about the prime minister, or he would tell a story about some event that took place there.

For those twenty-four hours, Peter downloaded all of his knowledge. We couldn't believe what we were hearing. Any place we went in the world, Peter could tell us about moments and events that were critical to that country's history. How and where he got that information, instantaneously, was mind-boggling. At times we couldn't even keep up with him.

PETER JENNINGS: Midnight in Indonesia is coming up on the island of Java. The largest Buddhist temple in the world in Central Java. We're celebrating now in the world's fourth most populous nation after China and India and the United States. You see these Javanese dancers now acting out the law of Karma, in which unworthy deeds are recognized by punishment and praiseworthy deeds, rewards of re-incarnation.

TOM YELLIN: I think if Peter Jennings were not the anchor at ABC, we would never have done the millennium show. That show was built on Peter's decades of experience, wandering the world, trying to figure out what the hell was going on. The thing that's so interesting about that program is, if you remember, people were very, very worried that it was going to be a very dangerous night and that something terribly tragic was going to happen. So not only did Peter have to prepare for these celebrations twenty-four hours around the world, he also had to prepare for the possibility that something terrible was going to happen, maybe even right outside our door in Times Square. Being able to figure out how to do that, and how to play it — so that the sense of the moment captures the danger and the possibility of danger, but also this extraordinary transition in time into a new millennium — is just a really, really, really hard thing to do. So you had his experience, his global experience, combined with his skill as a broadcaster, combined with his sensitivity to the particular moment all in play at once. It was an extraordinary performance.

I sat in that control room with others for twenty-four hours, helping to direct that program, and all of us were amazed at what Peter was able to do. The first thing he did that was extraordinary was that he was able to keep his attention focused for twenty-four hours. That was a broadcast in which, on the one hand, he had to do very sensitive interviews with people like Cornell West and other deep thinkers who were thinking about the past and the future, and connections between the past and the future, and where the world was headed. On the other hand, he had to do a bit with Dame Edna, he had to do comedy. And he had to introduce music, and he had to be able to talk to people about their hopes and dreams, and he had to interview world leaders. I mean, it was all on display there. To be able to do all of that with grace and with style and with thoughtfulness was really extraordinary.

I think you see the full Peter in that program. You see his grasp of the world, his understanding of the world. You see his appreciation for the diversity of culture around the world. You see his sentimentality. You see his loyalty to the people he worked with. At four in the morning, he thanked everybody, including one person in particular, Nancy Gabriner, who had been by his side as his researcher and his second brain for much of the past twenty years. It was an extraordinary moment. I don't think you could watch that program without seeing Peter project his own life experience and share it with the entire audience.

PETER JENNINGS: We're going to go to Africa now, and there's no continent on earth in which there's more business undone. Africa enters the new millennium, as someone put it, awash in *coups d'état,* awash in wars, and with a health epidemic that threatens to do greater damage to the ranks of the continent's people than centuries of slave trading actually did. We're going to go to Djibouti, on the horn of Africa, on the edge of the Red Sea.

MARC BURSTEIN: We had correspondents around the world. We had stringers around the world. Peter had been to probably every place that we were dropping in to. He knew the people. He knew the culture. He knew exactly what would go on in these places. As midnight approached or as midnight struck in these various places, and we went literally around the globe, starting with the first midnight at four a.m., you just knew as a viewer and as a producer that he was asking very incisive, insightful questions about an area that he knew something about but knew that most likely the audience didn't know anything about.

In one broadcast in one single day you saw more sides of Peter Jennings than you might have seen in watching him for years.

DAVID WESTIN: I think one of the times in the millennium broadcast that you really saw the genius of Peter Jennings — and for me,

it may be the most memorable moment —
was when there was a very large, beautiful
celebration in Red Square in Moscow. Peter
went to Red Square and talked about what
was going on in Russia and what had happened with the fall of the Berlin Wall and the
coming apart of the Soviet Union and the
ascendancy of a democratic government in
that country. Then we went immediately to
Jim Wooten in a refugee camp in sub-
Saharan Africa, where it was pitch black and
people were sleeping out in the cold. Only
Peter could understand both of these situations, could bring those to us and at the
same time, get out of the way of the story.
He didn't over-talk. As much as he knew, he
didn't try to prove to you he knew everything. He let the story play itself. And so,
when Jim Wooten simply held the microphone up, out in the dark, in the tents, in the
desert, Peter just let it play. That, for me, was
the most powerful moment in the entire millennium program. It showed Peter's enormous capabilities, his enormous range, and
his ear. He had a wonderful ear.

PETER JENNINGS: It's going to be midnight
all across Western Europe now. We want
to help you celebrate it in Paris and in London and in Rome. And we want to cele-

*January 1, 2000*

brate it in Poland, the Netherlands, the Czech Republic, and Italy, and Norway, and Sweden, and all those places. Let's just listen to Paris for a moment.

BOB IGER: I went down to our studio to say hello to him in the middle of that marathon telecast, and there he was in his tuxedo with the throngs behind him, having a gay old time. Totally immersed in it all and the experience. Not just as an anchorman, but as a person of the world.

PETER JENNINGS: In all sorts of other cities around the world they have — sensible people have gone to bed. It's already six-thirty, almost seven o'clock, in New Zealand, tomorrow. It's four-thirty, almost five o'clock, in Sydney, Australia. It's almost three o'clock in the morning in Tokyo. But there are celebrations to come in New Orleans and in Chicago, which are our next midnights.

DIANE SAWYER: He had the decathlon of broadcasts because Peter was live, he was throwing all over the world, he was changing clothes. He was both riding this wave of exuberance and watching out for terrorism. He was bringing philosophy and depth to people in paper hats with whistles. He got it all done. He started early in the morning, and he was thoughtful and a little bit reflective, and then, as Times Square started filling up, you could see the helium in him. To be able to keep that going all day long, with never a commonplace phrase, never a cliché, about something that was just basically a ceremony and a celebration but that had dimension in our world — it was the work of an Olympian.

# 9
# SEPTEMBER 11

*No event tested Jennings' anchoring skills more than the attacks of September 11, 2001. He was on the air for seventeen hours straight, guiding Americans through the horror. September 11 drew upon his many talents — as a reporter facing breaking news, an anchorman handling a live crisis, a Middle East expert providing historical perspective, all the while reassuring a nation in grief.*

PETER JENNINGS: There is chaos in New York at the moment. . . . There is chaos.

ROGER GOODMAN: [We] were boarding an airplane to go to London for a meeting. And just before we got on the plane, I looked up at a monitor and I saw some smoke coming out of the World Trade Center. I said, "Oh my God," we ran as fast as we could, not having any idea what was going on, got into

*In a moment like this the only thing you can be is yourself. . . .
You have no time to be anything other than what you are or
who you are.*

—Peter Jennings

a cab and raced to the city, going the wrong way down streets, going through the Midtown Tunnel. We showed our press passes and got to ABC about forty-five minutes after the first plane hit. I ran in as fast as I possibly could and sat down, where I stayed for the next sixty hours. The minute I said, "Peter, I'm here," he said, "Thank God."

DON DAHLER: It has completely collapsed.

PETER JENNINGS: The whole side has collapsed?

DAHLER: The whole building has collapsed.

JENNINGS: The whole building has collapsed?

DAHLER: The building has collapsed . . .

JENNINGS: My God! The southern tower, ten o'clock Eastern time this morning, just collapsing on itself.

ROGER GOODMAN: I remember after the first tower fell, looking at Peter's face. His face was just turned white. Everybody was so emotional. He tried to stay as calm as he could. And then the second building fell and he was quieting all of us down. When that second tower fell, he just wanted total silence. He wanted us all to sit back for a second and just reflect on what was going on. We could not believe what our eyes were seeing.

PETER JENNINGS: Let's look at the north tower quickly — quickly.

JOHN MILLER: The north tower seems to be coming down.

JENNINGS: Oh, my God!

MILLER: The second — the second tower.

JENNINGS: It's hard to put it into words, and maybe one doesn't need to. Both Trade Towers, where thousands of people work, on this day, Tuesday, have now been attacked and destroyed with thousands of people either in them or in the immediate area adjacent to them. This is — there is simply no way to accurately describe the emotion this evokes in people all over the world.

DAVID WESTIN: It started Tuesday morning, about a quarter-to-nine in the morning, and we were on nonstop until midnight, Friday night, without a pause, without a commercial break, with no break whatsoever. It was almost a hundred hours, and Peter was on the air for over sixty of those hours. So first of all, you just have to look at his stamina, his ability to keep his thoughts together and to keep his emotions in check as he did for the most part. Then he had to try to understand the scope, the range of the problem: Is this a military problem? Is this an intelligence problem? Is this a domestic terrorism problem? Is it something else? Are there more attacks to come? Where do we go?

There were — as there always are, but particularly in that event — initial conflicting reports. A lot of reports were wrong. A lot of hysteria set in. The government on that occasion basically shut down, decided that the best approach was not to say anything because they might get it wrong. So we were left to rely upon almost gossip. There were wildly fluctuating reports on what was happening, and casualty limits, and whether there would be attacks in Chicago or Los Angeles or wherever, or whether the plane in Pennsylvania was shot down by the U.S. military, or whether there was an attack on the Capitol. Try to put yourself back in the moment and think about the level of confusion.

Peter was sitting there in our newsroom, listening to all of this, watching some monitors, and trying to help us make some initial sense out of it. We all craved information. We just wanted to know what was happening. Peter wanted to get us as much information as we could without going too far, without jumping to conclusions. Even when people would come on and give some answer that we all yearned to believe, Peter would draw us back, and say, "Well, that might be right, but it might not be right, so let's wait and find out whether we get it confirmed." We saw that play on hour after hour after hour, as various reports came in, and the scope and the size and the magnitude of the incidents happened and the personal trauma happened.

ROGER GOODMAN: Peter held our hand through those sixty hours of 9/11. Once again, the information from that large encyclopedia, that large computer of his brain just downloaded, as he tried to ease us all through it. There were an awful lot of emotional moments during those four or five days. And Peter truly was the captain of the ship. We watched him — we watched his face, we watched his expressions — and he really led us through probably one of the

most difficult programs that I've ever covered, or moments that I've ever been involved with in my life.

The story was in our backyard. This story was right there. This was our home. This wasn't Europe. You could go outside and you could smell it. You'd walk outside that next morning, after we had been there for twenty, twenty-four hours, and the firemen and the policemen were in front of ABC holding candles.

DAVID WESTIN: New York was terrorized. Washington was terrorized. People were afraid, deeply afraid. Our loved ones, including Peter's loved ones — his wife and his children — were deeply shaken by this. And through all that, he maintained a steady balance, a center, an intelligence, and a way of informing us without misinforming us and without stoking up our already raw emotions any further. He maintained that throughout. I think he did a real service to the nation. I think Peter's sixty-plus hours on the air began part of the healing process, in coming to terms with a new world, because it was clear — and Peter understood that from the beginning — this was a new world. It would never be the same.

RUDY GIULIANI: The thing that stands out about Peter Jennings, in general, [is that he was] very calm, very sensible, very measured, very balanced. Now, many stories, that's easy to do. September 11, it's very difficult to be able to cover it in a balanced way because your emotions push you in so many directions. . . . That reminds me of what a lot of us had to go through. We had very, very strong emotions: anger, fear, concern, sympathy. But you had to control all that in order to do your job. I had to do that in my case; Peter had to do it in his. . . . Peter had to communicate to the whole world, and I had to communicate to the people that were working with me.

PETER JENNINGS: *I don't always keep my composure. I sometimes lose it. I try not to let the public see that I'm losing it. My friends and my family are always amazed when people say that I'm calm, because I'm not always calm by any means. . . . But I think it's probably true that the worse things get around me, the cooler I tend to be. I tend to focus very hard under pressure, which I think serves a journalist or an anchorperson pretty well.*

COLIN POWELL: It was an enormously emotional period for the nation, and there was sufficient emotion with the issue itself that anchors didn't need to plaster another layer on. That's what was so good about Peter. He could deal with a very emotional issue, yet do it with a certain confidence and calmness in his demeanor. And that confidence and calmness could help stabilize the situation and help bring the American people back to normalcy.

BARBARA WALTERS: During 9/11 he was close to tears several times. He was also exhausted. He was never off the air, but he knew that his presence whenever you tuned in, that his being there said something. It said, "We're going to be okay. We're going to get through this, and we're going to get through this together."

PETER JENNINGS: *For me, there was one very tough moment in the middle of the day. I turned around and on the desk behind me there was a message from my children, just saying they'd called. . . . And I just lost it. In fact, I even lose it sometimes telling the story. And I turned around to the audience and said, "Now we've all got to talk to our children. We must talk. You must call your children." And that was the only moment that I just thought, "Hey, get it together, Jennings. You're losing it here."*

LYNN SHERR: Peter wasn't just a great anchor on 9/11. He was, as usual, a great human being. One of the seminal moments was when he said to the viewers, "Why don't you call your children and see how they're doing?" That's a pretty amazing thing to say when the world is falling down around you. Of course, it's the first thing you want to think about. But he said it.

PETER JENNINGS: We do not very often make recommendations for people's behavior from this chair, but . . . if you're a parent, you've got a kid in some other part of the country, call them up. Exchange observations.

MARC BURSTEIN: I was sitting in the control room at that point, wondering about my own children. I don't think there was anybody watching who wasn't. All of a sudden, Peter gave you license to think about your children. It was okay to think about something less than the big picture because it was a very personal story on a completely different level.

ELIZABETH VARGAS: When you saw him urge our fellow Americans, you know, reach out, call your family members, if you have children, call them right now, you could see then that he was also a father, that he was also a husband, that he was also a friend, because he cared deeply about the people in his life and the people who worked for him and with him. And anybody who knew him knew that about him. It was an important thing, and you saw that really come through.

JOHN MCWETHY: Peter and I were often involved in live broadcasts of sad and difficult times for our country. He lost it a number of times. It didn't surprise me because he was pretty tender underneath his sophisticated surface. But it often terrified me because I was afraid he would throw it to me, and he often did. And I was often about to be a basket case myself. Peter would toss it to me, and I would have to cope in some way and give him forty-five seconds to get himself back together. I felt sometimes I was a safety valve for Peter in those difficult times when the country was struggling. . . . That's the nature of live television. Then Peter would get his act back together and — bang! — there we went. I would tell him later, "Don't do that; that's not fair." But he would keep tossing to me.

We were on the air September 11, 2001, for what seemed to be days. Peter never flinched. He just kept going. Somehow, he managed to make it original and interesting. He would constantly tell me, "Wake up, McWethy, we're coming at you." He would inject life into a broadcast that could have easily been dragging.

MICHELE MAYER: I think September 11 was difficult for all of us, but we knew what we had to do, and we just kept going. We were on the floor, keeping things under control so that Peter's line of sight was clear. There weren't people moving around a lot and making a lot of distractions. I made sure that his zipper was zipped if he had to get up from the desk and walk around. We made sure that those kinds of things were taken care of, and things were quiet on the floor for him when he needed to concentrate. If he was reading an obituary or something like that, everything had to be quiet, calm, under control. We are all very aware of what Peter needs, and that's what our job was: to make sure things went smoothly in the studio. Wherever else it was going crazy, whether it was in the control room or back in editing or anything like that, it was our job on the floor to make sure things were perfect for him.

JEFF GRALNICK: The worse a circumstance got, the uglier the story was, the calmer Peter became. He was the voice of sanity during periods of insanity, which is what a broadcaster needs to be. It's a unique skill to be able to talk knowledgeably for hours, to broadcast down a path that is constantly changing and never predictable without ever letting the viewer know that there is anything difficult going on anywhere around you. You know the story about ducks swimming? It looks easy above the water. Nobody knew what was going on under the water when

Peter was on the air. He was just steady. Steady and complete.

PETER JENNINGS: *One of the roles, I think, we can play is to give people information and perspective in a quiet, reasonably sober sort of way. Television is very inflammatory at times and can, at the same time, be very necessarily calming. When we have a national tragedy, we all turn on our television sets to be reassured that our lives are intact and that our lives have meaning. I have the privilege of sitting at the center for periods of time. And I'm very conscious of the fact that I don't want to be pushing my emotions on other people. My opinions, my analysis, my sense of context about why something is happening, yes. But I don't like pushing my emotions on people. . . . I think it's important to keep it together. If we don't keep it together at a time of crisis, who's going to?*

DON HEWITT: Television — sometimes it's a theater; sometimes it's a sports stadium; sometimes it's a chapel. It's where people go at times of stress to be. It was like after the Kennedy assassination: they didn't go to church. They went to their television sets, and the whole country held hands. At that time it was Walter Cronkite, and they said, you know, "Father Cronkite, tell us every-thing is going to be all right." Well, Peter was part of that at 9/11, which was "We're not going to go to church. We're not going to go to a synagogue. We're not going to go to a tabernacle. We're going to our television sets, and guys like Peter Jennings will calm us down and kind of point us in the right direc-tion."

VINNIE MALHOTRA: I think that in tough times people wanted to be comforted by Peter. They wanted to be comforted by his soothing voice, his soothing tone. He was a reflection, a lot of times, of how you were feeling sitting at home. I think 9/11 is a clas-sic example of that. . . . In a lot of ways, it was that connection that he had made with people that really stood out, that really made him who he was, and really developed a trust between the American audience and Peter Jennings.

JENNA MILLMAN: I remember seeing him in times of trauma and thinking "God, this guy really understands how I feel. I don't know how he understands how I feel, but he really understands how I feel and he's really giving me the information that I need to know." My grandmother was thinking the exact same thing about him. What a unique quality, to be accessible and attractive and calming and comforting to people spanning many generations.

PETER JENNINGS (2001): *I am not a minister. I am not a counselor. I am not a psychiatrist. I am at best a guide.*

CHRIS ISHAM: 9/11 was a different story, in a different category, partly because the scope of it was so enormous but also because it was striking all of us here where we live. It was an attack on our city. It was not an attack on the other side of the planet. It was not a bomb going off in a city in Israel. These were attacks that occurred right here. And so, there was an immediacy to it that I think Peter felt, and we all felt, working on that story. There was also a sense that we had entered a new dimension on this story. The stakes had just increased to such an extent that I don't think any of us had really grasped before. This was uncharted waters we were entering. Peter understood that immediately, tried to make sense of it. He did, I think, a brilliant job of beginning to bring some clarity to it. He fully understood the depth, the importance, and the scope of this.

I think 9/11 brought together all his skills,

including his ability to operate fluidly on the air in any kind of a news crisis. It brought together the depth of his understanding of the forces at play in the Middle East, of emerging Islamic fundamentalism and Islamic extremism, which he had already studied up close. It brought to bear his understanding of the struggle that the United States was involved in. And of course, it brought to bear his love of his city and of his country.

ALAN ALDA: His compassion didn't, in any way, take away from his ability to think critically and with his full intellect. When he talked for sixty hours on 9/11 with no script as the events unfolded and as he reacted to each new understanding of the depth of the attack and the tragedy, he was able to do something that few people can do. It was because of who he was as a person. He could respond to the events that were particular and daunting and horrific and report them in detail. And at the same time, he could think broadly and conceptually. He didn't need to go away for six months and stew about it. He got it all at once and was able to put that together with us and for us.

PAUL FRIEDMAN: I think a performance like that of 9/11 is the culmination of everything he had learned over the years about how to do this extraordinarily complicated, difficult thing, which is to be an anchor in a situation like that. I think he was terribly upset by it, but he knew how to compartmentalize that and shove that aside until he could get away from his responsibility of being on camera. To some extent, the fact that he had spent so much of his life in the Middle East, and so much of his life thinking about that kind of violence and terrorism, helped him see possibilities and put things together as they were happening and be properly cautious about not jumping to conclusions. He always used to point back to the Oklahoma City experience, where everybody jumped to the conclusion, "It was Middle Eastern terrorists, right?" And it turned out to be an all-American boy. You learn those things along the way, and there comes a point when you get to put them all together. And 9/11 was that point.

PETER JENNINGS (2004): *There's no such thing as living isolated by two oceans anymore. We're altogether too connected to the rest of the world, and the consequences are huge of being much more connected to the rest of the world than we have been in the past. But it sure makes it challenging for jour-nalists.*

DAVID WESTIN: He started to bring us that first rough draft of history that helped us start to feel the world hadn't just gone entirely insane. It was a terrible tragedy, it was awful, but maybe there was some way to make sense of it and go forward.

PETER JENNINGS ("ABC News Special: Answering Children's Questions"): This week, a tragedy unfolded before our eyes. America faced its greatest challenge in many, many years. . . . And as we attempt to come up with answers, questions from the children . . . What about you, Mara? Put the mic right up close, would you?

MARA: I don't — I don't really get, like, what did we do? . . . Like, we didn't do anything to them, but they did it to us. Why did they do it? Why did they do it?

JENNINGS: There's the toughest question that I've heard all morning. All right. Let's try to find some answers to that. Margot, do you have an answer to that question?

MARGOT: Well, I think that maybe they did

it because they feel that since we're not their religion and we don't — maybe we don't believe in the same God that they do, maybe they think that we were evil just because we're not like them and it's sort of prejudice.

JENNINGS: That's very interesting. . . . How do you comfort each other? Sierra, that's it, you take the microphone away from your mother.

SIERRA: Well, at first I didn't know what to do. I felt lost. . . . And the past few days we've just been talking a lot, and we watched the news, and we thought maybe we shouldn't because watching it so much wasn't really helping, like. It just brought, just like, more tears to see everything that was happening.

JENNINGS: That's interesting. I was doing the news all of these days, and I must, at some times, agree with you.

DAVID WESTIN: Everything that he had learned, everything he had studied, every skill he had developed, all of his personality — on the air and behind — all of his character, made him the best person to try to help us through that very difficult time. Peter and I never talked about this, but I always suspected that at some intuitive level — not consciously, because he would never think in these terms — he knew that he was the right person to do that story, and frankly, that we needed him. Not just ABC News needed him, but the country and his audience needed him to help us try to make sense out of that.

Now Peter would cringe at hearing that said. I can hear him saying to me, "That's just ridiculous, David," because he didn't think in those terms. It wasn't personal ego when something like this happened. At the same time, I think at some level he was savvy enough to understand that this was really what he was meant to do.

PETER JENNINGS: *It is forty years since I came to the U.S. and in my entire experience, nothing has quite moved me as much as the coming together in the wake of 9/11.*

*I am not particularly sophisticated. You find me in my most comfortable circumstances wearing shorts and moccasins and wool socks in the middle of summer . . . in the middle of, if not nowhere, somewhere that nobody cares very much who I am or what I do.*

—Peter Jennings

# 10
# THE MAN

*Peter Jennings was magnetic. People were drawn to him. Despite his celebrity, friends and colleagues say he was remarkably down-to-earth. One of his greatest pleasures was paddling across a quiet lake in his native Canada. Back in New York, he took on causes, such as the homeless and public education, with the same compassion and commitment that drove his career.*

TED KOPPEL: From the time I first met Peter forty-one years ago until our last meeting shortly before he died, I felt a thrill whenever I saw him. Not many people have genuine charisma, that sort of animal magnetism that makes it difficult to focus on anybody else in the room.

CHARLIE GIBSON: I suppose if you ask a dancer, "Why does Fred Astaire move so beautifully?" they really couldn't tell you. Part of it's innate. Peter just had a sense of carriage and manner that was innate. He knew, I think, that you noticed him when he walked in a room. He just had a presence — and I don't want to use the word "charisma" — but certainly an appeal and an elegance to the way he moved. He knew that. He had an effect on people, and he liked that.

LAUREN BACALL: He was kind of disarming. He behaved in a way you didn't quite expect all the time. Needless to say, that is one of the most attractive aspects of a human being, that touch of mystery. . . . I always found him interesting. I was always interested in what he said and the way he said it.

MIKE LEE: Was he cocky, informed, charming, dismissive? Yes, all of those and more. He was larger than life. I never spent one minute — and I have spent many days and hours with Peter — that I didn't feel either charmed or a bit intimidated, and most of all, informed.

LYNN SHERR: Peter had a reputation as a ladies' man, which is true — dare I say it, he was one of the sexiest guys around — but he really respected women's intelligence, and he totally respected what women could bring to the table, personally and professionally. I always used to tease him that I made some of the best girlfriends in my life through women I met through him. He had great taste. And he had that smile. He had a smile that could have powered the entire East Coast. Actually, I think it did.

SARAH JENNINGS: You might see Peter as this suave, debonair fellow, as he was called. I always laugh, because one never sees one's brother that way. I think Pete was totally unpretentious. I think that's partly a result of his upbringing. Our family wasn't snobby. It was down-to-earth. We had all sorts of interesting people from all walks of life going through our lives. So when Peter stepped off the stage, he wasn't pretentious about what he did. He didn't take himself as a diva. His children had to make their own beds. When they would come up to the cottage in the summer, they lived very simply. They didn't live a grand life. They led a very rich and a very full life, but I would say Pete was unpretentious about his success and who he was.

HAL BRUNO: Peter wanted his children to understand that what he was doing was something right, and that all of the things that went on with the celebrity that accrued as the years went on — that wasn't what was important. At times it was difficult. We used to ski together out in Colorado with our families. When we'd come in to the lodge and he'd take the goggles off, everybody would immediately recognize him. We'd all gather to have skiers' lunch, and people would keep coming up and asking for an autograph or trying to say hi. It was very difficult to get through lunch because of all the people coming up. Peter took it all in stride. He always was gracious in talking to people. I remember, he explained to Christopher and to Elizabeth that this was part of the job — and they were just little kids then — that "people want to come up and talk to us because of the work I do." It was never more than that. He went out of his way to make sure that they didn't think we were special people.

JOHN LEO: I've never met anybody who was that famous and handled it so well. He was just a normal person when he was off camera. He never called attention to himself. He never tried to pull rank or dominate the conversation. He was perfectly normal. He enjoyed the social interaction with friends without being a big man or a celebrity. Wherever he went, he'd cause a commotion, of course, and he always responded well. Autograph seekers would come over and officially drool over him, and he was very gracious, even if he was in the middle of a meal.

TOM BROKAW: I remember one night we were at dinner, skiing. A whole bunch of us were there and a woman came over to the table, leaned over, and said, "Can I have my picture taken with you?" I said, "Gosh, I just would rather not. How about if we just shake hands? Peter and I will shake your hand." Peter popped up and said, "No, no, no. We should have our picture taken. Come on, let's have our picture taken." I'm saying, "Peter, it's not necessary," and he said, "Look, Tom, she'd like to have her picture taken with us." I really don't remember how it turned out, but I just remember Peter thinking, "This poor woman has screwed up her courage to come over to this table and wants to have her picture taken with us." I'm not trying to shove her out of the way. I'm just trying to say it'll just draw more attention to us. He was perfectly happy and willing to do that kind of thing.

I remember being at a very expensive hotel in Los Angeles, checking out early in the morning. This very well-dressed couple turned, and they said, "Oh my God! I can't tell you how thrilled we are to be in your presence. We never miss you." I'm beginning to soar, and I'm saying thank you very much. They said, "Mr. Jennings, our life would not be complete without you at the end of every day." I went back and said, "Well, Pedro, I've been taking care of you with your fans again."

DAVID WESTIN: Peter Jennings was a powerful man. What he said could move news divisions, and it could change governments. But he always took great delight in telling the story of how my wife's grandmother never quite saw it that way. A few years back, my wife asked Peter as a favor to call her grandmother on her ninety-fifth birthday. Miss Leila Palmer Sandy lived at the time in an old farm house in northern Virginia, and she didn't watch all that much television, but she loved Peter Jennings. Peter agreed not only that he would call Miss Sandy, but he made something of a ritual out of it each year. He would pretty much do the same thing: He'd break away from preparing *World News Tonight* some time in the afternoon, and he'd place the call, and Miss Sandy would pick up the receiver, and she'd be duly impressed that her favorite anchor was on the other end of the line. They would talk for a very few minutes, and then Miss Sandy would announce that she had an awful lot to do, she would say goodbye, and she would hang up on Peter Jennings.

The point of that story is not so much that Peter took the time out of his busy schedule to make the call. It's not even that he truly enjoyed talking with this very self-reliant, independent, plain-spoken woman. The point of the story really is that Miss Sandy was pretty confident that her time was just a bit more valuable than Peter Jennings', and she wasn't afraid to tell him so. And the real point is that Peter just loved that. He thought that was terrific.

LINDA BIRD FRANCKE: To everyone who knew him outside the television world, Peter was just a regular guy. He would make his own phone calls, for example. You never got a phone call that said, "Please hold for Mr. Jennings." It would be Peter on the end of the line with that golden voice that he thought he had to identify: "This is Peter." Of course, he didn't, because his voice was his own caller ID, right?

MARTHA RADDATZ: When I was with Peter

in Iraq, he was doing his traditional sixteen-, eighteen-hour days, running around all over the country. He stayed at the main military base, Camp Victory, which is where I stayed. To watch him with the troops was wonderful. He was just energized. We'd go into the dining hall, he's very low key, doesn't seek attention. But pretty soon, word would spread throughout the dining hall: "Hey, that's Peter Jennings." There were a lot of anchor people over there at the time. Geraldo Rivera was there. I watched how various soldiers and Marines would come up and say, "Hey, how are you doing, dude?" And they would come up to Peter Jennings and say, "Hello, Mr. Jennings. How are you?" I mean, with utter respect. And Peter had time for everybody. He was just completely gracious.

RUPEN VOSGIMORUKIAN: I thought after becoming an anchor he would turn. On the contrary, the higher he went in his hierarchy, the softer he became. Maybe when he was young he had more of an ego, which later on he knew how to soften.

PETER JENNINGS: *Part of the challenge of being an anchorperson . . . is that you don't want people to know too much about what you really believe because they then tend to invest that in the things which you say and they make judgments, which may be totally incorrect, about what you're saying, let alone what you stand for. I am not by nature an evasive person. . . . I am very open for the most part. [But] I've learned to be somewhat more protective. I've been burned a few times and learned to be somewhat more private.*

PAUL FRIEDMAN: People were always very surprised when they met him. He had this image of being kind of icy and aloof on the air, and they were always surprised that he was so easy, and so down-to-earth, and so considerate and caring with people. He really enjoyed meeting people and talking to them. He was kind of embarrassed about this "Oh, here is the big anchor" treatment. He liked it because he had an ego, but he was also embarrassed by it.

You always had these cases where somebody's parents would be in town. The parents would come in to see where they worked. I have known stars who would say, "I don't want any part of that. Let me know when they are not around, and I'll come out of my office." Well, if Peter heard that somebody's parents were around, he would come charging out of the office and make an enormous fuss. "Oh, so-and-so is such an important member of our staff. What he does, or what she does, is so important to what we do." And, "You have raised a great kid." Those parents would leave that room all puffed up and proud. That is a part of Peter that people didn't see. He was very caring.

MARC BURSTEIN: One Friday night I brought in my daughter and her Brownie troop, about ten nine-year-old girls. They watched the broadcast come together for a couple of hours prior to six-thirty, and then they watched from the control room and the floor while the broadcast was going on. When it was over I was hoping that Peter would wait a couple of extra minutes. As I said, it was a Friday night, and it was after an especially long week. I can't remember exactly what the news events were that week, but I think Peter had been on the road and just gotten back. I was hoping he would just stick around long enough to say hi to the girls. Well, he didn't just say hi to the girls. He sat and talked to them for at least thirty, forty minutes after the program. He asked them questions. He let them ask him questions. He posed for pictures with every single one of them. Then he posed for pictures with all the moms. Then he posed for a group shot. When I got the pictures developed I brought them down to him, and he didn't just sign, "Best wishes, Peter Jennings." He wrote a particular inscription to each and every girl and each and every mom. That wasn't on camera. Nobody knew about that. He wasn't doing that to get ten or fifteen Nielsen viewers. I don't even think they count nine-year-olds in the Nielsen sample. But that was Peter. And that was his passion for children.

LYNN SHERR: I think our viewers knew him for a long time, certainly when he was in London, as James Bond in a trench coat — the sharp-looking guy running after stories. When he came back to this country and started anchoring in New York, I think they saw the soul of a genuinely good human being who cared for other human beings. There was nothing phony about that.

TODD BREWSTER: He was a very emotional guy. He would tear up pretty easily in a lot of instances. He was one of those men who sure tried, worked to hold it back. It wasn't something that you wanted to show too often or too much. And he was a quintessential WASP and had WASP sort of manners and traditions.

PETER JENNINGS: *I never thought it was my job to have other people know precisely how I was feeling about anything on the air. They have enough trouble dealing with their own feelings. . . . I just don't think it's — I think that crying on television is a bit demeaning to everybody, but mostly to the audience.*

TODD BREWSTER: There was a certain dignity to holding yourself together. I think he maintained that, but he felt every story very powerfully. . . . I've seen him weep and hug perfect strangers who were telling very intimate details about their lives, which they would do, by the way. They would open up to him because — that's the other journalistic talent he had — people wanted to talk to him. They wanted to tell him their stories. And I think that's the quality of a good journalist, too, to be able to create the environment in which people feel comfortable telling the truth.

PETER SHAW: He was a gentleman in a largely ungentlemanly world. Peter would talk to anyone, anywhere — in an airport waiting lounge, on a street corner. He'd go up and he'd strike up a conversation, just as easily as he would deal with a head of state.

And he could put both of them at ease and be at ease completely himself.

LYNN SHERR: It could drive you crazy sometimes. You'd be walking with Peter down the street, and he would stop and talk to people. All you wanted to do was get somewhere! It wasn't about ego — I mean, Peter had a reasonably-sized ego, and that's fine — but he really liked connecting with people. That's what made him so good at his job, and it's what made him such an extraordinary friend.

LAUREN LIPANI: I remember being in an airport — I think it was Atlanta — and he and I were walking toward the gate. He said, "Go ahead, I'm going to have my shoes shined." He sat down, and I went ahead. We started to board and I didn't see him, but we still had a lot of time. So I got on the airplane. I was sitting in my chair, and I kept looking up ahead of me, looking for him. He still wasn't getting on the plane. I was getting a knot in my stomach. I called his cell phone and he didn't pick up. I thought, "Well, maybe he's in the tunnel coming to the plane."

They might have called last call, or they said they were closing the door, and I thought, "Oh, no, where is he?" So I got up and I said to the flight attendant, "There's someone who needs to be on this airplane." I was reluctant to say who, as Peter would hate that, but I did. I called his cell phone, and finally he picked up. He said, "Oh, oh, I'm coming, I'm coming." He came onto the plane. I said, "Where were you?" He said, well, the person who was shining his shoes, "He was from Lebanon and I wanted to talk to him." He didn't care about making the airplane. He just wanted to talk to the person he met in the airport, whom he'll never see again but whom he found so interesting. That was a very Peter moment.

VINNIE MALHOTRA: If you were ever waiting in a line somewhere, waiting for a flight somewhere, Peter had this really wonderful way about him that he would just walk up and down the line. He would just stop and he would talk to people, just a random person waiting in line. He used to always ask people where they were from. I think a lot of that had to do with the fact that Peter traveled just about everywhere in the world. When he'd ask somebody where they were from, it was his way of immediately knowing a little something about them. If they were from England, if they were from Florida, wherever it was, Peter had been there at some point, and he had a feeling about that place. It always sparked a new conversation. He could go on for half an hour while he was just sitting there, waiting for a plane to take off.

SARAH JENNINGS: Peter wasn't exactly a linguist. He could pick up a few words of Italian or Arabic or whatever, but when you were with him in an Italian restaurant, you would never know he didn't speak Italian. He just had this way. What he didn't know in words and sentences, he would make up for with charm and connection with the people he was communicating with. It was really about communication. He certainly had that gift.

LYNN SHERR: Peter was the only man that I know who would address taxi drivers by name. You would sit in the back seat of the cab, Peter would read the ID thing, and he would say, "Oh, Mr. Green," "Oh, Mr. Khan, how are you today?" He wanted that connection. They were startled. They had no idea how he knew who they were, and then they figured it out. He did that all the time.

KAREN BURNES: When I was a kid, I used to

read his fan mail. I'd sit there reading through these huge piles of mail, and I kept noticing this same woman kept writing to him, saying, "I'm so in love with you, Peter, I can't live without you. I am pining away for you. I'm sick. I need your help." She would sign them "Honeysuckle Divine." I said, "Peter, this woman is sick. She needs your help." He would say, "Oh, no, no, no, no, lovey" — he always called everyone lovey — "No, lovey, I can't. She's all right." I would say, "No, no, we have to go help her." He would say, "No, no, no, it's okay."

I didn't know, of course, at the time, that fans could come in all shapes and sizes. I didn't know that Honeysuckle Divine was a stripper on 42nd Street. After a while, I said, "Honeysuckle Divine is going to commit suicide if you don't help her. We have to go see her." And because I was so sure she was going to kill herself, Peter, being a kind enough person, took me, this little girl, to 42nd Street. We actually went to a strip club, went backstage, found Honeysuckle Divine, pulled her out, and made sure that she was not, in fact, going to kill herself. She was so amazed that Peter Jennings had come all the way to see her that she later for years said it had changed her life. And that was Peter. He would do anything for anyone if they were in trouble.

TED KOPPEL: I remember walking down 67th Street with Peter — it must've been about forty years ago — and a panhandler stopped the two of us. We each gave him money, but Peter stayed and talked to the man for about ten minutes. He asked about his life, and he listened, and thereby he invested a damaged soul with dignity.

ALAN ALDA: He was very specific and active about his compassion. He personally went down to soup kitchens and fed people. Not as a show, but as something to do as a person. He didn't do it as a famous person; he did it as Peter.

KEITH SUMMA: The first time I met Peter, I worked with a homeless organization here in New York City, and he wanted to be one of our volunteers. One of the things we would do is go to the homeless shelters in New York to monitor the conditions and make sure that the homeless folks who were living there had a bed and a blanket and running water. Peter and I went out to a homeless shelter in one of the worst neighborhoods in the middle of the night, into one of these large armories where there are a thousand people on cots. It was a scary place.

When we walked in, it was clear to me that Peter had never seen anything like this. It struck me because Peter was a worldly reporter who had seen everything, and here he was, forty blocks from his own home, and he saw this third-world poverty. I think that struck him. And he spent the rest of his life trying to help homeless people in New York, handing out sandwiches to people under bridges, in the shelters, trying to raise money. And he never wanted anyone to know about it. He kept it very quiet. But he was intimately involved in trying to deal with the poverty right here in his own town.

GRETCHEN BABAROVIC: It opened Peter's eyes. Peter had been all over the world, but here it was in his own city, and he was shocked. And so nothing would do. He came back to the office and he said to me, "Look, Gretchen, this is really important to me." He said, "I really believe that we should awaken the powerful in this city to the plight of these people. It's terrible. What can we do?" Then he said, "Well, I think maybe what I'll do is invite some of the people I have access to. . . ." Peter never was presumptuous about who he was, and what he was. I don't think he ever totally accepted the power that he had. He said, "I'm going to see if they'd come out with me on the food truck."

And that's what we did. We sent letters and made phone calls, and we put these invitations out to various and sundry powerful people here in New York. One of them was his very own boss, the chairman of ABC, Tom Murphy. Tom is maybe ten years older than Peter. Peter took Mr. Murphy out on the food truck with him, and they went all through the food program in these very dire parts of the city. And lo and behold, the truck broke down. Who do you think pushed that truck? It wasn't Peter. Peter was up there orchestrating, as he always had to be in control. Mr. Murphy was pushing the truck.

PETER JENNINGS: *I always thought it was sad that we hide the homeless because it's a fact of life. I think it's incumbent upon us to recognize the homeless, to see the homeless, to look the homeless in the eye.*

MARY BROSNAHAN SULLIVAN: Peter would end his broadcast and literally run across town and hop in the van, and we would go out and deliver hot meals on the streets. The quality that will always stay with me about Peter is his sincerity. He was one of the most sincere people I've ever met, and I don't mean that in a maudlin or sentimental way. He just had this refreshing directness that was so surprising to people who met him for the first time. You can only imagine the look of shock and then profound gratitude from people on the street when Peter would show up and give them a carton of hot stew or some milk.

I remember one of the last times we went out on the feeding program. At the end of the run, we stopped at the Bowery flop houses to deliver our last meals. I remember taking Peter upstairs to the Providence Hotel and, after twenty minutes, having to practically drag him away from the table because he was so engaged with what those men had to tell him.

There's a feeding stop down near Housing Court near Chinatown. There's the men who live there in the homeless encampment, and then there's the Chinese grandmothers who come out with the small children from Chinatown. One night we went out, and Peter was doing crowd control because the two groups really don't get along. There was this adorable kid — he couldn't have been more than six or seven years old — and he was wearing a Yankees cap about two sizes too big. Peter leaned down and said, "Are you a Yankees fan?" The kid looked up and said, "Yeah." And he said, "Well, my wife is home right now watching the Mets play." Without missing a beat, the kid looked up and said, "A Mets fan?" He said, "Yeah." The kid said, "You need to find a better woman." I'll just always remember that grin on Peter's face as he looked out and said, "Kid, there is none."

PETER JENNINGS: *Almost every night in Central Park — I am a dog owner — I talk to someone I know who is homeless. It is no substitute for a home, but here in the people's park they feel safer — at least for a while — than they do on the streets.*

MARY BROSNAHAN SULLIVAN: [Peter's wife] Kayce told me about an encounter she had shortly after Peter died. She was sitting on a park bench, and the gentleman near her leaned over and offered condolences to her for her loss. She said, "Thank you." He said, "You don't know who I am, do you?" Kayce said, "No, I don't." He said, "It's me, Frank." Kayce said, "Oh." He said, "You still don't recognize me, do you?" She said, "No." Frank went on to explain that he was homeless and she probably didn't recognize him because he had gotten cleaned up recently and had a shave. He was sitting there with his girlfriend. Then Kayce knew immediately who it was. Frank went on to tell her how sad it was that Peter had died because it had meant so much to him and the other people who live in the park near their apartment because Peter would so often stop by and talk to them. More importantly, he had stopped to listen to what they had to say, how their lives were going. Few people realize what a great friend Peter was to homeless New Yorkers.

PETER OSNOS: Once you've been a star, you've been a star. The celebrity business is like anything else: Enough of it and you've got it. Peter knew what it was to be a celebrity a long time ago, with all of the virtues and privileges it carries. I think what motivated him particularly as time went on, were the things he thought were important. The things that he thought really mattered.

LINDA BIRD FRANCKE: He was really cheap. For years he only bought second-hand cars. And he would trundle his family around in these falling-apart cars that would die by the side of the road. So he became a favorite client of Dependable Taxi because they were always having to rescue him. He just was very anxious about money. He didn't want to be seen as anybody with money. And I think that he was so bewildered that he had money himself, he just didn't know how to deal with it.

PETER JENNINGS: *I don't think until my current job did it ever occur to me that you would make huge amounts of money from doing what we do. It didn't when I went overseas as a foreign correspondent in '69, '70. I had $400 in the bank. It didn't occur to me that I needed more at the time.*

TOM WOLFE: There is a German sociologist who defined guilt as the fear of being envied. Now I don't think Peter felt guilty about much, but I think he did have a fear of being envied. He did not want to be singled out as, "Hey, there's the famous Peter Jennings" and, "God, he makes ten million dollars a year." He didn't want that role for a second, and that's why he was never in the party pictures in the Hamptons. I mean, he publicized Jazz@Jennings because that was a big moneymaker for charity. But otherwise, he was not part of that.

GRETCHEN BABAROVIC: There was a group in the Hamptons called the Bridgehampton Child and Recreation Center. Peter's friend Linda Francke approached him because there was a child care center, which serviced the people who serviced the community, and they were struggling to make ends meet. Linda asked, would he host a gospel session? He just said, "Absolutely." He loved the idea of it. Then it segued into Jazz@Jennings. Peter loved it. He just loved it.

LINDA BIRD FRANCKE: One thing the Jennings did so brilliantly was to host Jazz@Jennings every June at their house, for the last nine years, to benefit the Bridgehampton Child Care Center. Most celebrities — if you want to call them that — would lend their names or their houses and then they'd go somewhere else. Not Peter. He was hands-on. We never sent out invitations because then we saved the cost of printing. A personal letter went to everyone on the guest list. He hand-wrote notes to each person. He allowed his tennis court to be torn up every year so he could put the tent up on the tennis court. He contacted the jazz musicians, all of whom played for free.

One of my tasks was to write the bios for the program of each musician. And every year Peter rewrote them, which was very annoying. But it was the most amazing event. In the nine years of this Jazz@Jennings, we raised — or he raised, let's put it that way — close to two million dollars for the center. It kept the center alive. This was the forgotten minority community in the Hamptons. I mean, you hear "the Hamptons" and you think everybody is rich and off on their yachts or on their helicopters. That's not true. There's been a longstanding minority population on the side called the Turnpike, which really had been overlooked. And Peter took that on as a cause.

BARBARA WALTERS: They had some of the greatest old-time jazz players. Peter adored it. He had the best time. This was not a big-deal, fancy, chic, charity event. This was people in their T-shirts and their sweaters listening to wonderful music. Nobody enjoyed it more than Peter.

DAVID WESTIN: For Peter, jazz was more than just a form of music; it was really an entire way of looking at life. And the jazz masters were more than musicians; they were truly great artists.

GRETCHEN BABAROVIC: He became totally engaged in the world of jazz. He would go out in New York, go to jazz evenings and jazz clubs, and sit and listen. He was so thrilled whenever one of the guys would call him and invite him to a jam session. He just loved that.

And singing, he loved to sing. If he went to church, boy, you could hear his voice booming out, singing those hymns. It just went right to his soul. And he embraced all kinds of music. One of the great honors of his life was to be asked to be on the board of Carnegie Hall. He was so pleased and proud to be part of that great institution.

GIL KAPLAN: I was on the board of Carnegie Hall and later Peter joined that board. We got to know a lot about music together. In fact, I currently host a show on WNYC Radio called "Mad about Music." It's about famous people who happen to love classical music. When I asked Peter to be my first guest, my guinea pig for a pilot, his first reaction was to be annoyed. He said to me that that was a show he had wanted to do but he had been turned down at ABC Radio because, as was Peter's wont, he wanted to feature every possible kind of music. That's not the way that radio audiences are organized; people listen to classical music or jazz. So instead he helped me, but he never let me forget that this had been his idea before mine. Whenever somebody would say something nice about the show, he'd turn to me and say, "My show, my show."

ALEXANDRA WOLFE: My first memory of Peter is when his daughter and I used to ride horses together. Peter would always be the father who got really involved. He would always get his hands dirty. . . . All the other parents would stand outside the ring or not come at all. But Peter would go right in the middle of the ring with our trainer and actually help teach the lesson.

I saw how important it was to Lizzie that he would always come, and he'd always be there. I'd see the look on her face, and I'd see her put that much effort into what she was doing. I think it was contagious. All of us sort of stood up straighter when he was in the room. You really wanted to impress him and wanted him to be proud of you, even if he wasn't your own father.

CHRISTOPHER JENNINGS: The same qualities which made my dad the journalist he was made him the parent he was. Whereas other children are encouraged to make way for the world of adults, Liz and I were always expected not merely to listen but to participate, to inquire, and most of all to learn.

LENA KAPLAN: Peter had an uncommon way of communicating with people and making them feel totally at ease with him. I saw it in the way he dealt with children. He was very much on their level. He spoke to them in the same language as he would have spoken to anybody, taking for granted that they would understand what he was talking about, but always quick to laugh with them.

GIL KAPLAN: He treated our children in an adult way, which was the way he did things. I'm not sure our kids always were happy about it at the time, because after all, they were being questioned as though they were adults, and they were twelve years old or something, having opinions on life and their school work. But that was Peter.

ALEXANDRA WOLFE: I think what speaks most highly of him are his children. Lizzie and Chris are two of the bravest, most intellectually curious people I know. I think because of his outlook on life, they care about the world that doesn't touch themselves. I mean, Lizzie goes to Bangladesh for the summer to help build houses. Who does that? I think they just see the world a different way because of how he was.

Dinner conversation used to be about interesting things. It wasn't, "How was tennis today?" and "How was going to the beach club?" It was, "So, did you hear about what happened in Bosnia?" It was really involved, but it was casual. It wasn't a forced "let's talk about the newspaper" conversation.

PETER JENNINGS: *Both my kids have this very heightened social conscience. I think it's because we spend a lot of time together focused on, Hey, let's not just talk about home; let's go meet a homeless person, alright? You don't give a homeless person money. If they're hungry, you help them get some food. I took my daughter to South Africa to the first election. I took my son to the fiftieth anniversary of D-Day, so that they would grow up with some sort of sense of what violence is — not just what it is on television. And in that respect, they're both quite privileged.*

KAREN BURNES: My father, Jim Burnes, was an anchor and a television correspondent with Peter, and he dropped dead suddenly when I was fourteen, and Peter . . . could've easily said, "Well, I've just lost my best friend, but you know, I'll check in with the daughter every so often." . . . Instead of that, he basically just adopted me. He took me in, he made sure I was going to school, he made sure I had everything I needed, he made sure I was reading, that I was doing my homework. . . . He really did not have to take in this lost young girl and stay in my life, my whole life, just because he'd once been my father's friend. That wasn't what I expected of him, but it's what he did.

PAUL FRIEDMAN: What people didn't get was that he had this quality of sweetness. To some extent, you could see it on the air because he did the kids' programs and you could see the way he interacted with kids. I have some video — which, no, I won't give you — of Peter and my children and his children. And they are all in the four- to eight-year range, playing with Peter in my house. And Peter is on the floor, pretending to be a horse, and these four kids are climbing all over him. It went on for an hour and a half. There is no question in my mind that he enjoyed it at least as much as they did. He just had this thing about kids.

CHRISTOPHER JENNINGS: I think Dad connected so well with children because he always maintained a childlike awe about the world.

KAREN BURNES: I think people saw him at work and said, "This is a demanding, tough, professional person." He was, as the *New York Times* called him, urbane. But he was kind and warm, and he was very whimsical. He once went to India to cover the Indo-Pakistan war, and he came back with an elephant for me that was the size of a — I mean, it was two hundred and fifty pounds. It was huge. He dragged that elephant from India to Beirut to New York and brought me this huge box for Christmas. I opened it up, and there was this magical creature with mirrors and beads. He knew that a child would like that. And he brought this two hundred and fifty pound box back from a war, just to please a little girl. That's Peter. Wherever Peter was, was magic. I think that's the best way I can describe it.

LYNN SHERR: He related to smaller people. He related to older people. He related to less privileged people in a way that was quite astounding, given his status in life. Once, I invited him to Thanksgiving dinner, and he joined our family. He paid more attention to an elderly aunt than he did to anybody else around the table — talked to her, listened to her. That's what Peter did. Peter listened. It was a miracle to see. He made her feel as if she was the youngest person in the room. That's the kind of effect he could have on people.

KEN AULETTA: If he went to a book party or a function where there were a lot of people in the room, including a lot of fairly famous people in that room, Peter would notice the most vulnerable people in that room — a child, a spouse who was not well known, who seemed awkward — and he would go right for those people and talk to them, ignoring all the famous people in the room, all the people who basically wanted to talk to Peter Jennings. You'd see him in a corner with some teenager talking, and listening, and asking the questions.

DIANE SAWYER: I remember a friend of mine telling me that she had gone to some boring, fancy party and there were all sorts of United Nations muckety-mucks there, and she looked in the corner, and sitting in the corner was Peter. He was talking to, like, the Third Assistant Deputy Secretary to the Zambian Minister of something or the other, with all the intensity and focus and curiosity that he would have talking to the Secretary General.

MIKE LEE: For some reason Peter and I became like brothers. I don't know why. I always thought he had mistaken me for someone else from the very beginning. I never felt special enough to be his friend. He adopted me somehow.

GRETCHEN BABAROVIC: I always think he was a little bit surprised at where he'd ended up, in terms of the so-called celebrity, even though he always had star quality. I think he was driven by that inner core of insecurity that so many people, who are so good at what they do, have.

LYNN SHERR: Peter always seemed so in charge. It always seemed as if he had it all together. In fact, he was as vulnerable as a two-year-old. A couple of years ago I invited him to a dinner party along with his wife, Kayce, who is also a close friend. It turned out Kayce was going out of town. Peter said, "Well, would it be okay if I came without Kayce?" I said, "Yes, of course, I'd love you to come." He said, "Phew, finally someone's invited me somewhere and not just for my wife." You know,

I really think he believed that, at least at that moment.

DIANE SAWYER: I think that Peter had this combination of absolute confidence and self doubt. He was restless, searching, learning, becoming. You always had the feeling that he was not one of the enameled finished products, who knows everything he thinks, and who knows what we should think. He was ready at any moment to learn something profoundly changing, profoundly altering in his life as well as yours.

PETER JENNINGS: *I've always thought that if you just rubbed management the wrong way, it kept you sharper. If you thought they were going to fire you tomorrow, right? I've always thought they were going to fire me tomorrow, since I was a kid. And, I don't know, it just makes me work a little harder.*

KEN AULETTA: There was a part of Peter that wanted to please. You hear this psychobabble about how he didn't graduate — you know, he didn't go to college and maybe he was insecure about that. Who cares about that? I think that a part of the makeup of a good journalist — and Peter was a good journalist — is a certain insecurity: Did I get the story right? Do I have all the facts? Do I understand the larger context? Maybe there's also an element of wanting to please people. That certainly ran through Peter, that: Am I right? Do I have it right? He was always questioning.

CHARLIE GIBSON: It is the nature, I think, of broadcasters to need reassurance. How many broadcasters does it take to change a light bulb? Five: one to do it and four to tell him what a great job he did. And that's true of Peter to a large extent. He was nervous about what he did. I began to realize how much Kayce meant to him when we did a broadcast once and Peter was on it, and we went to commercial. I wasn't finished with the tease for the next segment before Peter had finished dialing up Kayce to ask her how he'd done. "Do you think that was okay? Did I get the point across?" or whatever. Peter needed that reassurance because he was always nervous about what he did. In many respects that's very positive — that you don't get so cocky and so self-assured that you lose the ability to hear people tell you when you've done a good job and when you haven't.

TOM BROKAW: His insecurities — we all have them. I had them. Dan had them. I thought it was a job requirement if you were an anchorman: You had to be insecure. I thought there were two essential elements to being an anchorman. First, you had to have bravado — you had to be willing to go where the big story was and think that you could get it on the air. And the other essential element was fear that you wouldn't get the job done or you were not adequate to it.

I think that ran through Peter as it runs through me and as it ran through Dan when we were doing these jobs. Peter looked so supremely self-confident out there, but at the end of the day, I know he'd have a drink and he'd wonder whether he'd done the right thing on the story. Maybe he'd given too much emphasis to one aspect of it. Maybe we were a little better that day. We talked about this thing constantly.

KEN AULETTA: These are people, these anchors. Not only have they competed against each other for decades, and kept their eye on each other for decades and respected each other for decades, but they're also people. They're like ex-presidents. There are very few people who share the experiences that they've had, and very few people who can understand the experiences they've had the way each other can understand it.

I moderated the last public appearance that Peter, Dan Rather, and Tom Brokaw did together. It was right after Dan had made a mistake on the National Guard report on Bush. The bloggers were chewing on his leg, and everyone was really on his case. Peter and Tom both came to his defense in the most eloquent way possible. I'll never forget. Peter was the first to speak. He said, "I just want to say" — this was before a huge audience at the New York Public Library — and Peter said, "I just want to say Dan may have made a mistake or two here; we all have. But do not judge this entire man's journalistic lifetime by one mistake. This is a magnificent figure."

I remember Dan was sitting between Peter and Brokaw, and tears started rolling down his cheeks. Then Brokaw weighed in against the *jihad* against Dan Rather. And more tears started rolling down his cheeks. Then I looked at Peter, and Peter had tears in his eyes. They were defending Dan, both of them, very eloquently, but they were also defending themselves: "there but for the grace of God go I." They lived in this public arena, where every day they are exposed the way few other people are. One misstep, one mistake could expose them to the kind of ridicule and vitriol that Rather, in this case, was exposed to. And they didn't want to abide it.

DAN RATHER: Ken Auletta was doing a seminar for the *New Yorker*. It was a big audience in New York City. Ken was beginning to question me about a story that was in the news and was controversial. Peter interrupted him and spoke up in my defense. He knew that because there was an ongoing independent panel looking into that story, I couldn't and wouldn't say anything in my own defense. Peter spoke up. I never forgot that. It was so typically Peter. Peter was a loyal friend. Anybody who talks about Peter Jennings and doesn't talk about his loyalty, particularly his loyalty to his friends, just doesn't know him very well.

TOM FENTON: You know, there are not many people that you can speak frankly with in our business. I mean, really frankly, openly, candidly. You could do that with Peter. He was not a backstabber. That's also rare in this business. . . . He was a great colleague — class in a business that doesn't have a lot of class. In a business that doesn't have a lot of really straight shooters, Peter was a straight shooter.

PETER JENNINGS: *I tend to see the best in people and am surprised when they have other agendas. That may be less true the older I get. . . . I'm unquestionably more skeptical. And I think that both government and much more recently business have tended to add to my cynicism about public behavior. . . . I used to spend most of my life thinking I didn't have a cynical bone in my body. I think that's no longer true.*

ALAN ALDA: When Peter was your friend, he cared about how you were doing and made sure you heard about things that affected your life. And this was how tens of millions of people who never met him felt. He cared about how they were doing, and he made sure that they heard about things that affected their lives — not only heard about them, but saw more deeply into them. I think so many people responded to Peter the way they did because Peter was a truly authentic person. He was who he was, even though he was many things at once. He was complex and simple at the same time, knowledgeable and inquisitive, kind and tough. He was gracious and he was direct. Once, after dinner at our house, he stayed after the others had gone and he washed the dishes with us. We couldn't talk him out of it.

He did it naturally, without fanfare. He turned to me while he was drying a dish and he said, "Now that everyone's gone, if I were you, I'd send that wine back where you bought it. It's a little off." Graceful, yet direct.

HILARY BROWN: He was always an editor. He was always going through your scripts, of course, with a fine-tooth comb, but then he would go through everything. I mean, he used to edit my Christmas letter — you know, those things that you send to everybody, all your friends and relatives? He'd phone me up and say, "Oh, too many clichés once again, Hils. You've got to do something about that."

LYNN SHERR: Peter was a very loyal friend. Even better than being considered Peter's friend was being considered part of the family, although every now and then it had its drawbacks. He used to have a big Christmas party at his house out in the country. The very first year, hordes of people were invited. All sorts of people were there. They had this huge buffet line, and all of a sudden it looked as if there was not going to be enough food. Peter came running over to me in the buffet line, pulled me out of the line and said, "FHB, family hold back!" He was a great friend, but you did sometimes go home hungry.

GIL KAPLAN: We regarded Peter as an extended member of our family, but as a result, you had to accept his behavior. He was in the house, for example, and it was a warm day and he was perspiring, so I suggested that maybe he wanted a clean shirt of mine. He said that was a great idea, and he was quickly bounding across the room, heading up to my bedroom. I said, "I'll get it for you." No, not at all. Peter just went into my bedroom, opened a drawer, found a shirt he liked, and took it. Well, most people would regard that as bad manners, but in our home, once the signal was clear that this was family, he behaved like that. We came to accept that and actually adore it.

JOHN LEO: Peter loved ties. He particularly loved ties his friends were wearing. You'd go out to dinner with Peter and he'd admire your tie, and you'd say thank you and try to get back to the conversation. No, no, Peter would extravagantly admire your tie over and over until you took it off and gave it to him. And that's how he acquired a great many of his ties. At his fiftieth birthday party, we dummied up a slide show of all the events of his life that were likely to be embarrassing, such as emceeing the Miss Canada Contest and so forth. The one that got the biggest laughs was — he turned fifty in the Dukakis year — was of him stripping the tie off Dukakis during their interview. Everybody roared over that because every man in the audience had lost a couple of ties to Peter. He did send me six ties one year, to apparently make up for it. They were the six most hideous ties I've ever seen in my life.

LINDA BIRD FRANCKE: Every year Kayce and Peter gave a Christmas party on the Saturday before Christmas. This was a major local event. Everybody was invited, and I really mean it: the butcher, the baker, the candlestick maker, the electrician, the plumber, the ambassador, the Pulitzer Prize–winning journalist, the lawyer, whoever the Jennings had come in contact with and liked, because they were immensely friendly with everybody.

Everyone would gather and sing. There were song sheets, and we'd all sing Christmas carols and the more ecumenical "Frosty the Snowman." Peter loved it. He had a beautiful singing voice, but his own interpretation of the notes on occasion. He would call on people to do solos. We had to sit through the interminable "Twelve Days of Christmas" sung by some little kid. It was really, really fun. There were drinks and dinner and everybody laughed.

JOHN LEO: He thought the dandiest thing to do on New Year's Eve was to dress up in a kilt. I don't think there's enough money in the world to pay me to do that, but Peter enjoyed it.

SARAH JENNINGS: While he led this very public life, he did keep his private life private. He tried as best as he could to live an ordinary family life — have his children go to school like other people's children, and not to be idolized or adulated just because their father was a big star. In a society that is very heavy on celebrity culture, I think he did his level best to avoid being a celebrity. Of course, that's very, very difficult in the TV business. It's an odd thing to come to New York City and see your brother's picture on an enormous billboard coming in from the airport. But when you're in our sort of family, it didn't mean a thing. We're still family, and that was Peter's job and he had to do it, but it didn't mean that he was as big as a billboard.

Still, it was a very difficult job. Peter always took three weeks a year in Canada, and that was the touchstone of his year, I would say. We always used to joke: the first week he'd come in, he'd be insufferable; the second week he'd be coming down to earth; and the third week he'd turn back into a human being.

PETER SHAW: This was a fellow to whom bliss was to be paddling a canoe on a remote mountain lake in Canada, perhaps in the winter. Peter was very much a family person. In many ways, he was at his happiest when he was around the dinner table in the kitchen, as he was often with us, eating pasta, drinking wine, eating red peppers that had been sliced by my wife.

SARAH JENNINGS: When he came home he was able to enjoy the simple life. He lived in this marvelous city of New York and had this very rich diet of cultural events and famous and fascinating people, but he'd come home in the summer, and he could put on his shorts and pull on a pair of wool socks — by the way, he always bought his wool socks in the Byward Market in Ottawa, and he'd wait every year to come in and to pick up his supply of socks — and then come up into the country and enjoy the simple life. He loved to canoe. He loved to sail. He would go with his children out on the river, kayaking, or he'd go up over a chain of beautiful lakes. I find it lovely to think that someone who could lead such an intense and rich life could still come back and enjoy the beauty. Peter always loved Canada.

CHRISTOPHER JENNINGS: My dad was never as happy as when he was in his canoe. The two of us went on many canoe trips together. I cherish the memory of one particular trip, lying beside Dad under our canoe waiting out a freak summer hail storm on the Black River in Quebec. Amidst the roar of ice on fiberglass, the two of us laughed uncontrollably.

ALEXANDRA WOLFE: When I went to Canada with them, I was prepared for a vacation. I had never really been outdoors. I was raised in New York; the Hamptons to me are really rural. I went up to the farm in Ottawa and he said to me, "This is not a vacation vacation; this is a working farm." I said, "Oh no." Before dinner one night, he said, "Oh, we're all having chicken." I figure, we'll go to the grocery store, get some chicken. No. Instead we're going to eat the chicken out back. So he says, "First we have to kill the chicken." Kill the chicken! The only dead chicken I'd ever seen came cellophane-wrapped and was from Perdue.

So we're out in the backyard and I hear the chicken's neck snap. Out walks Peter with the chicken dangling in his hands. He says, "Ali, will you pluck the chicken?" And I mean, I gasped. I'd never seen anything like it before. He said, "You've really got to do this. I mean you can't be a city girl all your life." So he gives me this dead chicken and he says, "Take the feathers out." I'm shaking, I think it's so gross. I can't believe it. So he sits down with me with this bloody dead chicken in his hands, showing me exactly how to pluck the feathers out until I would actually feel comfortable enough to do it myself. Finally, I plucked the chicken and took a photo to prove to my parents that I actually did it.

PETER JENNINGS: *I find huge virtue in physical labor and am very pleased that my children both have discovered the virtue of labor, not merely intellectual pursuits.*

GRETCHEN BABAROVIC: He was a natural athlete. He'd skied since he was a small boy. And of course, you scratch a Canadian and you find a canoe, or a lake, or a hockey puck. And those were very much part of his athletic loves.

He also had a wicked sense of humor. He could laugh at himself, for the most part, except for maybe his hair. That was a bit of an Achilles' heel. But when you really tickled him, he'd throw his head back and his eyes would get all squinty, and he'd just let out this guffaw. He loved a good joke. And when you got him started, he was a wicked mimic. He could do accents like nobody.

CHRISTOPHER JENNINGS: My dad had this unique mix of cooking and dancing. We would turn up the music very loud, and as we chopped and stirred, Dad would swing me into his famous jitterbug. My father was an urbane and graceful man, but as a parent he never shied away from being deeply and fundamentally goofy.

BARBARA WALTERS: I think my most prized personal memory of Peter is not Peter on the air but Peter with Kayce, Peter in a sweater with his arm around Kayce, and Peter with his children. Peter didn't talk about himself privately ever on the air, except during 9/11 when he heard from his children and told the viewers that they should try to get in touch with their children. And you realized that he had fear himself about his children's lives then. Those were the moments that I will remember.

ALAN ALDA: He was very proud of his wife, Kayce, and I really got the impression that he was truly proudest of her because she knew the names of the homeless people out in front of their apartment building. When they were picked up in a roundup by the police, she went out and collected their belongings and put them in the basement of their apartment building until they could come back and get them. Peter told that story with such pride. I've seldom seen anybody so glad about another person's actions. That he could be married to someone who thought that way meant so much to him.

TODD BREWSTER: His devotion to Kayce and Kayce to him was just a wonderful thing to watch. Peter had had not the greatest success in marriage before Kayce, and yet there was nothing in their warmth and their life together to suggest that there was anything awkward in this union. They were devoted to each other and had a great time with each other and shared a wonderful sense of humor and an appreciation of friends that was very nice to watch.

LINDA BIRD FRANCKE: He was an immensely proud and loving husband to Kayce. He adored her, and she him. It was one of the magical unions. I think that his special love for her was obvious all the time. He looked to her, he reached for her, he touched her, and she him. I remember a wonderfully poignant scene. They came to my daughter's wedding in Baltimore. At the reception, I was out in back of the tent doing something, and there they were, the two of

*With wife, Kayce Freed, celebrating their marriage*

them, dancing on the lawn, off the dance floor. It was utterly romantic because they were beautiful together, both tall and graceful. There they were having their private, wonderful dance. It was a magical moment.

GRETCHEN BABAROVIC: It was like a boat that found its mooring.

DAVID WESTIN: For those of us who knew Peter at all well, he let down his guard whenever he talked about Kayce and about his children, Chris and Lizzie. We all knew that Peter took his job very seriously. He cared passionately about what he did at the office. But I think none of us suffered under any delusion but that ultimately he would judge his own success according to how good a father he was.

GRETCHEN BABAROVIC: His children were the very soul of his existence. He was so proud of his kids. He had expectations of his kids, but the kids were brought up pretty much as normal kids. They had to help with the dishes. They had to take the garbage out, walk the dog, and say please and thank you and I'm sorry.

JEANMARIE CONDON: Peter worked very

hard at being a good father to his children, Lizzie and Christopher. He loved them passionately, passionately. If those kids were in town from college and they wanted to meet him, he would cancel everything. He would bring them to screenings of our documentaries when we were working on them and ask them what they thought. He would value their input and would take their advice. We would hope that what we'd done would pass the Lizzie or Christopher test.

Actually, we sometimes enlisted them. We would tell them in advance, "He's having trouble with this section, but we think it's kind of good. If you think it's good, can you tell him that it works?" They would play along. Once, we were arguing that we should use this Christian heavy metal music in our St. Paul documentary. We were going back and forth about it and he kept complaining that he wasn't sure that people would understand the words. So I told Lizzie in advance: "Listen, he's having a lot of trouble using this rock 'n' roll music in this section. He says he doesn't know if people are going to understand all the words, and he's just a little intimidated about using it. If you like it, can you just tell him that?" Lizzie came to the screening and she watched the section. She dutifully said, "That's great. Great

*With son Christopher . . .*

*. . . and daughter Elizabeth*

choice of music." And he never said anything else about that song. That was it.

TODD BREWSTER: There was something about Peter that came alive when those kids were around — when they were younger and then when they went to college and right through. I think he was proud of both of them. I think that he saw achievements in both of them that he wished that he could have had in his own life. As remarkable as his life was, there were things that, as with all of us, he wished he could have done.

LINDA BIRD FRANCKE: Oh, he was an amazing father, almost to a fault. We all adore our children, but Peter took it to another level. He could not really talk about his children without crying. Peter cried a lot. He was immensely sentimental. We got used to his crying and just ignored it. Others would think, "Oh, my God, what's that?"

I remember at his last Christmas party, Christopher, his son, was about to graduate from Wesleyan, and Wesleyan, needless to say, had asked Peter if he would deliver the commencement address. So Peter had asked Chris how he felt about it and Chris evidently said, "Let me think about it." Christopher had gotten back to Peter just that day or something. Peter was telling me the story and he said, "And Christopher said, 'Just come and be my dad,' " and Peter burst into tears.

JEANMARIE CONDON: He worked very hard at being a dad and he loved being a dad. And characteristic of Peter, he never thought he was doing it well enough, and he'd beat himself up about it. He would talk to you about it. And he ended up with these two children who are every bit as intellectually honest and caring and courageous as he was.

# 11
# CITIZEN

*On May 30, 2003, Peter Jennings became an American citizen. He was inspired in part by his work with Todd Brewster on two books:* The Century, *a 608-page illustrated history of the twentieth century in America, which was an instant best-seller, and* In Search of America, *which examined the nation's founding ideals and their life in contemporary America. Both books were accompanied by multi-hour primetime documentary series on ABC. Jennings was also motivated by the attacks of September 11, which fostered an even stronger emotional bond to his adopted home. But as proud as he was of being an American, he retained his Canadian citizenship.*

BARRIE DUNSMORE: As a Canadian, I think I can say that Canadians bring a different perspective on the United States, and Peter

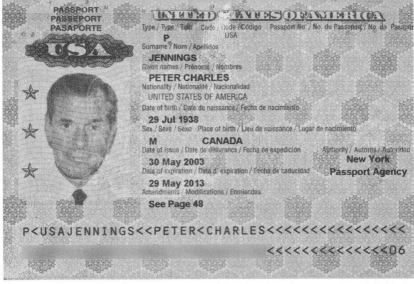

*My Canadian roots are very deep. My attachment to Canada is intense. My affection and admiration for the United States are also very intense. My gratitude for the opportunity to share in the American experience is boundless.*
—Peter Jennings

certainly had that. It's kind of a joke, but it's not exactly an accident of history that Canadians are the way they are, because Canadians are mainly United Empire loyalists who decided not to be part of the revolution.

PETER JENNINGS: *You know, in the United States we grow up with the notion of life, liberty, and the pursuit of happiness. In Canada you grow up to a greater extent with citizenship, good government, and never cross the street against a red light. I took my son up to a World Series game in Toronto when the Blue Jays won the World Series, and we had an awesome evening, and there was quite a lot of beer consumed. We all came out of the Sky Dome . . . and one cop on Front Street put up his hand, and we all stopped. And I thought to myself, boy, home again.*

BARRIE DUNSMORE: I think Canadians tend to see the world in a different light than Americans do, not that Canadians think that they're better than Americans or that they can do things better than Americans. On the contrary, most Canadians suffer from some degree of an inferiority complex towards the United States. But at the same time, there is a sense that there's a way of doing things up in Canada that might be more civil, that might be more conscious of minorities, and other such things. I wouldn't overstate that, but I think that Peter did bring some of that attitude — what you might call a social democratic view of the world. Not a radical left and certainly not a radical right view, but something along the social democratic lines that many Canadians have as a perspective on the world.

PETER JENNINGS: *My parents were deeply part of the Canadian establishment for whom being Canadian was a condition, not merely a nationality. I grew up when there was no need for Canadians to assert their national identity. There were no pretensions to a manifest destiny. We were quite proud of being Clark Kent rather than Superman. And we could never have imagined hockey being played below the Mason-Dixon line.*

BILL BLAKEMORE: I think the fact that he was a Canadian had a great deal to do with why he was so valuable to us in the United States. He was right on the edge of our society but fascinated by and attracted to America and working for the American Broadcasting Company. It meant he always had that little added bit of objectivity to help us see ourselves as others see us. When he was traveling overseas, he was very international, partly looking towards England culturally. He was very much at ease, going from culture to culture to culture. He took us along and helped us enjoy that access.

PETER JENNINGS: *As a journalist, being Canadian has always served me in unusual ways. In any number of places during my long period as a foreign correspondent for ABC I have sidled up to uncooperative people and whispered, "Actually, I'm Canadian." And it worked, even though neither the person being sidled up to nor I could define what I meant, except that I was somehow less threatening than an American.*

JONATHAN ALTER: I think the fact that he was a Canadian gave him a sense of detachment, and detachment is an important quality in a journalist. That little space between him and the country he came to love really helped his perspective. It gave him a little bit more depth and texture than you get from someone native-born. One of the greatest observers of our country was a Frenchman, Alexis de Tocqueville, and he also had that kind of distance where he could appreciate what was great about the United States but also look at it with a little bit of depth perception. Peter had that as well.

I also think it's true that first-rate journalists who are not American-born tend to have a little bit more of an international perspective. They realize that the sun doesn't rise and fall on the United States, so they see things a little bit more contextually in terms of the world. Peter's Canadian heritage helped him in that, and I think it helped him from being too much of a cheerleader.

PETER JENNINGS: *I remember my mother coming to see me once when I was living in England. At dinner one night an American made the mistake of saying that the U.S. had saved the world in World Wars One and Two. My grandfather had gone to France with the 48th Highlanders in 1914, had been captured in the first gas attacks, and was held as a prisoner for almost five years. When my mother's tiny fist hit the dining room table and lifted the silverware, the poor American was reminded in ways he would never forget that Canadians helped save the world, too.*

DAVID WESTIN: He was Canadian in the sense that, like some of our brothers from north of the border, he grew up somewhat in the shadow of the United States and somewhat distressed with the United States. We were awfully big, and we tended not to pay enough attention to Canada. He felt that slight a little bit, which gave him a healthy skepticism about America.

BARRIE DUNSMORE: His skepticism, which he might have brought with him from Canada, was something that was part of his personality. He would always look at things in a slightly different context than most Americans or, for that matter, most people.

PETER JENNINGS: *I was once criticized by someone in the Reagan administration when I was living in London because — this was during the Cold War — I was putting the Soviet position on the table and allowing people to judge. He said very critically, "But you're too fair." Now, that's very Canadian, to see America in terms of the rest of the world. Canadians grow up with a strong sense of influence. Americans grow up with an imbued sense of power. . . . I've never gotten over the fact that America is, in some ways, a foreign country on which to report.*

PETER OSNOS: Part of Peter's very strong moral dimension to the way he approached stories and people and issues came from being a non-American. Peter brought a cosmopolitan quality to most of the big international issues. I don't mean by that that he was anti-American in any way. In fact, he was, over time, totally devoted to this country. Peter spent his time traveling around the United States, meeting with people, and he loved it. But Peter was Canadian, and he could look at our kinds of issues without many of our superpower conventions. He had just enough of the sort of international cosmopolitan perspective to launch him into issues in a very distinctive way.

For example the Middle East: The Middle East was one of the great stories of his life and time, and it has always been a complex one for American reporters who try to press their way through it. The American view of the Middle East is very much dominated by our internal politics. Not having grown up with that in quite the same way, I think Peter was liberated from it. That meant that he was able, over the years, to bring a perspective to Middle East reporting that would have been tough or tougher for a lot of American journalists. And that went on right straight through to his reporting from Iraq, which again was liberated from the conventions of ordinary American patriotism.

DAVID WESTIN: At the same time, he loved the idea of America. He would say, "America is the only country in the world founded on ideas." He loved the Constitution. He loved the idea of a written constitution and a liberal democracy as practiced here — as much as he understood the flaws in it and recognized and reported on those flaws as well. But he loved it.

PETER JENNINGS: *You won't go anywhere else in your life where the Constitution has taken on the quality of a sacred text. You will not visit any other nation where the claim "that's unconstitutional" rings with the quality of accusation. Nowhere else you go will the "un" prefix be applied to a nationality, the way that we say something is un-American. You will discover — if you haven't already — that as you rub shoulders with the world, being German or Chinese, for example, is a fact, but to be American is an ideal. . . . One of the beauties of the American story is that it is itself a journey, that the founders conceived it to be one — and the ideals they set forth were just that, ideals — perhaps unattainable, but worthy goals for a nation of strivers.*

CHARLIE GIBSON: He became a student of the country, not just of its society, but of its history. He was fascinated by American history. He'd read an American history textbook the way some of us pick up a John Grisham or a John Irving novel. He loved it. He absorbed it.

TODD BREWSTER: I may have actually contributed to his interest in American history — I'd like to think so at any rate — because I have a passion and interest in American history and American culture and American identity. Although he loved Canada and always referred to himself as Canadian all through his life, Peter nonetheless had spent almost all of his professional life working for an American company or working in America. And I think he grew to realize . . . that America was this incredibly powerful, important force culturally, politically, economically. And that to understand America more deeply was to understand the world more deeply.

TOM BROKAW: I'm a product of the American West and the Great Plains, and it's always been important to me, heartland America. I would talk to him about that some. "Peter, you ought to get out there." And then, on his own, he did begin to get out there. He wrote the book, he began to take the show on the road across this country, and he would always come back with that same sense of discovery. I'd say, "Peter, I've known about that for a while." He came out to the American West, and the wolves were a big issue. They had been for some years. Peter said, "My God, do you know about those wolves?" I said, "Yes, I do." But I loved the idea that he never quit discovering his new adopted country.

BARBARA WALTERS: I think Peter struggled for many years because he was a Canadian citizen and loved his country so much, and yet America was where he had earned his stripes, really. When he reported on political events, if somebody wanted to attack him, that was his vulnerability: how can you report on this or that because you're a citizen of Canada?

I think, because of this Peter did more homework. He knew every Congressman in every district — where they went, where they came from. You couldn't spring anything on Peter that he didn't know, in part because he was saying, "I may be a Canadian citizen, but part of my heart is in this country, and this is where I have to bring the news." I think it was a conflict for him for quite a few years.

PETER JENNINGS: *In any number of circumstances when I questioned — or even appeared to question — the Wilsonian self-congratulation that inspires American thinking on world affairs, it was firmly suggested by some that maybe I should go back where I came from. And they often sent bus money.*

GRETCHEN BABAROVIC: When I first came to work for him, people were constantly saying, "Oh, he's Canadian, why doesn't he go home?" Whenever we'd come to a controversial point in the newscast, we'd get these letters from people who'd say, "What does he know? He's a Canadian." He did struggle with it because he did love this country and he knew that this country had given him a great, great deal, but being Canadian was very important to him. It was who he was. It was his roots. Yet, here was this adopted country, just sort of beginning to chip away, chip away.

TODD BREWSTER: He began to appreciate certain basic appealing aspects of the American identity that go all the way back to the country's founding. The project that he and I worked on, *In Search of America,* really was a path to that because he spent so much time reading the American founders, understanding the founding impulses, understanding what a terrific experiment the founders undertook when they started this democratic republic. I think he realized just how courageous these men were, how brilliant they were. He realized that in the work they had done they had created a personality and identity — you could even say a race of people — of which he had now become a part.

We felt that, going around the country, going from place to place. The whole idea of the project was that we were going to go around America, like Alexis de Tocqueville, the great French aristocrat who came in the nineteenth century to discover what America and democracy were. We were going to see if these American founding values were really there anymore. And we were going to see that at a critical juncture, the entrance into the twenty-first century, when there were so many elements that were working against it: the Internet, globalization, the worldwide acceptance of democracy and market economics. If everybody was going to act like an American, then what did it mean to be an American?

As Peter began to understand more of what it was to be an American — some of these very basic, pragmatic values, which put liberty at the top and equality very near it, and which put this element of egalitarianism throughout so many parts of American decision making — he came to feel that he was an American. We talked about being an American, being a kind of affirmative act: you declare yourself.

TED KOPPEL: Peter was enormously proud of working in the United States. Loved the American dream. Loved the American legal system. Loved the Constitution and everything that underlies the American system. He was tremendously grateful for the opportunities that he had been given here in the United States. But at the same time, he was very proud of having been born in Canada. Loved Canada. Loved the Canadian people. And he felt it would somehow be disloyal to Canada if he gave up his Canadian citizenship and became a U.S. citizen.

CHARLIE GIBSON: As he came in greater and greater measure to respect this country, we also wondered why he waited on citizenship. I never had any doubt that eventually he would do it. Maybe it was to honor his Canadian parents that he kept his Canadian citizenship solely for so long. But then I think after 9/11 he felt that it would be wrong not to express the bond that he felt with this country for having gone through what it did.

GRETCHEN BABAROVIC: I will say that his mother really didn't want him to become an American citizen, and she had told him that in no uncertain terms. She died in 1991, so then it was okay. She probably was turning over in her grave, but he made his decision.

He came to me one day and he said, "You can't tell a soul. You must swear on the Bible. You cannot tell a living soul, but I have decided that I want to become an American citizen. And I've been thinking about it for a long time."

We put the process in place. We had to gather all the information that the immigration services wanted. Just like everybody else, they had to approve of his papers. And he had to wait his turn — no jumping the queue. Then the call came that he was able to go to immigration. And he was just thrilled, beyond thrilled.

PETER JENNINGS: *I cried a little bit — my kids didn't cry, but I cried a little bit — but I'm a fairly emotional character anyway.*

TODD BREWSTER: I remember a very distinct moment. Peter had always said to me,

"Be careful in the prose that we use together that we don't say 'we Americans' because I'm not an American." He would say, "You're an American, and I'm a Canadian. People don't like me pretending I'm an American when I'm not." So I was always very careful to be certain that we never used that phrase. Then one day in 2003, a couple years after *In Search of America* had come out, he and I were traveling together to Gettysburg, I believe to give a lecture. He started saying, "Well, we do this and we" — meaning in the collective "we, as Americans" — and I turned around and I said, "Peter, you're violating your own rule. What's going on here?" He looked at me and he said, "No, I'm not." I said, "What are you telling me?" He said, "Well, yes." And I said, "Did you become an American citizen?" He hadn't wanted to tell, but he sort of whispered it to me. Of course, he couldn't keep a secret. He whispered it to Justice Scalia the next night, I think at this event in Philadelphia. He was totally charmed by the idea of becoming an American.

PETER JENNINGS: *It was actually . . . on the night of [July] 3rd. I'm sitting at a table with Justice Scalia. And he gave the toast to the founding fathers, and I gave the toast to the country. And when I finished, I sat down, and he said . . . "Not bad for a Canadian." So I got down on my knees, and I said, "Well, actually, I'm an American, but can you keep it a secret?" I now realize how stupid it was to ask a Supreme Court justice if he could keep a secret.*

ANTONIN SCALIA: I was surprisingly impressed by that. It made me feel really good to know that here was a man, having been in this country this long, had acquired enough of a love for it that he wanted to become a citizen. He certainly wasn't doing it for ratings purposes or he would have done it a lot sooner. He just finally decided that this was the country he wanted to be part of. That made me feel very good. A couple of weeks later, I sent him an American flag to celebrate his joining the brotherhood and sisterhood of American citizens.

GRETCHEN BABAROVIC: I think he kept it private because he did not want people to think that he was using his citizenship for any other reason than that he was proud to be an American, that he felt that he wanted to become an American citizen, that he had fallen in love with his adopted country, and that he truly respected her. This was his way of showing his respect. I really, really believe that. He didn't want people to think there were any ulterior motives.

PETER JENNINGS: *It is fascinating for me to have two passports now. One of them is the evidence of my roots. The other may tell you something about the love I have come to feel for my adopted home and its ideals. . . . I thought my timing was perfect: Just when America seems to be most misunderstood — both to the world and, at times, even to herself — just when the shock of a foreign attack has jolted the nation into a dramatic shift of behavior — some of it laudable, some of it frightening. Just when America, fresh from leading the free world to victory over the Communist menace of the twentieth century, is faced with leading the free world against the menace of terrorism and fanaticism in the twenty-first century. I thought it was a good time to be an American, to embrace the ideals that made the nation in Lincoln's words, "the last best hope of mankind." For at her best, she still is.*

DAVID WESTIN: I remember when he came to tell me that he'd become an American citizen. He'd kept it a secret for quite a while. It was in July of 2003. We both had birthdays coming up — we share a common birthday

— and he came up to tell me he'd done this. We ended up, both of us, with tears in our eyes. He was so emotional about the importance to him of having taken this large leap into a country that he truly loved and, because he loved, questioned.

PETER JENNINGS: *There is another reason to become an American: To play my own small part . . . to see that America, so laudable in her infancy, remains committed to the ideals that made her great.*

JON BANNER: He was a kid in a candy shop. He was so giddy over the idea of being able to vote in his first presidential election. He was so excited to go serve on a jury. And then he was so excited to go vote. I mean, his passion for everything extended to the passion that he became an American citizen. It was just unbelievable. The summer he became an American citizen was my first summer as his executive producer, and I was trying to think of something to buy him for his birthday. He was so passionate about his citizenship, and it had just been made public, so I called up and had a flag that had flown over the Capitol put in a box. On the bottom of the box I put: "Peter Jennings, who went in search of America and found it."

COKIE ROBERTS: I love the fact that he could be sentimental about it, and corny. On election nights, for instance, he would like to wax philosophical about this country and the American experiment and the whole notion of American democracy. He would always come back to why it mattered and why it was all important.

PETER JENNINGS: *The United States is the only nation in the world founded on a creed. Being American is not a matter of birth. It is an ideological commitment.*

COKIE ROBERTS: He took so much flak for not being an American citizen and for doing so well by this country without being an American citizen that, when he actually became an American citizen, I think he was just delighted by it. He was almost like a little kid about it. He just liked the fact that he got up and went to vote in Election 2004, when the rest of us mailed in our absentee ballots so we could be in New York to be on the set. He was just thrilled to show up at the polls.

PETER JENNINGS: *I aspire to be a good American. And I aspire to stand for the best American values. That's not easy. It takes work. I know of no people on the Earth who are more generous, who are more open, sometimes to the point of distraction. I know of no group of people who mean better. That doesn't mean that we do the best. If there's an international disaster — and I've found this all the time I've been a reporter — almost the first people on the ground all the time are the Irish or Australians or New Zealanders or Canadians. Americans are not always the first to be there, but when Americans show up you can feel the shift. The effort takes on a certain momentum. . . . So, I aspire to be a good American means to see the best of America, but it's also to see the bad, and to work in a responsible way to try to make that which is bad better, and to relish the best in the country. It is an exceptional country. . . . At its best, it's a joyous experience, a really, truly rich experience. I've never had any richer experiences in any other part of the world. And maybe that's because I feel more a part of it.*

CONDOLEEZZA RICE: I think he enjoyed the cacophony of America. America is big and complicated and noisy and difficult. Nothing about America is tidy. I suspect that he wanted to be a part of that untidiness that is the United States. Canada is a wonderful place, but it's a smaller and more homogeneous population. There's something about America that is complicated. You either like its complications and its cacophony or you find it overwhelming. And Peter liked its cacophony. He liked its complications.

AL SHARPTON: I think that the fact that he was not born naturally to America gave him two things: a sensitivity to people that felt like they were outsiders, and a thirst for learning all he could about America at every different level and every different experience. You never felt that he just was talking to you about the story. He really was trying to understand different aspects of American life. He made you feel like this mattered to him. Even after he had his interview, and the camera was off, he really wanted to understand what Americans of all shades, of all economic backgrounds, of all religions — what it really was all about.

I remember he did a special on Gary, Indiana. I interviewed with him, and we talked about what Gary was like in 1972, during the National Black Political Convention when I was there at eighteen, and then how it was years later. He really wanted to talk about the changes I saw in black America, and what it meant, and why I had grown, and what that meant. We talked as much off camera as on. I remember saying to the people that were with me when I was leaving, "This guy really cares about what's going on in the country."

I think that Peter had a sensitivity for issues for people of color. Because he looked at America as this great coming together of different cultures, he seemed to have that sensitivity more than most. Maybe it was because he wasn't born here and could look at it differently, maybe because he was such a passionate student of history. I think that he clearly was more sensitive than most to black issues, Latino issues, and other issues. He did it in a way that you didn't feel that he was being phony, or that he was doing it because he wanted applause or plaudits. He made you feel he did it because he really believed that there needs to be a real story about everybody: I'm doing it because I really think this is America and that's my job, to show what America's about.

TODD BREWSTER: One of the things that I always found interesting is the degree to which people tried to paint Peter along one ideological path or another and how he really didn't fit in any of them. He could make liberals angry at him. He could make conservatives angry at him. What he really was, was

465

a curious person. He was looking for what was surprising and different and interesting. If this story wasn't being reported over here, then he went after it. And if this other story over here wasn't being reported, he went after that one.

ALAN ALDA: Once, Peter gave me a copy of the Constitution that you could carry in your pocket, and he said, "I carry this around with me everywhere I go. Carry it around with you. When you're in an airport and you have a few minutes, take it out and read it." I kept it by my bedside instead of carrying it around. I'm going to carry it around from now on. I'll remember him by it. He's right, you know. If you just open that up and look at it, you find out a lot about who we think we are and who we are meant to be. He contributed to that in the most personal way. He was the way we understood what was happening to us and what we did to one another.

PETER JENNINGS: *The late Chief Justice [Warren] Burger was the one who encouraged me to carry a copy of the Constitution in my back pocket, as he always did. On the July Fourth weekend I was asked to read the Declaration of Independence aloud to a group cel-*

*ebrating, somewhat rowdy friends. As I did, the room sank quickly into silence as they absorbed the meaning of that eloquent insistent declaration by Jefferson that the new Americans sought justice. Today, in the midst of the global revolution, one of the most challenging questions is whether the durable language of a handful of American eighteenth-century intellectuals will continue to provide the framework for a successful twenty-first century government.*

TODD BREWSTER: To this day, I carry the Constitution in my backpack because Peter gave me a copy just like the one he had. . . . He had this fascination with a nation that was built around a document. The fact that you could take that document — short enough to read in fifteen or twenty minutes — and stuff it in your back pocket and carry it with you as a sort of guide to living or recipe for good behavior, was very appealing to him.

PETER JENNINGS: *People come to America with a strong sense of where they came from. We all have some strong sense of the past. But I think the sense of the future is just overwhelmingly powerful in America. That's a very, very beautiful thing.*

*I started smoking when I was thirteen, and I remember very clearly how we guys thought it was the cool thing to do. It never occurred to us for a second that we were ever going to become addicted.*

—Peter Jennings

# 12
## "I HAVE LUNG CANCER"

*Peter Jennings died on August 7, 2005, from lung cancer. He announced his diagnosis to the public in a taped segment that aired on* World News Tonight *on April 5, 2005. He had been a smoker for many of his sixty-seven years.*

SARAH JENNINGS: When we were up at our summer cottage and our father was away in the city working, one of the things to do was to get hold of Granny's cigarettes and have a puff. I can remember — actually, it's as clear as yesterday — Pete was about eleven and I was eight — and all he did was say, "Now, Sarah, all you have to do is breathe in," which I did immediately. And, of course, I had this tremendous coughing fit. I was traumatized. I was never, in later life, able to inhale. I used to have a marvelous fake inhale, but I was never able to take smoke into my lungs again.

Peter, on the other hand, started to smoke at the age of thirteen, and he did become heavily addicted to cigarettes. I was at a dinner party recently with an old classmate of Peter's from his junior school. This man is now a justice of the Supreme Court of Canada. He came over to ask how Peter was. He said, "I remember when we were in grade eight, going on a canoe trip and puffing away, puffing away, as we paddled down the river." So at that time, it was the thing to do. Unfortunately, he got severely hooked on it. He smoked heavily all his life until he had his children, and then he was able to give it up, through a tremendously strong effort. He used hypnosis and other methods.

TOM YELLIN: When he was in London he used to have a pack of little Player cigarettes, with the green stripe, always open on the desk. He smoked at least a pack a day, often more. He gave up smoking when his children were very young. I think it was enormously difficult for him. He went through a variety of different steps in order to give up smoking, and eventually he did succeed. I was shocked, actually, because he was such a smoker. It was so much a part of his personality and his persona — this glamorous foreign correspondent with a cigarette in his hand.

PAUL FRIEDMAN: When I came back from London to be executive producer with Peter, it was about that time that Peter had gone to a hypnotist, to stop smoking — one of the many times he stopped smoking. I was a smoker at that point. Peter went through a difficult period of withdrawal. Then he insisted that my wife and I go up to see this hypnotist to kick the habit. He set it up, and kind of forced us to go.

I have a hundred dollar bill, encased in plastic, signed by Peter, which represented his paying off a bet that we made. It was a bet over whether I could quit smoking. The inscription is, "Never thought you had the self-control." It's so typical of him, to put it in plastic, so it couldn't be spent.

MATTHEW MYERS: One day, I was coming over to ABC for an interview and I bumped into Peter outside, smoking. I think he was horrified. He was truly like a young teenager being caught doing something he knew he shouldn't have been doing. He sheepishly stepped back, actually, and smiled at me and immediately changed the subject as to what I was coming to talk about. It was clear that his struggle with how hard it was to quit smoking was one of the reasons he was so committed to telling the tobacco story honestly and fairly.

DAVID WESTIN: Peter loved to cover stories. He hated being the story. For a man who was so public and so widely recognized, he just hated the idea of being the center of attention. He was a very private person, and he valued that privacy. When he discovered he had this illness, I think he was very brave. I learned when I was out in San Francisco, actually at an event that Peter was supposed to be with me for. I called back, and he told me over the telephone that the biopsy had come back and it had confirmed the cancer. I flew back on the plane very upset, but also thinking, "How can I persuade Peter he has to announce this?" Knowing how private Peter was, I was sure he was going to say, "We just have to keep this quiet." At ten-thirty the next morning, he came up to my office and said, "Here's the announcement I want to make. What do you think? I think we have to announce it and we have to call it lung cancer." He was ahead of me throughout the entire process.

TODD BREWSTER: I got a call early the morning of his announcement. He started talking, and he said, "I'm not going to beat around the bush, I'll come right to it: I have lung cancer." He said it as if he was delivering a piece of news that was not his own. It was an extraordinary example of his appreciation for manners and his willingness to exhibit them. He was calling close friends of his to tell them so they wouldn't have to learn this news the wrong way, which is to say, with the rest of the world. He felt this extraordinary responsibility to those he loved — that he needed to take care of them in that moment even more than taking care of himself. He was himself to the end. He was a gentleman.

I asked him in that phone call that morning, "Are you going to retire?" He said, "Absolutely not. It's the worst thing I could do."

JON BANNER: He brought the senior staff of the broadcast together, in my office, and informed us. It was a very emotional time for all of us, and also for him. He could barely get through telling us. I think there was just shock. I think we all sat there with our mouths open in disbelief. Part of it was that those of us who have known him for so long had always seen him as indestructible. Nothing could happen to this guy. We just sat there for, I don't know, ten, fifteen minutes afterwards, just speechless. I went into his office afterwards. I gave him a hug, and he said, "If you don't make me cry, I won't make you cry." It didn't work. I mean, it was so unfair. This guy was on top of his game, and he had a beautiful wife, two beautiful children, and he was an institution. I mean, he was ABC News. I think it sort of made us all aware of our own vulnerability because here was this guy who was indestructible, and if he was like that, we all just sort of, I mean, it was just heartbreaking.

DIANE SAWYER: I think your first reaction is to say, it's impossible — it's impossible in logic; it's impossible in the destiny of ABC News; it's impossible that the world has to rearrange itself so suddenly. Peter's indestructible. Peter is the captain. The center. The muscular core of ABC News. We have seen him go into war zones. We have seen him take enormous chances in his reporting for such a long career, that to be felled, to be enduring something like this seemed simply incomprehensible.

MICHAEL CLEMENTE: Even though I knew Peter as a friend, as a colleague, as a person, as a father and a brother and a son and all that to his family, he seemed invulnerable.

And suddenly, he was hugely vulnerable. It was upsetting. It was shocking. I thought, "All right. We'll help him get through it, somehow. We'll get all the information. We'll get the specialists. We'll figure it out. And we'll get past it." We sort of lost track of the fact that he is human, also.

BRIAN ROSS: People who were taping his piece came out of the edit room in tears because he didn't do the piece in one take. It took many takes, and a lot of them didn't go well, and he was upset with himself because — perfectionist that he is — he wanted it to be just right. I guess I knew then this is, this is very bad.

ELIZABETH VARGAS: That was probably the hardest evening for all of us. We were watching him tape his announcement that he had cancer, and we could see him struggling to speak. That was deeply upsetting, I think, to everybody in the news division who was watching. I think there were a lot of us who were worried that we wouldn't be able to get through the show that night. And then, you had to put it into perspective and think, "This man is fighting the fight of his life. We need to be there for him and to do our jobs as well as we can because that's what he would want us to do." And so we did.

I remember I went into his office; we were fifteen minutes before air. I had raced over from my office when he finally decided that he couldn't do the show. He was still concerned with taking care of us. It really struck me. He'd just announced that he had cancer, and yet he was still in the leadership role, making sure that those of us who were working on the broadcast that night were all okay. I think that talks about what a consummate professional and a consummate human being he was, even in the face of so much adversity and so much stress in his own life.

PETER JENNINGS: Finally this evening, a brief note about change. Some of you have noticed in the last several days that I was not covering the Pope. While my colleagues at ABC did a superb job, I did think a few times I was missing out. However, as some of you now know, I have learned in the last couple of days that I have lung cancer. Yes, I was a smoker until about twenty years ago. And I was weak and I smoked over 9/11. But whatever the reason, the news does slow you down a bit. I've been reminding my colleagues today, who've all been incredibly supportive, that almost 10 million Americans are

*His final broadcast, April 5, 2005*

already living with cancer. And I have a lot to learn from them. And living is the key word.

The National Cancer Institute says that we are survivors from the moment of diagnosis. I will continue to do the broadcast on good days. My voice will not always be like this. Certainly it's been a long time, and I hope it goes without saying that a journalist who doesn't value deeply the audience's loyalty should be in another line of work. To be perfectly honest, I'm a little surprised at the kindness today from so many people. That's not intended as false modesty. But even I was taken aback by how far and how fast news travels. Finally, I wonder if other men and women ask their doctors right away, "Okay, Doc, when does the hair go?"

At any rate, that's it for now on *World News Tonight.* Have a good evening. I'm Peter Jennings, thanks and good night.

TOM YELLIN: What particularly struck me about the way that he made that announcement was that he came as close as he's ever come in my experience of working with him and watching him, of injecting himself into reporting a story. It was almost him being openly emotional on television. But if you look carefully at the language, if you look at the way it's phrased and you study it as a piece of writing, he was exceptionally careful. It really was quintessential Peter. It was, "I know this is about me, but I want to still have a little bit of distance from it because I'm reporting it to you." As a reporter, he always felt that having a little bit of distance from the story, no matter how personal it was — and what's more personal than reporting your own illness? — was essential. In that way, he had just enormous respect for viewers. He never, never gave in to the easy, sentimental path.

DIANE SAWYER: I suspect I had the reaction most people had, which is: It was all Peter — Peter's cadences, Peter's humor, Peter's diffidence, Peter's "don't you dare think of me," Peter's "let's set the tone here together, and remember that the world is what matters, not me." Yet in his voice was all of our fear and hope and anxiety and fate.

BARBARA WALTERS: Peter believed in telling the truth. Peter believed in facts. He didn't sugarcoat them. It was so typical of him to announce that he had lung cancer, to say it himself, to not gloss it over. He had already begun to lose his voice. He didn't want people to feel sympathetic or even maudlin. He wanted to say, "There is hope. I'm going to lick it. I'm going to be part of it and I'm going to be back," and we all felt, until the day he died, that he would be back. It was *World News Tonight with Peter Jennings*.

BARRIE DUNSMORE: If you consider that here is a man who was absolutely at the pinnacle of his career, and all of a sudden he discovers that he has a disease, which might be the instant end of it, it would have been so easy just to fold the tent and go away and see what could be done through chemotherapy or whatever. The fact that he wanted to go in front of the millions of people who had watched him for twenty years or thirty years or more and explain to them personally what was happening, and do so in a voice that he would have on almost any other occasion found totally unacceptable, it was a real act of courage. I think that it also demonstrated the enormous sense of respect that he had for the people who had watched him over the years — that he felt that it was his responsibility to tell them personally what was happening.

TOM BROKAW: When I saw Peter's announcement that night in what I thought was for Peter a pretty fragile condition, I thought he was being brave, but I was deeply concerned about him. . . . There was so much of Peter in it. That line: "Well, Doc, when do I lose my hair?" And "Americans *living* with cancer" with the emphasis on the word living.

He could deliver his lines with such élan, and he did that night. But just beyond that you could see what he was dealing with.

TIMOTHY JOHNSON: As a friend, I was shocked. He seemed to me to be larger than life, indestructible. It just seemed impossible that this very vibrant, vital person could have something like that. But as a physician, I knew that this was going to be a terribly tough fight because I understand that this is a very, very tough, brutal cancer.

Quite frankly, I was surprised when I was watching the news that night. Even though I knew about his smoking history, I was surprised when he made it public in his announcement. I was very pleased that he did so. I thought it was very courageous to share something like that because I think it will help a lot of people to focus on their own smoking and to say, "My goodness, if that man can get lung cancer from smoking, I could, too. Maybe I should quit while I still have time." I hope that's what happens for a lot of people.

MATTHEW MYERS: The tragedy and the irony hit me like a rock. For Peter Jennings, someone who has done more to educate the American public about the hazards of smoking, to succumb to his own addiction was the ultimate lesson that the best way not to die from a tobacco-related disease is never to start. Peter struggled with his addiction to tobacco; it's one of the things that helped give him a real feel for what a difficult problem this was.

When I saw the announcement that he had lung cancer, I sat down almost immediately and I wrote him a personal note of support. I thought that it was important for him to understand that even as he was suffering through the difficulties of lung cancer, he should be aware that he had probably done more than anybody else in his field to make sure that fewer people would suffer from lung cancer and fewer kids would start smoking.

SARAH JENNINGS: I was enormously proud of him. That was a tremendous effort. It was a physical effort at that time because he was already having difficulty with his voice. The fact that he decided he would meet it head on, and share it with the public, I think, is very characteristic of Peter's work. He knew what the facts were, and he put them out there for people to see them as clearly as they could. I was enormously proud that he did that.

DAVID WESTIN: He was very concerned that he remain personally involved in *World News Tonight,* that he had a say in what was going on in the broadcast, and who was on the broadcast, and how we were doing the work. As always, he wanted us to be covering the news first and foremost, and he didn't want to be the news for very long. He wanted to move on from there quickly.

ALAN ALDA: When we went to visit him just a few weeks after he announced his illness, he'd laughed, he'd joked, told us what his feelings were in a very dispassionate way — the same way he would report on tragedies around the world. It wasn't a tragedy to him. He wasn't scared. He wasn't complaining. He just told us what was happening.

He was surprised by two things, I think. He was surprised by the fact that he didn't feel scared, and he was surprised by how moved he was by the reaction of the people, not just in his workplace, but around the country. The mail he was getting really moved him. And it surprised him that it moved him, and I think that's because he was really a modest person.

April 15, 2005

Dear _____,

I really hope you can understand what your note meant to me. I abhor the whole idea of one response for all — but it is really important for me to say thank you in a hurry — to each of you.

Some of you have made me laugh like hell — thank goodness that doesn't hurt. Some of you — many of you — have made me cry, in the very best sense, which out of a slight sense of embarrassment I immediately blame on the steroids. Some of you have reached out of the past so distant that it's nice to know we are both still kicking. Others, not always strangers, have reminded me of connections unknown or forgotten by me until now. These are the ones that often make me cry — which I then blame on the steroids.

As one friend said quite accurately, it is like being hit by a truck. He then said he was glad that I was willing to stand here and slam right back.

Truth be told, I think you have given me more strength than I thought I had. I write as I begin chemotherapy because I want you to know that — and to say thank you.

As for the steroids — no, not that kind — they have given me an appetite for calorie intense ice cream, which is what the doctor ordered. Damn, we need a bigger fridge.

As always . . .

Peter

KEN AULETTA: He went through the most aggressive chemo and radiation program that Sloan-Kettering devised. It was like playing tennis with Peter. If you played tennis with Peter, he was always trying to beat you and hit that ball. It was great sport. I mean, you'd go and you'd have a cup of coffee later or a Coca-Cola, and you'd sit around and you'd talk about the world, including tennis. But on the tennis court he was always trying to blow one by you with an ace or trying to smack that ball in a corner you weren't, and oftentimes he would over-hit or hit the net because he got a little too aggressive, so you'd just volley back and try to keep the ball in play, and hoped that Peter wouldn't be overly aggressive. As aggressive as he was on the tennis court, that's how he was in fighting this disease. He was determined to beat it.

---

April 29, 2005

Yesterday I decided to go to the office; I live only a few blocks away. I got as far as the bedroom door. Chemo strikes.

Do I detect a knowing but sympathetic smile on many of your faces? You knew this was coming.

Senator Arlen Specter of Pennsylvania wrote me a note to say that the only way to get through chemo is to "work your way through it." He's a tougher man than I am.

I assume there are a few others out there who, like me, are going with the flow until the day gets better.

Incidentally, Hamilton Jordan, former Chief of Staff in the Carter Administration, sent me his book *No Such Thing as a Bad Day*. He's had cancer four times. He tells me, as have many others, that when it gets really bad, it will get better. Phew!

Thousands of you have spoiled me

---

rotten with your attention in the last couple of weeks. Whether you have a cancer connection or not, your anecdotes, mementos, home recipes, and general all-purpose guidance and concern have all been so deeply appreciated. I hope you know.

So many experiences have meant something special. A woman in my building, who is a cancer survivor, showed up at our front door so that we could see that bald really is beautiful. She's right.

I won't soon forget an encounter as I was leaving the hospital. A middle-aged couple was going into the building and as they passed me, I heard my name and turned. The woman stepped right into my face and said, "Me too. Lung cancer." Instinctively, immediately, we gave each other a hug . . . a real hug . . . and went on our respective ways knowing that we had been strengthened by the connection.

So thank you for all of the connections. And finally, if you would, add a friend of mine to your prayers. The jazz legend Percy Heath, whose bass anchored the Modern Jazz Quartet for four decades, died of bone cancer on Sunday. He was 81 and we will sure miss him.

As always,

Peter

LAUREN LIPANI: I was lucky enough to spend some time with him when he was sick. My day often involved people coming to me and asking me to please tell Peter that they missed him and they loved him and they couldn't wait to have him back. I tried so hard to convey that to him. And, well, I hope I was successful. But he would react like, "Oh, I don't know, I don't believe you." I think he melted a little bit. He started to get it, but he was surprised by the reaction. I don't know why. Maybe because it was so enormous you couldn't get your head around it.

CHARLIE GIBSON: That is *World News Tonight* for this Monday. I should mention that Peter Jennings was in the office this afternoon helping to put tonight's broadcast together. We had a great time, a lot of laughter. He was keeping us on our toes, as usual. For Peter and all of us at *World News Tonight,* I'm Charles Gibson. Have a good night.

TOM NAGORSKI: We arranged to have a better-than-usual [speakerphone] system just for our morning conference calls so that we could hear Peter better. His voice had gotten really pretty weak and raspy. On the morning of the bombings in London, he was of course on the line. And it was just one of those days where it hit home — man, we need him here. He was very succinct and very detailed about some points he wanted us to make. One was a simple one: he wanted to make sure we gave a very, very vivid picture of where these bombings had happened. He said, "Don't forget, Americans know London. Give them some feel. Don't just show where those four attacks happened, but show them where Buckingham Palace is or where Big Ben is as a reference point." Then he said, "Don't leap to conclusions about who did it," which was a point he always made, and not just about terrorism: it's just better to get it right than to get it first.

CHARLIE GIBSON: Peter Jennings spent more than fifteen years working and living in London, a city he loves. He sends a note tonight to point out what he says is the obvious. And I'm quoting Peter:

"We are all Londoners this week. And, once again, we are stronger for it. I recognize that eloquent, stoic determination never to give up, as Winston Churchill said during the War. I have been in London and other British cities when they've been attacked with unrestrained violence. The perpetrators have always been the losers."

And then, in typically gracious fashion, Peter closes by writing:

"On behalf of all my colleagues at ABC News who did such a terrific job covering this story, goodnight."

CHARLIE GIBSON: The entire time in the months of Peter's illness that you did *World News Tonight,* you had three different audiences in mind. Number one, the audience at home, for whom the broadcast is normally done — and you want as large an audience as you can get. Number two, you were doing it for the staff, to show the staff that there is stability here and that, while there is this huge absence, things would be okay. But then, third, you were doing the program for an audience of one: How is Peter reacting to this? What does he think of the lineup tonight? What does he think of each individual story? How does he feel that was written? You're always thinking about that: an audience of one. And on nights when you heard that he'd called in and thought it was a pretty good show, you felt pretty good about yourself.

KEN AULETTA: I marveled at this guy who had this ability to always be a gentleman. My wife and I visited him in Long Island about a month before he died. He lived up the road from me, but I hadn't seen him in several weeks. He was sitting on the deck with his children and with his wife, Kayce, and we had a drink sitting on the deck. He was obviously weakened by the chemo and the radiation. But after an hour of a very sociable visit and chatting and jokes and talking about kids, and a little bit about his health and treatment, he insisted on getting up and walking us to the door because that's what Peter Jennings did. It was quite extraordinary. My wife and I said, "No, no, you don't have to do that." He said, "No, I want to do that." He was just a gentleman.

BILL BLAKEMORE: I saw him in his apartment just before I left on a trip. He was already too weak to get up from his couch, but it was classic Peter. He was still the elegant Peter. He wanted to hear all about this trip to the Arctic and the study of global warming that I was about to do. We reminisced over a few things in Beirut. It brought a smile to his face to remember those things. And then he started asking some pointed questions about what we were really going after, up there in the Arctic, and how we were going to look for signs of global warming. The elder brother he was to all of us, it came out. "We'll be keeping an eye on you," he said.

TIMOTHY JOHNSON: What I was most struck by was the way in which, in the midst of his own terrible battle against this awful cancer, he was so aware of the needs of others around him. He was really sweet about asking about how others were doing and thanking them for their care and their love toward him. It was really quite striking.

TOM NAGORSKI: The last time I saw him he was very frail, but he took the time to ask about a book I was working on, he asked after my mother's health, he asked after Natalie and William, our children. He called him William; we call him Billy. He always let us know that he felt "William" was preferable. I always told Peter — and I did that last time — that he could edit his broadcast all he wanted, but he couldn't edit our son's name.

Sometime later I found an envelope at home and realized that this was the last correspondence we'd had from Peter. It was actually a letter for our daughter. She had sent him a get-well card in April. What would Peter do? He would always find the time to write a note like this one: "Dear Natalie, That was a wonderful, wonderful letter. The colors really cheered me up. Whenever an adult is sick, there is nothing like a young person's kindness to make him feel better."

ANNOUNCER: From ABC News, this is a "Special Report."

CHARLIE GIBSON: Good evening. From ABC News headquarters in New York, I'm Charles Gibson. And it is with a profound sadness and true sorrow that I report to you Peter Jennings has died tonight, of lung cancer.

Peter died in his apartment here in New York. With him was his wife Kayce, his children Elizabeth and Christopher. His sister Sarah was also there. His family, just a moment ago, released a statement, and I want to quote it: "Peter died with his family around him, without pain, and in peace. He knew he had lived a good life," end quote.

LAUREN LIPANI: He was too much a part of our day and our lives to ever be gone from *World News Tonight*. Especially when he was sick, I would have my head down, maybe at my desk, but I'd feel someone coming around the corner, walking down the hallway, and I'd lift it up, thinking it was him, walking in, carrying his briefcase. Without him as a leader here, a lot of people wonder how we'll be able to do our jobs. I think that the way to get through that is to just think about what he would do. That's what everyone is going to try.

KAREN BURNES: At ABC, it's like we had this force we didn't even know we had and suddenly the force is gone. We had someone who was the conscience of the place, the drive, the discipline. He brought so much to this entire news organization. He was such a unifying force here. And it's gone.

CHARLES GLASS: Peter was the best man at my wedding in 1977. But he was also one of the best men in my life. . . . I'll miss that moral support he used to give, and I'll miss the loyalty. And I'll miss that completely childish sense of humor that he had.

LYNN SHERR: He was magical. There was an aura about him. There was a radiance about him. Everybody wanted to be near Peter — men, women, children. When Peter left the room, the room was not as much fun. With Peter not on this Earth, the universe is not as much fun.

KAREN BURNES: I look at his kids now, and I think, how can I ever give them what he gave me? You know, I want to give back, just a tiny bit of what he gave me. And I wouldn't even know where to begin. . . . The void is so great; it's so great. It's as if the sun has gone out.

*The following month, Peter's children, Christopher and Elizabeth, spoke at his memorial service.*

CHRISTOPHER JENNINGS: Not long after

he became sick he gave me a pocket watch engraved with the phrase, "Loving deeply gives us courage." As his health began to slip, my love for my father made the prospect of his death all the more terrifying. Loving deeply, it seemed, made courage impossible. The words on the watch struck me as the false promise of a parent offering out of love that which they cannot give. After all, in the darkest moments, Kayce and Dad and Lizzie and I would all repeat that false mantra of the terrified — "It's going to be all right, it's going to be all right" — knowing, of course, that it would not be all right.

Later, hugging my father towards the very end and feeling his thin embrace across my back, that promised courage filled me, almost as if physically conveyed. What had changed was what I needed to be brave for. Earlier I had interpreted this courage as the ability to press on without him, the courage to greet his death with some understanding or peace. In fact, the courage my father offered to me on the back of my watch and in his final embrace was the courage to continue to love him with the same intensity as I had before, while knowing that to do so would surely crush me with grief. So, instead of recalling my father with a vast but expired love, I will allow myself to give him the love which he always had for us, a love which lives in daily acts and chores, an earnest and present love from the gut. The only way that I know how to give my father that sort of love, now that he is gone, is to do the things which would have made him proud. I am so fortunate that he made it very clear what those things are.

ELIZABETH JENNINGS: I looked for a poem that would capture somehow the pain of losing someone who illuminated every moment that we spent together, because without him I find myself stumbling around in the dark. The words I came back to in the end were his own. This is from the speech he gave when I graduated from high school:

"I am very mindful," he told us, "that I don't want to badger you from here about what I perceive to be the right formula for living a meaningful and caring life in this extraordinary age. I am only too aware that life can change on you in the twinkle of an eye. But I hope that as you go, wherever you go, that your tolerance for one another does not become indifference. Once you are clear about what your values are, you must always stand up for them. There is nothing worse than sliding through life with a conventional wisdom. It's a way of reminding ourselves that every day we step off the cliff into very large questions about life. Have a good trip."

Loving him so much and not having him with me is the hardest thing that I have ever done. Remembering him well will be the most important thing that we do.

# 13
## LEGACY

TOM YELLIN: What I think really distinguished Peter as a journalist was his commitment to truth. What distinguished him as a broadcaster was not just his skill and his command of the craft but his profound respect for the intelligence and the thoughtfulness and the curiosity of the people with whom he was communicating. He believes — I'm sorry — he believed that if you present a story well, and it matters, people will watch it, people will care about it, people will understand it. That sounds like a simple idea, but it's not necessarily something that many broadcast journalists believe.

KEN AULETTA: He was someone who understood that he was invested with authority and that his success depended upon people trusting him. He wasn't going to impose his opinion. He wasn't going to make wisecracks. He was going to try and dig deeper

*I grew up in a household where to be a journalist . . . was seen as an opportunity to be a public servant. . . .*
*I think of myself as a broadcaster who has the privilege of access to the public airwaves.*

—Peter Jennings

to help you because he worked for you. He didn't work for ABC. He really worked for the public. And he understood that.

I think the best journalists, be they in print or electronic media, understand that someone signs their checks, but that's not really their boss. I think the public understood that Peter worked for them and that he was their representative, trying to ferret out the truth.

TIMOTHY JOHNSON: From my standpoint, his legacy will be what I think the heart of science is, namely, the pursuit of truth, at all costs and with no effort spared. He just was doggedly determined to find out the truth about whatever subject he was exploring.

TOM YELLIN: I think Peter's greatest strength is that he was able to live a journalist's life with the right values. He believed that the truth matters, and when you find it, keep looking. And that's really, really hard to do. It's really, really hard to do.

SARAH JENNINGS: I've heard Pete in an interview talk about whether he was able to be objective. I think his answer was, "Probably that's impossible. But it was very important to be fair." I think those were the standards that were imposed on us by our father: integrity in broadcasting. These people were very poorly paid, so they really did do it for the love of the work and out of dedication to the work. I think those values definitely affected how Pete saw his work, and how he did it.

PETER JENNINGS: *I conduct myself no differently as a broadcast journalist today than I would have had I been working for the CBC. Our job is still to keep eyes and ears open on behalf of the public, to take the public places they might not otherwise go, to examine subjects of both interest and importance to them. So it doesn't really make any difference to me whether it's NPR or PBS or ABC. We all should conduct ourselves — and can conduct ourselves — in the same way. Don't always, but we could. I am not modest about this notion that journalism in general and broadcast journalism specifically — because so many people pay attention every day — is a truly important function in this society.*

BARBARA WALTERS: We hear a great deal these days about the public not having respect for the news men and women. I don't think anyone ever doubted Peter Jennings when it came to respecting him. They knew that he was the consummate journalist. They knew that he presented facts with a beauty, and a knowledge, and an integrity. He cared passionately, he did not suffer fools gladly, and he defined our world.

HANAN ASHRAWI: I think the world has lost a first-rate mind and journalist, a man who in his pursuit of the truth never lost sight of his humanity or the humanity of others — somebody who wasn't easily intimidated. . . . His humanity, the gentleness of his spirit, his warmth, his sense of humor, his intelligence — I'm going to miss all of these. The world has lost a journalistic phenomenon, and I don't think you have many of those.

HILARY BROWN: I think that Peter Jennings was far and away the best TV news anchor on the air anywhere in the world. The flawless performance that he turned in — day in, day out, whether he'd had no sleep at all, or a good night's sleep, whether he was in the studio or out in the field — he was absolutely unmatchable. And I think that that is going to be a benchmark for generations of journalism students and journalists.

JON BANNER: I think his legacy for journalists is to listen to your gut. Report stories. Don't be afraid to go to some place that nobody else is. Seek the truth. Pursue stories passionately. Tell them well. Another part of his legacy is: Don't be afraid to take a stand on a story. If you think you see a story where there's something that's not right, don't be afraid to say it's not right.

MICHAEL CLEMENTE: He leaves a huge legacy of broadcasters, writers, producers, journalists of all sorts who think and act and try to behave journalistically like he did. We'll hear him, we'll feel him, we'll understand the world a little better simply because there are a lot of other journalists out there — certainly many broadcasters — who are trying to achieve what Peter was able to achieve.

BOB IGER: We owe him an extraordinary debt of gratitude for being the primary face of ABC, for taking us on and off the air during so many significant world events, for creating a standard and teaching it to a generation of people, for taking us to so many places and simplifying so many complicated issues, and really changing our lives. I'm only sorry that I didn't have a chance to express that enough to him.

AL SHARPTON: I think Peter Jennings probably was one of the last of the giants of broadcast news. . . . We never really understood the overwhelming shadow of Peter Jennings until it wasn't there any more. It's like laying under a tree and getting the shade, and not realizing that the tree was shading you until the sun comes burning through because the tree's not there. Peter had a way of being overwhelming without appearing overwhelming. Then all of a sudden you're there without him and you say, "My God, I was overwhelmed by Peter."

BILL CLINTON: A lot of people have forgotten . . . how deeply the American people thought that after the Berlin Wall fell, we just wouldn't have to fool with the rest of the world. Peter Jennings thought we should become more involved with the rest of the world at the end of the Cold War, and he was right on that big, big question. He was right. I think the way he talked to us about the world will be his enduring legacy.

GEORGE STEPHANOPOULOS: He would fight, fight, fight for international coverage. Now we all know how important that is. Now we know as the world's only superpower that we can't afford to let our guard down for a moment, to ignore any region, any corner of the world. That was something that Peter had been fighting for forty years.

DAVID GELBER: Peter should know that, as one of his legacies, a lot of people are alive today in Bosnia who might not have been had it not been for his determination and passion for that story.

STU SCHUTZMAN: I think he made the world a much smaller place for Americans. I think he brought the world into American homes like no one else ever has.

CHRIS ISHAM: He believed very strongly that journalism could not be detached from the world and from people; that journalism was part of the ebb and flow of human events and of people. He had an ability to communicate to people why they needed to care about things that were going on on the other side of the planet.

MIKE LEE: When it came to foreign news, he had the clout, the imagination, and he made it happen.

JONATHAN ALTER: You might say a lot of people do international reporting, but that's not true. It's a kind of dying species of journalism at exactly the moment we need it most, when the world is most interconnected, when the threats from abroad are serious. . . . Peter Jennings is a reminder that people who think that they can sort of be educated citizens without knowing more about what goes on in the rest of the world are mistaken, and that we need to place more importance on international reporting even if it's not as sexy as something that is happening in a courthouse in the United States somewhere. We need to remind ourselves of it every day. The best way to honor Peter Jennings' memory is for people to stay focused on international coverage as he stayed focused on it over a long period of time.

MARTHA RADDATZ: We're losing a man who had seen and known everything he talked about. He had lived it. You cannot replace that experience. You can't do it. I worry about our business. Part of what I worry about is that reporters no longer get to learn, get to go, get to see with their own eyes. That's what you can't replace. Peter Jennings was history himself. He had seen it, he had lived it, he had reported it. He was history.

PETE SIMMONS: I won't talk about the

legacy to the industry or the legacy to America. But the legacy for correspondents is this: Know your story. Read, read, read. Find out everything you can and get your arms around that story before you get on that airplane. If there's a legacy, that's a Peter Jennings legacy: get your arms around that story.

BOB WOODRUFF: Peter's journalistic legacy is that preparation and depth of knowledge is often the best way to simplify a story into something that people can understand generally. What Peter Jennings taught us by his profound knowledge of the stories that he was reporting on is that you can tell a story simply without telling a story simplistically. Peter knew so much about every story. Most of it never got on, but because he knew the context of what he was talking about, he could tell it more succinctly and more simply and more understandably.

JEANMARIE CONDON: For his generation, he set the gold standard. There was no one who fought harder to do real important journalistic stories on network television. He was a fighter, and he expected the people around him to be fighters.

PETER JENNINGS: *The truth is that life —
which is in a corny way, what we cover — is
not simple. While we have an obligation to emphasize clarity, we do have to struggle against
making everything simple-minded, good or
bad. The truth of the matter is that how our
consciences guide us every day in the littlest
of things — not the grandest of things —
makes a difference between whether we con-
tribute to the country's well-being or not. This
is how we set an example. How much time we
give to O.J. How much we decide that the private lives of public people really matter to the
common good. It may sound a trifle high-
minded to some, but if we enable people to
understand more about their neighborhood
and their town and their country and their government, as a result of us they are more likely
to make more meaningful appraisals of the
people they send to the school board, the
county supervisor's office, to Congress, and
the White House. This is our direct contribution to democracy.*

JONATHAN ALTER: Peter understood you
need to give people not just what they want
to know but also what they need to know to
be informed citizens, and that's part of our
mission. He thought of it as a mission, a calling. This is something you don't hear too

much in our business anymore.

I think the way to honor Peter is not to build him a monument someplace but for people in the news business to try to stay focused on reporting a larger share of foreign news, even if it doesn't get ratings, and for the consumers of news — the viewers — to say, "I'm going to watch a little less junk, and I'm going to watch a little more news that's about complicated international events." If they do that, they'll really be striking a blow for Peter and he'll be up there noticing it.

KEITH SUMMA: I worked with Peter most closely on issues about public health, specifically tobacco. When you look at the public health reporting that Peter did, it's amazing, the impact that it's had. There are all kinds of public policy issues in this country that are different today because Peter decided that they were important issues, they were important stories, and they needed attention.

CHARLIE GIBSON: To be a good anchor you have to be a good reporter. You have to understand what it is to be a correspondent. Peter taught himself that brilliantly. Every young reporter should look at that and realize that what's key is not being on television.

So many young reporters think, "Well, it's the performance aspect of it. It is the being on television that is important." It's not. It is the curiosity. It is the ability to report and tell a story. I suspect Peter would think that's as great a legacy as any he could have.

BOB WOODRUFF: I think everybody should take a page from Peter Jennings' script: go out there and learn about the world before you start reporting on the world.

BILL BLAKEMORE: Peter's legacy will surely include this disciplined elegance. He was always jousting with you, but he was also always very sensitive to what your feelings were. He was trying to give you your best shot, inveigle you into revealing interesting thoughts, but he wasn't giving you an easy ride. He was always very tough on us correspondents. We knew we were working for him. He was the leader who set the tone. But central to his style was this insistence on fairness and politeness, which was quite consciously one of his journalistic tools. He would insist, especially in a bad crisis, on calming things down and having everybody speak civilly. He was trying to do what all great journalists do, which was to improve the quality of the conversation in the society. He was the master at that.

BARBARA WALTERS: The legacy he gave each of us who worked with him is to strive to be as caring, as thorough, as passionate about our work as he was.

CHARLES GLASS: I would say he lived for excellence as a friend, as a father, as a journalist, as a man. He lived his life, his adult life, as the voice and the face of a television network. But more importantly, he was its conscience, probably a conscience that will be needed more and more in the future. He was a permanent reminder not of what we are but what we as journalists have a duty to be.

TODD BREWSTER: I think Peter's legacy comes in a couple of places. He was part of a world that sadly is fading, a period of journalistic dominance of certain central organizations like networks and major newspapers that spoke through one voice. That won't happen again, I don't think. There were certain good things that came from that and certain bad things that came from it. The good things were that if you had the right person, he could be a terrific vehicle through which to understand the world. Peter was that.

The other thing is: Peter had very high standards. I would like to believe that the people that worked around him raised up to a new level of performance, which is what he demanded of everybody. His legacy is the rest of us, who now carry that on and hope to find ways of reinterpreting that kind of standard for the new journalistic and media world that we're entering in the twenty-first century.

BARRIE DUNSMORE: Peter was an extraordinary force for good in television journalism. His incredible desire to get the story and get it right and get it with nuances so that it wasn't just being thrown out there as raw meat for people to eat without any understanding — all of those things were enormously positive for ABC and for television journalism generally. The carryover effect is a little harder to judge because we don't know where the future of television news is going.

DAVID WESTIN: His death has sadly focused us on what he was and what he did, in a way that perhaps we took for granted just a little bit when he was among us. I think, certainly a commitment to international coverage. And a commitment to documentaries, which is something Peter believed in passionately and kept alive in broadcast television across the board. No one was doing them anymore, and Peter stayed with them throughout. And uncovering the unpopular story, which nonetheless is important.

In trying to do what is right with this wonderful power that we have in broadcast journalism, Peter realized the ideal that was possible and always strived to attain that. Sometimes he fell short. Sometimes he felt we fell short — and told us so. But the reason he did that is because he always saw the ideal. He saw how great it could be, and how powerful it could be.

CHRIS ISHAM: The thing that really will stay with all of us about Peter is that he loved life. He loved the news. He loved the world. He loved the pace of events. He loved traveling around the world and opening up new horizons. He loved the big things, and he loved the small things. He loved sitting down with heads of state. And he loved sitting on the beach with his kids and his dog. He loved a cookout in the evening and watching the sun go down. And he loved talking about the biggest ideas that we could all come up with at the time. He had an undying love of life.

BRIAN ROSS: I think, in many ways, he helped hold the barbarians at the gates — those who wanted to diminish the news or do it in a softer way. I think he stood for integrity, and that will be his legacy. I think it would be very hard for us to do anything but a newscast that he would be proud of.

TOM NAGORSKI: He is so with us in everything we do. As journalists, he's not just in the back of our minds, but he's in the front of our minds and he's in our ears. Those of us who've worked with him for all these years, I think, can't imagine ever approaching a big story, certainly not a major trip overseas somewhere without hearing him. Even more so probably now that he's gone, I can't imagine ever doing anything without thinking, "Would it be up to snuff with Peter?"

JOHN LEO: I think he stood for a kind of civility in broadcasting that may be on the way out. Regardless of what he thought, and what problems he had, he didn't impose his personality on the material to the point where he became the story. I think that's an important gift in journalism now.

PAUL FRIEDMAN: The important legacy, as far as I am concerned, is that he achieved this body of work with class, with dignity, with fairness. He never pandered. He never pulled any tricks or stunts the way you see other people doing. He never intentionally made himself more important than the story — and in many cases, he was as important as the story, because he was there. But that wasn't of his making. He didn't contrive things to make himself more important than the story. He always considered the story the most important thing — getting the story and describing it skillfully. That's a great legacy. I guess the worry is whether that will be treated seriously by journalism students and by the people in newsrooms around the country, whether that will be continued. I guess Peter would say, "Not worth speculating about. We'll just have to wait and see."

# 14
## "Finally, This Evening . . ."

*On April 14, 2004, in a speech to an audience of journalism students at the Edward R. Murrow School of Communication at Washington State University, Peter Jennings shared his ideas on how to improve network news. He gave the speech almost exactly one year before he was diagnosed with cancer.*

PETER JENNINGS: For those of you thinking about journalism — and I assume that's a reason to attend this university — I do want to say this: there is a real joy in doing it well. I jest sometimes that journalism has enabled me to see the world on the company's money, which is true. But I know nothing so satisfying as doing a story — and by that I mean any story — and knowing that you presented it fully, contextually, and understandably to a large number of people. That is really the definition of making a difference.

So it's probably only fair that I end by saying what I would do if I could.

I would do a weekly review of the news every week at a time when the public might be expected to watch, which means prime time, so the public could be given some sense of context of the week we've just been through and what we're facing for the week ahead.

I would make documentaries a regular part of the prime-time schedule . . .

And I would include regular programming from other countries — how they see us and why. How did it get to be that 55 percent of the people in Great Britain, our closest ally, believe that the United States is a threat to world peace?

I would make network news an hour every night.

And if I could, I would institute the change that my late boss Roone Arledge came to believe in after he discovered the downside of news as a profit center. I would make news and information programming exempt from the ratings system . . .

Finally, my wife asks the toughest question. "Will you," she said the other day, "tell these young people at Edward Murrow's alma mater, to go into journalism or to do something else?" Tough question. The answer is, if you believe what Murrow stood for and what my father stood for — that broadcasting is a public service — then please, come into the business. We need you.

# ACKNOWLEDGMENTS

In August 2005, Lynn Sherr called me. She suggested that the interviews conducted for "Peter Jennings: Reporter," the ABC News special that aired three days after Peter's death, be published in book form. I said no. She said, "Think about it." I said okay, but no. I was skeptical; there had already been many wonderful tributes to Peter and to his achievements and there would be many more. At the time, Peter's children and I felt that was enough.

A year after that phone call — almost a year to the day that Peter died — a beautifully bound volume containing lightly edited transcripts of the eighty-one interviews appeared at my door. Lynn had quietly created a few copies just for Peter's family, his most intimate friends, and his closest colleagues. I stayed up through the night reading, and by morning I knew Lynn had been right: there *was* a book in these interviews, and it wasn't just a tribute, though it would pay tribute to Peter's life. And it wasn't just about Peter, though it would chronicle his career. It would also be a book about journalistic values. I hope that *Peter Jennings: A Reporter's Life* will serve as a guide for young reporters, that it will confirm their best instincts and ease them away from someone else's worst. I hope that it will inspire other young people to come into the profession by showing them that this is a noble calling, which is why so many of us love it. I hope they will be tempted by the fun and the responsibility and the adventure and the challenge that made Peter's life the remarkable ride it was.

I have many people to thank.

To start with, of course, Lynn Sherr, a great journalist, but an even better friend. Long before I shared her vision of a book, Lynn understood the value in this flood of memories — for me and for Peter's children, to be sure, but also for his children's children, who will one day meet their grandfather in these pages and maybe understand themselves just a little bit better.

To Kate Darnton, a masterful editor, who learned quickly to interpret "newspeak" and who shaped a mass of words into a compelling narrative. To Peter Osnos, who gave us support and encouragement and who helped make sure this book happened. And to his colleagues at PublicAffairs, especially publisher Susan Weinberg, assistant managing editor Melissa Raymond, director of publicity Whitney Peeling, and Timm Bryson, who designed this book, for his effort and creativity.

To David Westin and ABC, first for supporting our family during the hardest months, and then for supporting the book, generously allowing us the use of ABC material and news division resources.

To Nancy Gabriner (Peter always introduced her as "my brain") and to Lauren Lipani (who somehow managed to both keep up with Peter and keep him under control) for giving their time, their energies, and their love to Peter and the project.

To Jill Greenwald in the ABC News legal department and Kate Bolger at Hogan & Hartson for their tremendous help and true diligence.

To the staff of the ABC Photo Department for their help in tracking down images for the book.

To Nola Safro who, with Lynn, took time out from the demands of *20/20* and the commitments of life, for excising the "uhs" and "ers" from the original transcripts so that we might more easily read the voices.

To Tom Yellin, my friend and teacher and production company partner, who demonstrated his brilliance again in leading the huge team that produced "Peter Jennings: Reporter" under impossibly difficult and painful circumstances.

To Talleah Bridges, Jeanmarie Condon, Alan Goldberg, Linda Hirsch, Sarah Koch, Jordan Kronick, Mark Obenhaus, Richard Robbins, Martin Smith, Gabrielle Tenenbaum, Terry Wrong — and others I may never know about — who conducted the interviews for the ABC special.

To the team that tracked down the eighty-one people interviewed and got them in front of the cameras and the cameras in front of them, including Karin Weinberg, Dan Woo, Carla DeLandri, and Joan LeFosse Paulsen.

To Phyllis McGrady, who helped get "Peter Jennings: Reporter" on the air with style and substance — and endorsed this book project from the beginning.

To all those interviewed for sharing your memories.

To the camera crews, editors, producers, LDs, APs, PAs, DAs, directors, engineers, assignment desk, transport desk, the folks in the studio, translators, fixers, drivers, bureau managers, bureau secretaries, and interns: Peter understood he couldn't do what he did without you, and I think you know that.

To those of you who helped keep Peter's life in order and the rest of us sane, most importantly two who were there for Peter whenever he called: Gretchen Babarovic, Peter's good friend, first line of defense, and indispensable administrative assistant; and Ray Dunn, Peter's driver, protector, and "little brother." Both Gretchen and Ray did everything Peter asked of them, and so much more. They became Peter's family; they remain mine.

To Lisa Freed, the most loyal, most giving sister — and, as Peter quickly realized, the most loyal, most giving sister-in-law.

To my mother, Judy Freed, who has always wanted the best for me and who realized when she got to know Peter that he was that.

To Sarah Jennings, Peter's sister, for the love, care, and support she gave her big brother, and for all she continues to give me.

And, finally, to Lizzie and Chris. They became my family by chance, but they are my friends by choice, and they are the best friends I could have hoped for. They are Peter's true legacy.

KAYCE FREED JENNINGS
*July 29, 2007*
*The Gatineau Valley*
*Canada*

# NOTES

## 1. A Canadian Childhood

"Both my parents . . ." From the uncut interview with Peter Jennings and *Reader's Digest* (Frank Lalli) on August 7, 2002. Reprinted with permission from *Reader's Digest*. Copyright © 2002 by The Reader's Digest Assn., Inc.

"My father was . . ." Interview by Larry King, *Larry King Live,* CNN, December 14, 1999.

"One of my earliest meaningful memories . . ." Lalli, *Reader's Digest.*

"I knew that my father . . ." Lalli, *Reader's Digest.*

"[My father] was pretty angry . . ." Lalli, *Reader's Digest.*

"I loved sports . . ." Lalli, *Reader's Digest.*

"I was bad in school . . ." Interview by Norman Atkins, "The A-B-Cs of Peter Jennings," *Rolling Stone,* May 4, 1989, p. 65.

"My parents were very disappointed . . ."

Lalli, *Reader's Digest.*

"I think I still . . ." Quoted in Elizabeth Kaye, "Peter Jennings Gets No Self-Respect," *Esquire,* September 1989, p. 176.

"One of my first jobs at CBS Radio . . ." Lalli, *Reader's Digest.*

"I had only been to New York once . . ." Lalli, *Reader's Digest.*

"And so I said 'no' . . ." Atkins, "The A-B-Cs of Peter Jennings," p. 65.

## 2. Boy Anchor

"I am one of those Canadians . . ." Speech before the joint convention of the Canadian Newspaper Association and the Newspaper Association of America, Toronto, Ontario, May 1, 2001.

"I was a twenty-something-year-old . . ." From "In Search of America: A Reporter's Challenge," a speech given to the Canadian Institute for Advanced Legal Studies, Cambridge Lectures Meeting, University of Cambridge, Cambridge, England, July 21, 2003.

"ABC was in bad shape . . ." Quoted in Mark Dawidziak, "Anchor's Stellar Career Came against the Odds," *Cleveland Plain Dealer,* August 9, 2005, p. E1.

"I don't care who watches . . ." Quoted in Jack Batton, "A Phenomenon Named Jennings," *MacLeans,* July 24, 1965, p. 14.

"I mean, it was ludicrous . . ." Interview by Norman Atkins, "The A-B-Cs of Peter Jennings," *Rolling Stone,* May 4, 1989, p. 65.

"I almost didn't recover . . ." Speech before the National Association of Canadian Clubs, Hamilton, Ontario, September 30, 2000.

"We went to a lunch . . ." Interview by Terry Gross, *Fresh Air,* NPR, November 17, 1998.

"It was a little ridiculous . . ." Quoted in CTV.ca News Staff, "Jennings Remembered as 'the Best of the Breed,'" CTV.ca, August 8, 2005.

"I realized . . ." Interview by Terry Gross, *Fresh Air,* NPR, November 17, 1998.

"I have not been chopped . . ." Quoted in Robert E. Dallos, "ABC Replacing Peter Jennings," *New York Times,* November 14, 1967, p. G5.

"I was the youngest anchorman . . ." Commencement address, Nightingale-Bamford School, New York, New York, June 11, 1998.

## 3. The Talking Trench Coat

"For all my failure in school . . ." From the uncut interview with Peter Jennings and

*Reader's Digest* (Frank Lalli) on August 7, 2002. Reprinted with permission from *Reader's Digest*. Copyright © 2002 by The Reader's Digest Assn., Inc.

"I was in Rome . . ." Lalli, *Reader's Digest*.

"I had, as my responsibility . . ." Interview by Terry Gross, *Fresh Air,* NPR, November 17, 1998.

"There are nineteen countries . . ." Interview by Norman Atkins, "The A-B-Cs of Peter Jennings," *Rolling Stone,* May 4, 1989, p. 65.

"For six years . . ." Quoted in Marc Gunther, *The House That Roone Built: The Inside Story of ABC News* (Boston: Little, Brown, 1994), p. 66.

"Somebody in the superstructure . . ." Lalli, *Reader's Digest*.

"Having lost all faith . . ." Courtesy of ABC News, "Palestine: New State of Mind," June 1, 1970.

"Having lived in the Middle East . . ." Lalli, *Reader's Digest*.

"Roone Arledge called . . ." Courtesy of ABC News, Alan Ives, producer, "Trust Is Earned" promotional campaign, ABC News, 2004.

"Peter Jennings is inside . . ." Courtesy of ABC News, ABC News live coverage, September 5, 1972.

## 4. Roving Anchor

"I've been reminded . . ." Answer during question and answer session after speech upon receiving the Lifetime Achievement in Broadcasting Award, Edward R. Murrow School of Communication at Washington State University, Pullman, Washington, April 14, 2004.

"a commercial for Dramamine . . ." Tom Shales, "Follow the Bouncing News with ABC," *Washington Post,* July 11, 1978, p. C1.

"Mr. President, quite frankly . . ." Courtesy of ABC News, "Sadat: Action Biography," December 19, 1974.

"As you're driving . . ." Courtesy of ABC News, "Sadat," December 19, 1974.

"I learned how to cover a funeral . . ." Interview by Terry Gross, *Fresh Air,* NPR, November 17, 1998.

## 5. Flying Solo

"It is a very big job . . ." Quoted in Sally Bedell Smith, "Jennings Named Sole Anchor," *New York Times,* August 10, 1983, p. C23.

"My first instinct . . ." Interview by Norman Atkins, "The A-B-Cs of Peter Jennings," *Rolling Stone,* May 4, 1989, p. 65.

"With me, Brokaw, and Rather . . ." Smith,

"Jennings Named Sole Anchor," p. C23.

"I was so instinctively resistant . . ." Speech before the Center for Research in Women's Health, Toronto, Ontario, February 9, 2001.

"I had not covered . . ." Quoted in Charles Kenney, "Why Peter Jennings is So Good," *Boston Globe Magazine,* November 6, 1988.

"It is nine-thirty in the East . . ." Courtesy of ABC News, election night coverage, November 6, 1984.

"ABC News now projects . . ." Courtesy of ABC News, election night coverage, November 6, 1984.

"The flags are at half staff . . ." Courtesy of ABC News, ABC News Special, "The Shuttle: Disaster in Space, 10:00 p.m.," January 28, 1986.

"When they hired me . . ." Alex S. Jones, "The Anchors: Who They Are, What They Do, the Tests They Face," *New York Times,* July 27, 1986, p. SM12.

"transformed the normally spirited competition . . ." Jones, "The Anchors," p. SM12.

"I have always found . . ." Speech upon receiving the Paul White Award, Radio and Television News Directors Association, New Orleans, Louisiana, September 9, 1995.

## 6. Making the News

"I don't set out . . ." Courtesy of ABC News, Alan Ives, producer, "Trust Is Earned" promotional campaign, ABC News, 2004.

"By the time . . ." Ives, "Trust Is Earned."

"I don't think you could ever . . ." From the uncut interview with Peter Jennings and *Reader's Digest* (Frank Lalli) on August 7, 2002. Reprinted with permission from *Reader's Digest*. Copyright © 2002 by The Reader's Digest Assn., Inc.

"I'm always looking . . ." Ives, "Trust Is Earned."

"One of the things I think . . ." Ives, "Trust Is Earned."

"Maybe it started with the Robert Bork . . ." Speech upon receiving the Lifetime Achievement in Broadcasting Award, Edward R. Murrow School of Communication at Washington State University, Pullman, Washington, April 14, 2004.

"Television interviews . . ." Lifetime Achievement in Broadcasting Award speech.

"You love history, sir . . ." Courtesy of ABC News, "Primetime Special Edition," November 18, 2004.

## 7. World News Tonight

"I get up every day . . ." Courtesy of ABC

News, Alan Ives, producer, "Trust Is Earned" promotional campaign, ABC News, 2004.

"There are a lot of people . . ." Ives, "Trust Is Earned."

"I think that all of us . . ." Ives, "Trust Is Earned."

"If people want sports . . ." Speech upon receiving the Fred Friendly First Amendment Award, Quinnipiac University School of Communication, Hamden, Connecticut, May 15, 2001.

"The U.S. is pretty much . . ." Speech upon receiving the Lifetime Achievement in Broadcasting Award, Edward R. Murrow School of Communication at Washington State University, Pullman, Washington, April 14, 2004.

"I fear that . . ." Fred Friendly First Amendment Award speech.

"Where's the restraint? . . ." Speech upon receiving the Paul White Award, Radio and Television News Directors Association, 1995.

"I may surprise you . . ." Speech upon presenting the forty-third annual Silver Gavel Awards, American Bar Association, Annual Meeting, New York, New York, July 11, 2000.

"We're guilty in journalism . . ." From the

uncut interview with Peter Jennings and *Reader's Digest* (Frank Lalli) on August 7, 2002. Reprinted with permission from *Reader's Digest*. Copyright © 2002 by The Reader's Digest Assn., Inc.

"I wanted to go to Sarajevo . . ." Courtesy of ABC News, *Peter Jennings Reporting,* "The Land of the Demons," March 18, 1993.

"And now the voice of experience . . ." Courtesy of ABC News, *World News Tonight,* February 7, 1994.

"The story of the Bosnian tragedy . . ." Courtesy of ABC News, "While America Watched: The Bosnia Tragedy," March 17, 1994.

"This is the country . . ." Courtesy of ABC News, "The Peacekeepers: How the U.N. Failed in Bosnia," April 24, 1995.

"When the Serbs . . ." "The Peacekeepers."

"I like doing what I'm doing . . ." Ives, "Trust Is Earned.

"I spent twenty-five years overseas . . ." Commencement address, Amherst College, Amherst, Massachusetts, May 25, 2002.

"I'm sometimes referred to . . ." Ives, "Trust Is Earned."

"I do have this notion . . ." Lalli, *Reader's Digest.*

"I ask whether . . ." Lifetime Achievement in Broadcasting Award speech.

"You have argued . . ." Courtesy of ABC News, *World News Tonight,* March 13, 2003.

"It is always difficult . . ." Lifetime Achievement in Broadcasting Award speech.

"This is an ABC News Special Report . . ." Courtesy of ABC News, "ABC News Special Report," July 1, 2004, 7:14 a.m. EST.

"I've been a reporter . . ." Ives, "Trust Is Earned."

## 8. Enthusiasms

"ABC has always encouraged me . . ." Speech upon receiving the Paul White Award, Radio and Television News Directors Association, New Orleans, Louisiana, September 9, 1995.

"This broadcast is about AIDS . . ." Courtesy of ABC News, "Growing Up in the Age of AIDS," February 2, 1992.

"This hour is about cigarettes . . ." Courtesy of ABC News, *Peter Jennings Reporting,* "Never Say Die: How the Cigarette Companies Keep on Winning," June 27, 1996.

"This is one of the classic . . ." "Never Say Die."

"I think what comes as a surprise . . ." From the uncut interview with Peter Jennings and *Reader's Digest* (Frank Lalli) on August 7, 2002. Reprinted with permission from *Reader's Digest.* Copyright © 2002 by The Reader's Digest Assn., Inc.

"In the overwhelming majority . . ." Speech at Harvard Divinity School, Cambridge, Massachusetts, November 15, 1995.

"I was fascinated . . ." Harvard Divinity School speech.

"There is a fundamental difference . . ." Harvard Divinity School speech.

"It is the man who inspired . . ." Courtesy of ABC News, *Peter Jennings Reporting,* "The Search for Jesus," June 26, 2000.

"The gospel stories . . ." Courtesy of ABC News, *Peter Jennings Reporting,* "The Search for Jesus," June 26, 2000.

"Don't be confused . . ." Interview by Steven Waldman, *Beliefnet,* beliefnet.com, June 15, 2000.

"Now, this program . . ." Courtesy of ABC News, "Peter Jennings Town Meeting: Kids, Parents, and Straight Talk on Drugs," March 30, 1997.

"Good morning, everybody, . . ." Courtesy of ABC News, "War in the Gulf: Answering Children's Questions," January 26, 1991.

"Good morning, and welcome . . ." Courtesy of ABC News, "Prejudice: Answering Children's Questions," April 25, 1992.

"Kids have given me . . ." Interview by Larry King, *Larry King Live,* CNN, September 8, 2003.

"Good morning and welcome . . ." Courtesy of ABC News, "ABC 2000," 4:51 a.m. EST.

"Midnight in Indonesia . . ." ABC News, "ABC 2000," 11:43 a.m. EST.

"We're going to go to Africa now . . ." ABC News, "ABC 2000," 9:05 a.m. EST.

"It's going to be midnight . . ." "ABC 2000," 5:55 p.m. EST.

"In all sorts of other cities . . ." "ABC 2000," 12:53 a.m. EST.

## 9. September 11

"In a moment like this . . ." Quoted in Lori Robertson, "Anchoring the Nation," *American Journalism Review,* November 2001.

"There is chaos in New York . . ." Courtesy of ABC News, ABC News live coverage, September 11, 2001.

"It has completely collapsed . . ." Courtesy of ABC News, ABC News live coverage, September 11, 2001.

"Let's look at the north tower quickly . . ." Courtesy of ABC News, ABC News live coverage, September 11, 2001.

"I don't always keep my composure . . ."

Courtesy of ABC News, Alan Ives, producer, "Trust Is Earned" promotional campaign, ABC News, 2004.

"For me . . ." Interview by Larry King, *Larry King Live,* CNN, April 10, 2002.

"We do not very often . . ." ABC News live coverage, September 11, 2001.

"One of the roles . . ." Ives, "Trust Is Earned."

"I am not a minister . . ." Robertson, "Anchoring the Nation."

"There's no such thing as . . ." Ives, "Trust Is Earned."

"This week, a tragedy unfolded . . ." Courtesy of ABC News, "ABC News Special: Answering Children's Questions," September 15, 2001.

"It is forty years since . . ." Speech upon receiving the Lifetime Achievement in Broadcasting Award, Edward R. Murrow School of Communication at Washington State University, Pullman, Washington, April 14, 2004.

## 10. The Man

"I am not particularly . . ." From the uncut interview with Peter Jennings and *Reader's Digest* (Frank Lalli) on August 7, 2002. Reprinted with permission from *Reader's Digest.* Copyright © 2002 by The Reader's

Digest Assn., Inc.

"Part of the challenge . . ." Lalli, *Reader's Digest*.

"I never thought it was my job . . ." Interview by Terry Gross, *Fresh Air,* NPR, November 17, 1998.

"I always thought it was sad . . ." Interview by Tom Snyder, CBS, April 24, 1998.

"Almost every night in Central Park . . ." Essay for the one-hundred-fiftieth anniversary of Central Park, New York, New York, July 2003.

"I don't think until my current job . . ." Lalli, *Reader's Digest*.

"Both my kids . . ." Lalli, *Reader's Digest*.

"I've always thought . . ." Interview by Larry King, *Larry King Live,* CNN, December 14, 1999.

"I tend to see the best in people . . ." Lalli, *Reader's Digest*.

"I find huge virtue in physical labor . . ." Lalli, *Reader's Digest*.

## 11. Citizen

"My Canadian roots . . ." Speech to the National Association of Canadian Clubs, Hamilton, Ontario, September 30, 2000.

"You know, in the United States . . ." Interview by Terry Gross, *Fresh Air,* NPR, November 17, 1998.

"My parents were . . ." Speech before the joint convention of the Canadian Newspaper Association and the Newspaper Association of America, Toronto, Ontario, May 1, 2001.

"As a journalist . . ." Canadian Newspaper Association and the Newspaper Association of America speech.

"I remember my mother . . ." National Association of Canadian Clubs speech.

"I was once criticized . . ." From the uncut interview with Peter Jennings and *Reader's Digest* (Frank Lalli) on August 7, 2002. Reprinted with permission from *Reader's Digest*. Copyright © 2002 by The Reader's Digest Assn., Inc.

"You won't go anywhere else . . ." Commencement address, Amherst College, Amherst, Massachusetts, May 25, 2002.

"In any number of circumstances . . ." Speech before the third annual gala in support of the Centre for Research in Women's Health at the University of Toronto, Ontario, February 9, 2001.

"I cried a little bit . . ." Quoted in Peter Johnson, "Jennings Speaks His Peace on TV News and His Role," *USA Today,* March 12, 1996, p. D3.

"It was actually . . ." Interview by Larry King, *Larry King Live,* CNN, September 8, 2003.

"It is fascinating . . ." From "In Search of America: A Reporter's Challenge," a speech given to the Canadian Institute for Advanced Legal Studies, Cambridge Lectures Meeting, University of Cambridge, Cambridge, England, July 21, 2003.

"There is another reason . . ." From "In Search of America."

"The United States . . ." Centre for Research in Women's Health speech.

"I aspire to be a good American . . ." Lalli, *Reader's Digest*.

"The late Chief Justice [Warren] Burger . . ." Speech upon presenting the forty-third annual Silver Gavel Awards, American Bar Association, Annual Meeting, New York, New York, July 11, 2000.

"People come to America . . ." Courtesy of ABC News, Alan Ives, producer, "Trust Is Earned" promotional campaign, ABC News, 2004.

## 12. "I Have Lung Cancer"

"I started smoking . . ." Courtesy of ABC News, *Peter Jennings Reporting,* "Never Say Die: How the Cigarette Companies Keep on Winning," June 27, 1996.

"Finally this evening . . ." Taped announcement, courtesy of ABC News, *World New Tonight,* April 5, 2005.

"That is *World News Tonight* . . ." Courtesy of ABC News, *World News Tonight,* May 23, 2005.

"Peter Jennings spent more than . . ." Courtesy of ABC News, *World News Tonight,* July 8, 2005.

"From ABC News . . ." Courtesy of ABC News, "ABC News Special Report," August 7, 2005, 11:41 p.m.

"Not long after . . ." From Christopher Jennings' memorial speech, given at Carnegie Hall, New York, New York, September 20, 2005. Reprinted with permission from Christopher Jennings.

"I looked for a poem . . ." From Elizabeth Jennings' memorial speech, given at Carnegie Hall, New York, New York, September 20, 2005. Reprinted with permission from Elizabeth Jennings.

## 13. Legacy

"I grew up in a household where . . ." Speech upon receiving the Paul White Award, Radio and Television News Directors Association, New Orleans, Louisiana, September 9, 1995.

"I conduct myself . . ." From the uncut interview with Peter Jennings and *Reader's Digest* (Frank Lalli) on August 7, 2002. Reprinted with permission from *Reader's*

"The truth is that . . ." Paul White Award speech.

## 14. "Finally, This Evening . . ."

"For those of you thinking . . ." Speech upon receiving the Lifetime Achievement in Broadcasting Award, Edward R. Murrow School of Communication at Washington State University, Pullman, Washington, April 14, 2004.

# CHRONOLOGY OF PETER JENNINGS' LIFE

July 29, 1938: Born in Toronto

1947: At age nine, becomes host of Saturday morning children's show on CBC Radio called *Peter's People*

1952: Moves with family to Ottawa

1955: Drops out of high school at age sixteen; goes to work as a bank teller for the Royal Bank of Canada

1959: Gets a job with CFJR Radio in Brockville, Ontario

1960: Moves to CBC Radio

1961: Joins CJOH TV in Ottawa as a reporter, where he reads the news and hosts a teenage dance program and the Miss Canada pageant

1963: Named co-anchor of *CTV National News*

1963: Marries Valerie Godsoe (divorced 1970)

1964: Joins ABC News in New York

1965: Becomes anchor of *Peter Jennings*

*with the News;* at age twenty-six, is the youngest national network news anchor

1967: Replaced as anchor of evening news and returns to being a field reporter

1970: Moves to Rome for ABC News

1971: Establishes first American television news bureau in the Arab world in Beirut

1972: Reports live from the Olympic Games in Munich on the kidnapping and killing of Israeli athletes by Arab terrorists; works with Roone Arledge, then president of ABC Sports, for the first time

1973: Father, Charles Jennings, dies

1973: Marries Anouchka Malouf (divorced 1979)

1975–1976: Becomes news anchor for *A.M. America,* predecessor of *Good Morning America,* based in Washington, D.C.

1977: Roone Arledge is named president of ABC News (while remaining president of ABC Sports)

1977: Moves to London; becomes chief foreign correspondent for ABC News

1978: ABC News renames its evening broadcast *World News Tonight* and institutes a three-person anchor team: Frank Reynolds in Washington, Max Robinson in Chicago, and Peter Jennings in London

1979: Marries journalist Kati Marton (divorced 1995); daughter, Elizabeth, is born

1982: Son, Christopher, is born

1983: Named sole anchor of *World News Tonight* and moves to New York City

1986: *World News Tonight* begins a decade on top in the ratings

January 28, 1986: Space shuttle *Challenger* explodes

1990: *Peter Jennings Reporting,* a series of prime-time documentaries dedicated to covering challenging issues, debuts

1991: Mother, Elizabeth Jennings, dies

1997: David Westin replaces Roone Arledge as president of ABC News

1997: Marries ABC News producer Kayce Freed

1998: First book, *The Century,* co-authored with Todd Brewster, is published; twelve-part companion television series airs on ABC the following year

December 31, 1999–January 1, 2000: Anchors "ABC 2000"; is on the air for twenty-three hours straight, covering the dawning of the new millennium

September 11, 2001: Anchors breaking news coverage of the 9/11 terrorist attacks for seventeen hours straight; logs more than sixty hours on the air that week

2002: Second book, *In Search of America,* co-authored with Todd Brewster, is published; six-hour companion television series airs on ABC

2003: Becomes a U.S. citizen

January 2005: Completes final overseas trip, reporting from Iraq

April 5, 2005: Announces he has lung cancer on *World News Tonight*

August 7, 2005: Dies from lung cancer

# SELECTED DOCUMENTARIES AND NEWS SPECIALS

**Peter Jennings Reporting (ABC News)**

Out of Control: AIDS in Black America — 8/24/06 (aired posthumously, completed by Terry Moran)

Breakdown: America's Health Insurance Crisis — 12/15/05 (aired posthumously; reported by Peter, narrated by Charlie Gibson)

UFO: Seeing Is Believing — 2/24/05

No Place to Hide — 1/20/05

From the Tobacco File: Untold Stories of Betrayal and Neglect — 9/8/04

Guantanamo — 6/25/04

LAPD — 6/1/04

Jesus and Paul: The Word and the Witness — 4/5/04

Ecstasy Rising — 4/1/04

How to Get Fat without Really Trying — 12/8/03

The Kennedy Assassination: Beyond Conspiracy — 11/20/03

Tragedy — 3/17/94
The Land of the Demons — 3/13/93
The Cocaine War: Lost in Bolivia — 12/18/92
The Missiles of October: What the World Didn't Know — 10/27/92
Who Is Ross Perot? — 6/29/92
Men, Sex, and Rape — 5/5/92
From the Heart of Harlem — 7/25/91
The New Civil War — 11/01/90
From the Killing Fields: Beyond Vietnam — 4/26/90
Guns — 1/24/90

## In Search of America (ABC News)

Headquarters — 9/7/02
Streets — 9/7/02
God's Country — 9/6/02
Homeland — 9/5/02
The Stage — 9/4/02
Call of the Wild — 9/3/02

## The Century (ABC News)

Facing the New Millennium — 4/10/99
Live from Tehran — 4/10/99
Picture This — 4/8/99
Nothing to Fear — 4/8/99
Searching for the Promised Land — 4/5/99
Innocence and Rebellion — 4/5/99
The Fall — 4/3/99

The Great War — 4/3/99
The Race — 4/1/99
Evil Rising — 4/1/99
First Step — 3/29/99
Lindbergh's Journey — 3/29/99

## Peter Jennings Town Meetings (ABC News)

9/11: Answering Children's Questions (first anniversary of 9/11) — 9/11/02

9/11: Answering Children's Questions — 9/15/01

Peter Jennings Town Meeting: Kids, Parents, and Straight Talk on Drugs — 3/30/97

President Clinton: Answering Children's Questions — 3/19/94

Kids in the Crossfire: Violence in America — 11/6/93

President Clinton: Answering Children's Questions — 2/20/93

Prejudice: Answering Children's Questions — 4/25/92

Growing Up in the Age of AIDS — 2/2/92

War in the Gulf: Answering Children's Questions — 1/26/91

## Other ABC News Specials

ABC 2001 — 12/31/00
ABC 2000 (The New Millennium) — 12/31/99 — 1/1/00

A Line in the Sand: What Did America Win? — 9/12/91

A Line in the Sand: War or Peace? — 1/14/91

A Line in the Sand — 9/11/90

Capital to Capital: Leadership in the '90s — 5/7/90

Capital to Capital: The Environment — Crisis in the Global Village — 9/12/89

Drugs: Why This Plague? — 7/11/88

Drugs: A Plague Upon the Land — 4/10/88

Capital to Capital: Questions and Charges of Human Rights Abuses — 10/14/87

Liberty Weekend — 7/4/86

45/85 — 9/18/85

Palestine: New State of Mind — 6/1/70

## Other Specials (WGBH)

AIDS Quarterly — 6/12/91 (renamed "The Health Quarterly"), 11/26/90, 5/23/90, 4/3/90, 1/31/90, 9/27/89, 4/25/89, 2/28/89

*Close-Up (ABC News Documentary Series)*

Illiteracy in America — 9/3/86

After the Sexual Revolution — 7/30/86

The Fire Unleashed — 6/6/85

To Save Our Schools, to Save Our Children — 9/4/84

War and Power: The Rise of Syria — 6/14/84

JFK — 11/11/83

The Consumer Offensive: Who Speaks for the People? — 11/29/75

Crisis of Price — 6/27/75
Sadat: Action Biography — 12/19/74

# PHOTO CREDITS

## 1. A Canadian Childhood

Page 30: Courtesy of the Jennings family.

Page 33: Courtesy of the Jennings family.

Page 34: Courtesy of the Jennings family.

Page 41: Courtesy of the John D. Burns Archives at Trinity College School. Boy on right is David Cape; boy on left is Ernest Rogers. Photograph taken in 1951.

Page 44: *(top)* Copyright © 1959 CTVglobemedia.

Page 44: *(bottom)* Courtesy of the CBC Still Photo Collection.

Page 50: Courtesy of CTV.

## 2. Boy Anchor

Page 56: Copyright © American Broadcasting Companies, Inc. Photograph circa 1965.

Page 59: Copyright © American Broadcasting Companies, Inc.

Page 61: Copyright © American Broadcasting

Companies, Inc. Photograph circa 1965.

Page 62: Courtesy of the Jennings family, circa 1965.

Page 66: Photograph by Rick Baughn.

Page 69: Photograph by Milo J. Pesak, circa 1965.

Page 78: *(top)* Copyright © American Broadcasting Companies, Inc. Photograph taken in mid-sixties.

Page 78: *(middle)* Copyright © American Broadcasting Companies, Inc. Photograph taken in mid-sixties.

Page 78: *(bottom)* Courtesy of the Jennings family. Photograph taken in mid-sixties.

## 3. The Talking Trench Coat

Page 82: Courtesy of ABC News. Photograph taken in Lebanon, February 29, 1972.

Page 84: Photograph by Anouchka Jennings.

Page 91: Courtesy of Anouchka Jennings.

Page 94: Photograph by Anouchka Jennings, circa 1973.

Page 99: Copyright © 1981 by Robert Azzi. All Rights Reserved. Reprinted with permission.

Page 105: Photograph by Charles Glass.

Page 109: Courtesy of ABC News. Broadcast in Bombay, India, November 21, 1972.

## 4. Roving Anchor

Page 130: Copyright © 1982 Joe McNally/American Broadcasting Companies Inc.

Page 134: Copyright © 1978 American Broadcasting Companies, Inc.

Page 139: Copyright © 1981 Joe McNally/American Broadcasting Companies, Inc.

Page 147: Courtesy of the Jennings family. Photograph taken circa 1983.

## 5. Flying Solo

Page 158: Copyright © 1984 Donna Svennevik/American Broadcasting Companies, Inc.

Page 168: Copyright © 1984 Donna Svennevik/American Broadcasting Companies, Inc.

Page 175: Courtesy of ABC News.

Page 189: Copyright © 1997 Lorenzo Bevilaqua/American Broadcasting Companies, Inc.

## 6. Making the News

Page 194: Copyright © 1985 Donna Svennevik/American Broadcasting Companies, Inc.

Page 197: Copyright © 1998 David Burnett/American Broadcasting Companies, Inc.

Page 229: Copyright © 2005 Donna Svennevik/American Broadcasting Companies, Inc.

Page 247: White House photo. Photograph taken December 13, 1995.

Page 249: Courtesy of American Broadcasting Companies, Inc. Photograph taken June 3, 2003.

## 7. World News Tonight

Page 254: Copyright © American Broadcasting Companies, Inc.

Page 257: Copyright © 1991 Dirck Halstead/American Broadcasting Companies, Inc.

Page 260: Copyright © 2001 Virginia Sherwood/American Broadcasting Companies, Inc.

Page 278: Photograph by Stu Schutzman.

Page 281: Photograph by Doug Vogt, 1994.

Page 296: *(top)* Courtesy of the Jennings family.

Page 296: *(bottom)* Copyright © 1994 Les Stone/American Broadcasting Companies, Inc.

Page 311: Copyright © 2004 Benedicte Kurzen/American Broadcasting Companies, Inc.

## 8. Enthusiasms

Page 318: Copyright © 1994 Gwendolyn

Cates/American Broadcasting Companies, Inc.

Page 340: *(top)* Courtesy of ABC News, *Peter Jennings Reporting,* "The Search for Jesus."

Page 340: *(bottom)* Courtesy of ABC News, *Peter Jennings Reporting,* "The Search for Jesus."

Page 348: Copyright © 2001 Virginia Sherwood/American Broadcasting Companies, Inc.

Page 364: Copyright © 2000 Ida Mae Astute/American Broadcasting Companies, Inc.

## 9. September 11

Page 368: *(top)* Courtesy of ABC News. Broadcast on September 11, 2001.

Page 368: *(bottom)* Courtesy of ABC News. Broadcast on September 11, 2001.

Page 373: Courtesy of ABC News. Broadcast on September 11, 2001.

## 10. The Man

Page 388: *(top)* Photograph by Kayce Freed Jennings.

Page 388: *(bottom)* Photograph by Kayce Freed Jennings.

Page 437: Courtesy of Denis Reggie, 1998.

Page 440: *(top)* Photograph by Kayce Freed

Jennings. Photograph taken in the Okavango Delta, August 1997.

Page 440: *(bottom)* Photograph by Kayce Freed Jennings. Photograph taken in the Gatineau Valley, Canada, 1996.

## 11. Citizen

Page 444: *(top)* Photograph by Kayce Freed Jennings, 2003.

Page 444: *(bottom)* Courtesy of the Jennings family.

## 12. "I Have Lung Cancer"

Page 468: Copyright © 1998 David Burnett/American Broadcasting Companies, Inc.

Page 477: Courtesy of ABC News. Broadcast on April 5, 2005.

## 13. Legacy

Page 500: Copyright © 2004 Virginia Sherwood/American Broadcasting Companies Inc.

## 14. "Finally, This Evening . . ."

Page 518: Copyright © 1998 Michael O'Neill/American Broadcasting Companies, Inc.